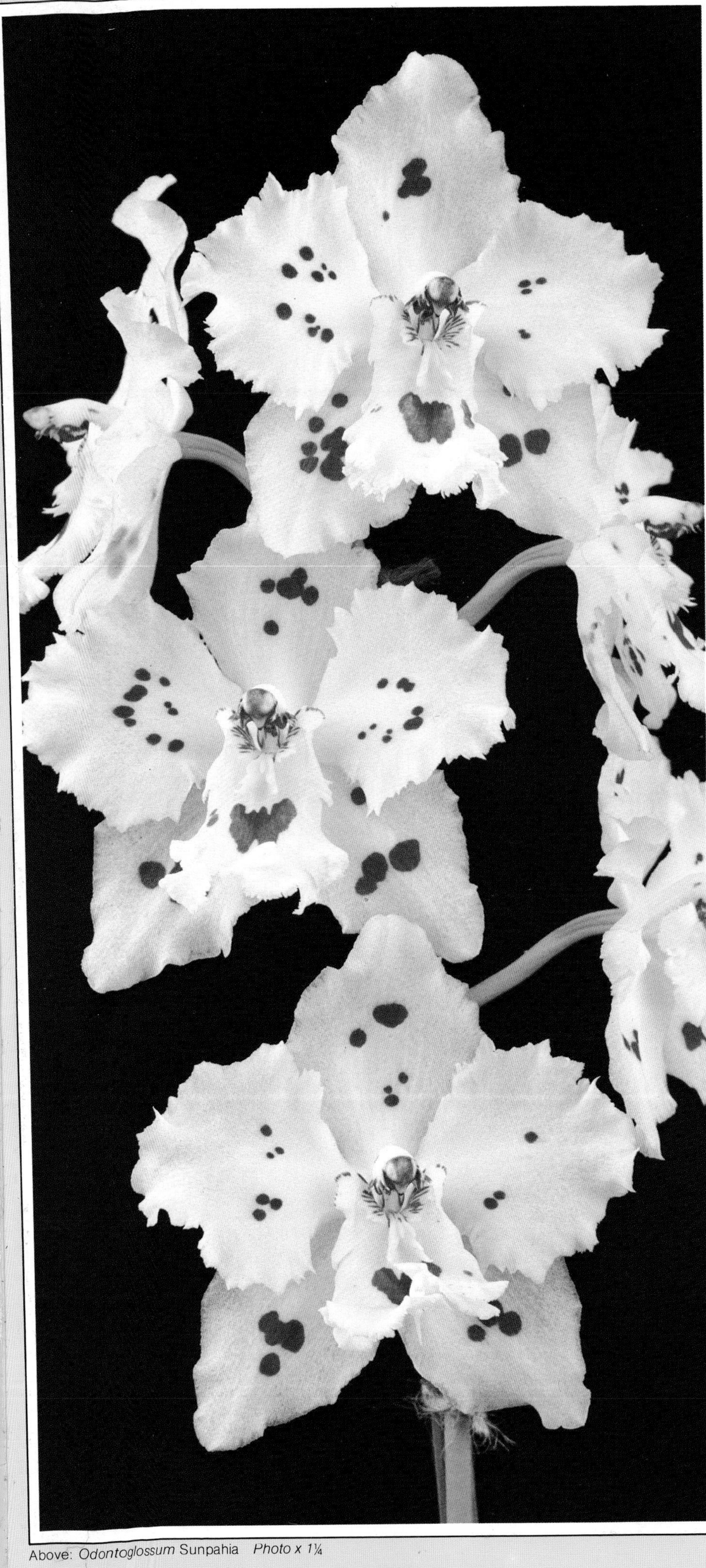

ORCHIDS
for everyone

Above: *Odontoglossum* Sunpahia *Photo x 1¼*

Above: *Miltonia* Peach Blossom *Photo x 1½*

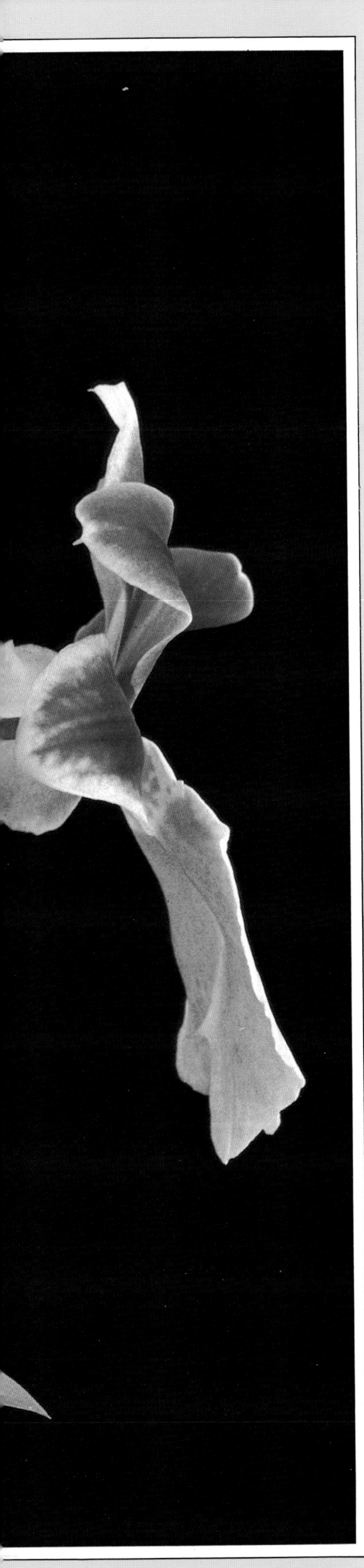

ORCHIDS
for everyone

A PRACTICAL GUIDE TO GROWING AND CARING FOR OVER 200 OF THE WORLD'S MOST BEAUTIFUL PLANTS

CONSULTANT:
JACK KRAMER

SALAMANDER

A Salamander Book

Published by Salamander Books Ltd.
8 Blenheim Court
Brewery Road
London N7 9NT
United Kingdom

© Salamander Books Ltd., 1980, 1997, 2003

A member of Chrysalis Books plc

ISBN 1 84065 535 6

All rights reserved. Except for use in a review, no part of this book may be reproduced, stored in a retrieval system or transmitted in any form or by any means, electronic, mechanical, photocopying or otherwise, without prior permission of Salamander Books Ltd.

All correspondence concerning the content of this volume should be addressed to Salamander Books Ltd.

Credits

Editor: Valerie Noel-Finch
Designers: Mark Holt, Roger Hyde
Colour reproductions: Scansets Ltd., Middlesex, England
Monochrome: Modern Text Typesetting Ltd, Essex, England
Printed in China

Above: *Coelogyne intermedia* Photo x 1¼

THE AUTHORS

Brian Williams A professional horticulturist, over many years Brian Williams built up an extremely varied private orchid collection, which won numerous cultural awards. A former Editor of The Orchid Review (UK), the world's oldest orchid journal, he has lectured to national and international societies on the subject of orchids and orchid growing.

Peter Dumbelton worked for many years as a professional orchid grower in commercial horticulture. He has lectured to a wide range of societies and has also been a noted judge at orchid shows throughout the UK.

Ray Bilton is an acknowledged expert on the breeding and culture of a wide range of orchids. He has contributed to conferences and periodicals throughout the world and is currently Vice-Chairman of the Orchid Committee of the Royal Horticultural Society, UK.

Wilma Rittershausen is Editor of The Orchid Review, which is the orchid journal of the Royal Horticultural Society, UK. In conjunction with her brother, Brian, she has written numerous orchid books and she is a regular contributor on orchids to the UK's bestselling horticultural magazine, *Amateur Gardening*.

David Stead is an experienced professional grower with a particular interest in breeding odontoglossums. He is a former Chairman of the British Orchid Growers' Association, UK, and a regular contributor to orchid journals and international conferences.

Paul Phillips is one of the world's foremost breeders of paphiopedilums and chairman of The British Orchid Growers' Association. He has lectured in many countries and has written for orchid magazines in the USA, Germany, Australia and the UK. He is a member of both the Orchid Judging Committee and the Orchid Registration Advisory Committee of the Royal Horticultural Society, UK.

Keith Andrew recently retired after 45 years as a commercial orchid grower. His special interest is in breeding phalaenopsis and miniature cymbidiums. He has given papers at conferences in California and has exhibited orchids in Germany and in the UK. In the past few years he has spent time growing orchids in Hawaii and in New England, USA.

Alan Greatwood is now retired after 40 years as the curator of a large private orchid collection. He is currently a member of the Orchid Committee of the Royal Horticultural Society, UK.

THE CONSULTANT

Jack Kramer is a well known and highly respected horticulturalist and writer. His personal collection of orchids is extensive and he has written and contributed to many orchid books appealing to a wide readership. He now lives in California, USA.

PHOTOGRAPHY

The majority of photographs in this book and those on the back of the jacket have been specially taken by Eric Crichton.

Above: *Pleione formosana* 'Iris' *Photo x 2¾*

CONTENTS

Part One: 10-99

Orchids in Cultivation

Part Two: 100-197

Orchids in Close-up

Key to symbols
Temperature categories for growing orchids:
● = Warm—minimum 15.5°C (60°F)
◑ = Intermediate—minimum 13°C (55°F)
○ = Cool—minimum 10°C (50°F)

❀ = Flowering season

Above: *Cymbidium* Gymer 'Cooksbridge' *Photo x1¼*

FOREWORD

What the late Eric Young had to say in his foreword to the first edition of this book is as true now as it was then. Orchids are much easier to grow than many people think, and the orchid-growing world is truly a worldwide one. The plants themselves are the reason. Quite simply, they are fascinating – not only beautiful (at least in many cases) but also strange and ingenious.

The growing of orchids began in Britain during the first half of the nineteenth century. That was a time when the merchant ships, coming into London and Liverpool from the newly discovered parts of the world, brought with them a flow of novelties and new marvels. Orchid growing became a particular hobby for rich men – and a prestige hobby at that. However, those rich men knew their plants. They were interested in them for their own sake. They encouraged, and in many cases financed, collectors and taxonomists to find and classify orchid species from all over the globe.

There were some very large and expensive collections in Britain at that time. The rich orchid fanciers were often very rich indeed, and they gave full rein to their hobby. That was perhaps the Golden Age of orchid-growing. If World War I gave a shock – and the Great Depression which followed – World War II finally put paid to that era. Fuel was nonexistent during that war; new taxation bore down heavily; and gardeners became very expensive to employ on a full-time basis.

Yet the fascination of orchids remained, and a new kind of orchid grower emerged in the postwar years. These were not rich men but ordinary men – and, increasingly, women – who were interested in plants and who found in orchids a mystery and a mystique not to be found in any other group of plants. Local orchid societies began to spring up, drawing support and membership from people who were both enthusiastic and, increasingly, expert about the great family of Orchidaceae. This was a worldwide phenomenon, as anyone who has had the opportunities of travel which I have enjoyed can attest. I doubt whether there is any branch of horticulture so vibrantly international as orchid growing.

Developments in science have helped. So much has been discovered in the past forty years about the cultivation and the propagation of orchids that many things which would have been speculative or simply difficult before are now routine. The result is that plants of the highest quality are now available at prices well below what would have been charged in earlier decades. The real price of good orchid plants has gone down dramatically, and the hobby is now within the reach of many more people than before. The still all-too-common idea that orchids are a rich man's hobby is quite untrue. They are the most interesting group of plants in the world, and they are now within the reach of almost every serious gardener. Orchids, indeed, for everyone.

The contributors to this book are all experts. They know what they are talking about. They have been growing orchids for years and have, in many cases, well-established international reputations. It is a privilege and a pleasure to be asked to write this foreword.

Alasdair Morrison
Chairman, RHS Orchid Committee
President, British Orchid Council

Part One
Orchids in Cultivation

Orchids are parasites. They are also carnivorous, insectivorous, and possess mystic — usually evil — powers. Additionally they are extremely expensive and need to be grown in very hot and humid conditions which are costly to provide. In cultivation orchids are short-lived plants.

These are just some of the many myths that in the past have surrounded orchids, and inhibited all but the very wealthy from growing what is surely nature's most extravagant family of flowering plants. With an almost worldwide distribution that includes every conceivable ecological niche, orchids stand supreme in the plant kingdom for their beauty and diversity, and are unrivalled for their willingness to adapt to a wide variety of conditions under cultivation.

This adaptability is one of the main reasons why orchids are fast becoming *the* plant, not only for greenhouse owners but also for apartment dwellers — many of whom are growing orchids very successfully as pot plants. With their long-lasting flowers and often attractive foliage, many of the more compact growing orchids are ideal plants for the windowsill. With a greenhouse at your disposal, all 70,000 species and hybrid orchids are potentially available to you, whilst a few genera may be treated as 'alpine' plants and grown without heat. In subtropical, tropical and equatorial areas of the world, a far wider range of orchids may be grown as garden plants, thus adding another dimension to the uses of this great family.

As decorative plants, orchids are without peers. Although in the past many non-ornamental uses — including both contraceptive and aphrodisiac qualities — have been ascribed to them, there is but one 'orchid of commerce', *Vanilla planifolia*. This primarily Central American species, a vine that can in nature climb to 15-23m (50-75ft), produces seed pods that are the beans of true vanilla. Although now largely replaced by artificial flavouring, Vanillin, it remains an important crop in many tropical countries.

But it is to lovers of flowering plants that this book is dedicated, especially those who yearn for perennial plants that produce their flowers during the dull days of winter, as many orchids do.

This first part of the book opens with an introduction to the botany of the orchid family. Then follows a brief historical look at orchid collecting and breeding, which leads on to a detailed practical guide to the successful cultivation of these fascinating plants. The first consideration in this section is where to grow orchids, with discussion of greenhouses, their ideal shapes and sizes, and their correct positioning in the garden. This is followed by a review of the greenhouse equipment and gadgetry available to assist the amateur grower, not forgetting the garden lover without the space for a greenhouse, for whom there is guidance on cultivating orchids on windowsills, in growing cases, cellars and lofts.

The provision of temperature and light requirements prefaces the section on how to cultivate orchids, which compares the merits of the various composts, discusses methods of potting and vegetative propagation and provides instructions on watering, feeding and pest control. For those interested in the decorative uses of orchids, there is a section on corsage-making and preparing plants for exhibition, and for the more ambitious, the final section gives instructions on artificial pollination, seed raising and tissue culture.

The aim of this first part is to whet the appetite for the cultivation of these wonderful flowers, by introducing new growers to a few of the many methods currently in use. One word of warning: although orchids are not parasitic by nature, they do have the infectious habit of growing on the casual onlooker.

Left: Orchids can be grown almost anywhere, providing a few basic requirements are met. Many — like these paphiopedilums — flower in winter, brightening your home on the dull days.

UNRAVELLING THE LEGEND

Orchids are seldom mediocre: people either love them or loathe them. However, once they have become acquainted with orchids, most people are fascinated by them—occasionally to the point of obsession. Loathing often stems from an ignorance of the enormous orchid family and may be based on an elementary fear or dislike of the unknown. Of course, some orchid growers do give up, but almost certainly not because the flowers repulse them.

Over the years orchids have been the focus of many stories, some of which descend to the depths of absurdity. One such, recounted by a former orchid grower exhibiting at a Chelsea Flower Show in the 1930s, alleges that an elegantly dressed lady, misled by a newspaper article on orchids, enquired the whereabouts of 'the meat-eating orchid'. Without hesitation the exhibitor apologized for the absence of this orchid from his stand, explaining: 'It has gone to lunch!'—a reply which appeared to satisfy the gullible enquirer. Considering the strength of the myths about orchids at that time, her innocence was at least partially understandable.

The aims of this book are to unravel the web of legend and half-truths surrounding orchids and to encourage a better understanding of the characteristics and attractions of the astonishing orchid family.

Above: This spectacular terrestrial species of *Caladenia* comes from Western Australia. Although not in general cultivation, there are many species, all brightly coloured.

Above: *Calypso bulbosa* is a terrestrial orchid found wild in North America, Europe and Asia. It produces a single leaf and flower.

What is an orchid?

There is no simple answer to the question 'What is an orchid?' No clearcut statement is possible: there is no single country of origin, no single habit of growth, and no single shape and colour of flower.

The Orchidaceae form the largest family of flowering plants known to science. Estimates of the number of native species range from around 15,000 to as many as 35,000, but it is generally accepted that there are at least 25,000 native species, derived from approximately 750 genera grouped in numerous tribes and subtribes. And, despite intensive exploration of large areas of the world during the past 200 years, new species are still being found. Most of these are members of established genera, but occasionally even a new genus is discovered.

Orchids are perennial plants found growing in a wide variety of situations and with different growth habits. Members of one large group grow in or near the surface of the ground and are known as *terrestrials.* Plants in the other of the two main groups grow on trees or shrubs and are known as *epiphytes.* The name is derived from 'epi' (above or on), and 'phyte' (plant), hence epiphyte: a plant growing on another plant. Members of

Right: The leafless orchid, *Epipogium aphylla,* thrives on the decomposing leaves of the forest floor. It is found from Europe to Japan.

Above: This large epiphytic *Epidendrum* from Mexico has heavy leaves and pendent stems. An attractive species, it is easily cultivated.

Left: Epiphytic cattleyas growing on trees near the light in a Florida forest. Aerial roots anchor the plants and search for food.

Below: Although this African orchid, *Ansellia africana* is found as an epiphyte in trees, it also grows on rocks as a lithophyte.

this group are not parasites; they do not draw food from their host, but merely obtain anchorage. They draw moisture and nourishment from the air and from humus collected in the angles of branches or in the crevices of the bark. Occasionally, epiphytic orchids are found growing on rocks, when they are more correctly termed *lithophytes.* In general terms, most orchids from temperate zones are terrestrial, whereas most coming from the tropics are epiphytic.

Orchids' flowers vary in size from those requiring a magnifying glass to appreciate their full beauty, to blooms up to 20cm (8in) in diameter. And flowers may vary considerably in size and shape within a single genus, thus complicating species identification, even for an expert. Although all orchid flowers are made up of six basic segments (see page 16), there are countless variations on this pattern. Breeders of hybrids have produced a large number of varieties, introducing new colours or broadening the segments of the flowers to produce a more rounded shape.

'New' orchids to fascinate the grower are constantly being created by hybridization between two different species or two or more different genera. Those crossed between more than one genus are known as *inter-* or *multigeneric hybrids.* Up to the present a maximum of seven different genera have been combined, over several generations, into a single multigeneric hybrid. Doubtless the future will yield even more complicated breeding.

Growing orchids

This extreme diversity is one of the main attractions of orchid growing, and maintains the fascination indefinitely. However long a grower has been cultivating orchids, there are always thousands more that will present a challenge to his growing skills and eventually delight him with yet a different shape or colour combination. Most amateur growers prefer a very mixed collection, but this will really test cultural abilities; invariably requirements of one group must be compromised to satisfy the needs of the majority. New growers would do better to limit the range of orchids they grow at first; it is advisable to master the basic skills needed to cultivate one group before progressing to another. This does not mean that the initial choice must be made between one or two types, for such is the variety available that there is bound to be a group just right for any particular set of growing conditions.

Patterns of Growth

To the layman, orchid plants often present a bewildering variety of shapes, but in reality they have only two basic types of growth: sympodial and monopodial.

Sympodial orchids

The majority of orchids have a sympodial growth pattern. These plants produce their new growth from the base of previous growths, rather in the manner of most herbaceous perennial plants. Many sympodial orchids have *pseudobulbs,* so called because they are not true bulbs (as in narcissus, for example), but are merely thickened stems that have become adapted to store moisture and food. These pseudobulbs enable the plant to withstand periods of dryness, and indicate that in nature the species grows in an area of seasonal drought.

Pseudobulbs show great diversity. The common egg-shaped ones of, for example, *Lycaste, Cymbidium* and *Odontoglossum* may vary from a few millimetres to 15-20cm (6-8in) in height. They can be very flattened, as in some *Oncidium* species, or almost round, as in several species of *Encyclia.* At the other end of the scale there are the thin, cane-like pseudobulbs of *Dendrobium* and *Epidendrum* which, although they may seldom exceed 3-4 cm (1.2-1.6in) in diameter, will frequently grow to 2 or 3m (up to 10ft) in height. In between these are the club- or spindle-shaped pseudobulbs of cattleyas and some laelias, which may range in height from 5-30cm (2-12in), but are generally comparatively plump.

As if this variety were not sufficient to cause confusion, even to growers beyond the very early stages, the rhizomes (the woody parts of the rootstock that join one pseudobulb to the next) may vary even within one genus from practically non-existent to 15cm (6in) or more in length. The pseudobulbs of *Coelogyne cristata,* for example, are produced very close together; a mature specimen frequently has the appearance of a bunch of large, shrivelled grapes. By contrast, the rhizome of *Coelogyne pandurata,* which grows in warmer conditions, scrambles over the surface of the ground, producing a new pseudobulb only every 10cm (4 in).

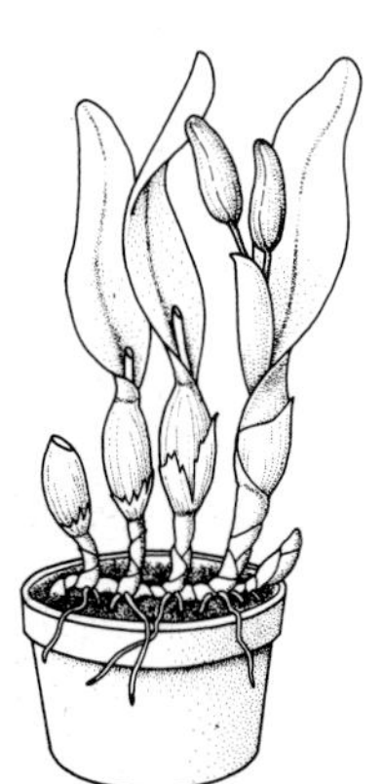

Left: The typical sympodial orchid has several pseudobulbs joined by a rhizome, which is not always visible between them. Each bulb may support one or more leaves.

Above: Pseudobulbs vary greatly in size and shape. Each is beautifully suited to its environment, having adapted to varying habitats.

Right: Paphiopedilums have no need for pseudobulbs. They grow in the ground in moist climates where drought conditions do not occur.

Right: *Coelogyne cristata* produces many closely packed pseudobulbs. When a few leaves are shed the old bulbs survive to provide food for the younger ones.

There are also sympodial orchids without pseudobulbs. Generally speaking, these inhabit areas where the seasonal supply of moisture is more constant. Perhaps the best known of these are *Paphiopedilum* from Southeast Asia and the related *Phragmipedium* from South America. Although both these groups may be deciduous in nature, they are seldom so when grown under glass. They produce large fans of leaves with the flower stem emerging from the centre.

Despite their apparently different growth habits, *all* sympodial orchids have at least one thing in common: the new growth is always produced from the base of previous ones.

Monopodial orchids

The principal direction of growth of monopodial orchids is upwards, new growth being an extension of the growth of previous years. Leaves are produced alternately on either side of a central stem, the interval between the leaves ranging from minimal to many centimetres. Although growth variation is less obvious among monopodial than sympodial orchids, it still exists. One extreme is shown by the genus *Arachnis,* which is often described as having a climbing habit, the vigorous stems reaching the higher tree branches 10 or even 20m (33-65ft) above ground. Such vigorous *Arachnis* species from tropical areas of Asia are not suited to pot culture in temperate zones, but the related genera *Phalaenopsis* and *Doritis* are ideal. In these, the broad leaves are produced from an abbreviated stem, and the plant remains compact for many years.

Occasionally, certain monopodial orchids will freely produce side growths from the leaf axils; some species of *Aerides* and *Angraecum* are particularly noted for this and often develop into bushy, multi-lead plants. But always the new growth is an extension of previous years, and pseudobulbs are never present.

Right: The typical monopodial grows from an upright stem from which the leaves grow outwards in pairs. New leaves are produced from the apex. Aerial roots grow from the sides and base. The plants vary in height according to genus. Vandas, as illustrated, can grow to more than 1m (3ft) while phalaenopsis are usually restricted to three or four leaves on a plant at any one time

Orchid roots

The roots of orchids, particularly epiphytic orchids, are usually much thicker than in other plants, and the root system may appear compact when compared with the fibrous root system of a more familiar plant. Many terrestrial orchids possess a comparatively finer root system and some spherical tubers (sometimes incorrectly called pseudobulbs). This is particularly the case with temperate species, many of which are herbaceous. These underground tubers enable the plant to survive periods of cold weather, with a resurgence of new growth when conditions are favourable. Terrestrial orchids from warmer areas usually produce the thicker roots characteristic of epiphytic orchids. Epiphytes need strong, thick roots for several reasons; they secure the plant to its host, and their thickness helps the plant to survive temporary periods of drought.

Above: Exposed aerial roots can only exist in warm moist climates. The green tip shows that the root is active and absorbing moisture.

The roots of monopodial orchids are produced at intervals between the leaves on the main stems, whereas in sympodial orchids the roots develop from beneath each new growth. The outer layer of the root, called the *velamen,* consists of several layers of spongy cells that are capable of absorbing and storing considerable quantities of moisture. Recent research on monopodials has shown that nutrients can also be absorbed in this way.

The growing tip of the root is often green (or white if under the surface of the compost) for the first 2-3cm. Away from the tip the velamen gives the root a whitish or tan colour, although when saturated it will assume a greenish hue. When the orchid is in its least active stage of growth or resting, the velamen will completely cover the growing point.

Above: An odontoglossum hybrid which shows the typical well balanced flower with all segments similar in size. Right: A non-typical orchid shape is represented by the masdevallia whose kite-shaped flowers consist of enlarged sepals fused together at the base to form a tube. The petals and lip are diminutive and remain hidden at the centre of the flower.

Foliage and flowers

The leaves of orchid plants vary in size from microscopic to 1m (39in) or more in length. They can be broad or pencil-shaped and range in texture from thin, papery leaves designed to last a single season, to thick, almost succulent leaves that persist for a great many years. In some orchids the leaves are attractively tessellated — marked into small squares like a mosaic — and in the 'jewel' orchids, such as *Haemaria, Macodes* and *Anoectochilus,* the velvety leaves in shades of rich brown or green with a contrasting network of silver, gold or reddish veins, become the principal attraction. The flowers of these orchids are generally whitish or grey-green, and are small and relatively insignificant.

Most orchids, however, are grown for the intricate beauty of their flowers. The variety of flower form is far greater than that of plant habit, with almost every colour except black represented — even a true blue is found. The flowers may be flat to almost tubular; in most the petals are the showiest parts but in others these segments are reduced and the sepals become the dominant feature. Flowers may be spotted, blotched or striped with a contrasting colour, or they may be a pure single colour. The lip is usually the most colourful and spectacular part of the flower, and has often developed an intricate, occasionally even bizarre, shape.

These adaptations are part of an efficient design that helps to ensure reproduction of the species (see page 18). Scent, which is present in many species and may vary from slight to overpowering, is another part of this mechanism.

The Orchid Flower

The typical orchid flower has six segments: an outer ring of three sepals and an inner ring of three petals. These six segments are all coloured, whereas in most flowers—a rose, for example—the protective outer sepals (here called the calyx) are green and like small leaves or bracts beneath the significantly more conspicuous coloured petals.

The uppermost, or dorsal, sepal of an orchid is symmetrical and slightly larger than the other two. This has been exploited by plant breeders with considerable success, particularly in the genus *Paphiopedilum.* The two lower, or lateral, sepals are equal in size and shape, usually separate and held at an angle between the petals. In *Paphiopedilum,* however, and also in its cousins, *Cypripedium* from the northern hemisphere and the South American *Phragmipedium,* the two lateral sepals are usually fused together to form a ventral sepal behind the lower petal. In certain other orchids, such as *Masdevallia,* all three sepals are united for the greater part of their length to form a tube. But these are exceptions. The majority of horticulturally interesting orchids have three separate sepals spaced symmetrically at the back of the flower.

The inner ring of segments consists of three petals, the lowest of which is frequently greatly enlarged and highly coloured. This larger petal is known as the *labellum,* or lip, and is the principal visual attraction for pollinating insects. Some genera, including, among others, *Coryanthes, Paphiopedilum* and *Acineta,* have developed the lip into a bucket or pouchlike structure. Once a visiting insect has climbed or fallen into this the only exit is past the sexual parts of the flower and pollination is assured. This natural tendency to elaboration of the lip has been developed by plant breeders into the most significant part of hybrid flowers. Indeed, many judges at orchid shows have commented that, with cymbidiums in particular, the absence of a brightly coloured lip precludes consideration!

At the bud stage the lip is the uppermost petal but as the bud develops to flowering the lip becomes the lowest segment by a 180° twist of the flower stalk, or *pedicel.* This process is known as *resupination* and is common to most orchids, although in most encyclias, among others, the lip remains uppermost.

The other two petals are usually held across the horizontal axis and are the most variable of all the segments. In some species the petals are broad, often frilled, and extremely flamboyant.

A distinctive feature common to all orchid flowers is that they can be divided into two equal halves in a vertical plane only. This feature has been one of the criteria used by botanists in deciding whether a flower new to science is a member of the orchid family.

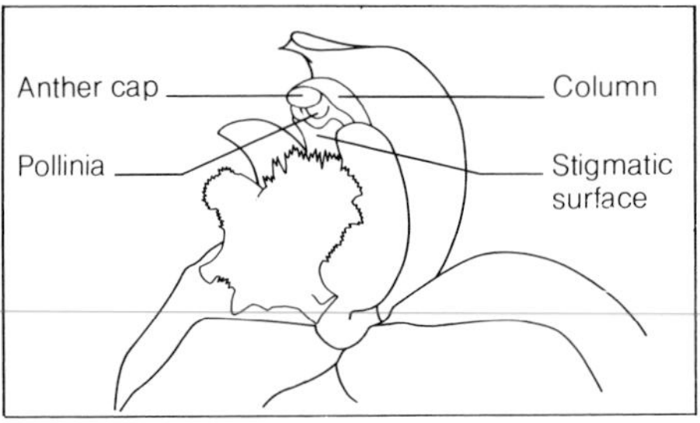

Above: This close up of *Cymbidium traceyanum* clearly shows the structure of the column, which carries the reproductive organs of the flower.

The reproductive system

The most significant difference between orchids and other flowers is in their reproductive apparatus. Like most flowers, the majority of orchids are bisexual, the male and female organs being present in each flower, but the structure and operation of the reproductive parts are different from the conventional system.

In a more familiar flower the female part of the flower (the pistil with the receptive stigma) is situated in the centre and the male parts (the stamens, each with anthers containing pollen grains) are arranged in a ring around it. In an orchid flower, however, the male and female sexual parts are combined into a fingerlike structure in the centre called the column or, more correctly, the *gynostemium.*

The pollen grains, the male part of the flower, are usually at the front end of the column. They are combined into waxy masses called *pollinia* and protected by a cap that represents the anther of 'conventional' flowers. The female part of the flower is represented by a stigmatic surface situated on the underside of the column a little way back from the tip. The relative position of the male and female parts is of critical importance for insect pollination to be successful.

Although most orchids have bisexual flowers, many species of the genus *Catasetum* have unisexual flowers, with male and female organs on separate flowers or even on separate inflorescences. These male and female flowers are often superficially different and early taxonomists named them as different species. As these peculiarities have become known, revised botanical names have been ascribed to many of these plants.

The Structure of an Orchid Flower
The drawings on this page show the typical flower shapes of six groups of orchids widely grown around the world. They share the following features common to all orchid flowers:

1 **Sepals** Usually three of approximately equal size—the uppermost or dorsal sepal, and two lateral sepals below.

2 **Petals** Always three—two similar petals either side of the centre and one lower petal which has become the lip.

3 **Lip or Labellum** Formed from the lower petal, this is the most ornamental segment of the flower. It acts as a 'landing platform' for pollinators.

4 **Column** The fingerlike structure that carries the reproductive parts—the pollinia and stigmatic surface.

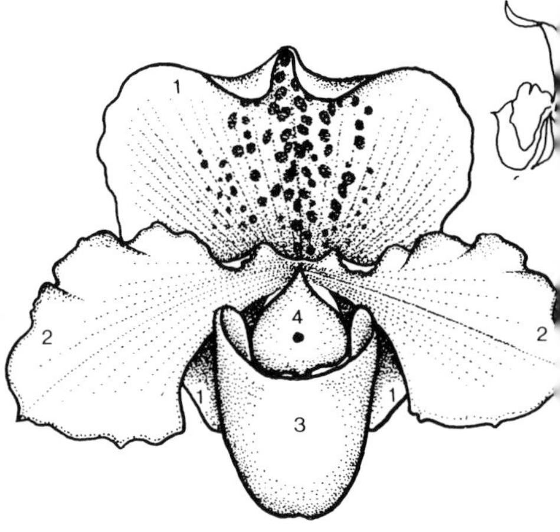

Paphiopedilum
Above: Heavily textured, almost 'varnished' blooms with a distinctive pouchlike lip and fused lateral sepals. Most flowers are borne singly on a strong 15-25cm (6-10in) stem and will remain on the plant in good condition for a period of three months or more.

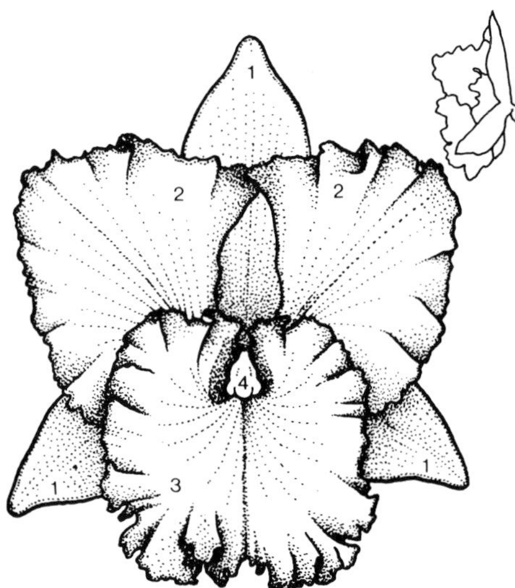

Cattleya
Above: The broad petals and large, wavy lip, which is often of a contrasting colour, combine to produce blooms of up to 15cm (6in) in diameter. Cattleya flowers are often heavily scented but tend to be weak in texture; they seldom last for more than three weeks.

Cymbidium
Below: Carried on tall, arching spikes of 10 to 15 or more, the 10-13cm (4-5in) diameter flowers are available in a wide range of colours, usually with bright lip markings. Of good texture, the flowers will last on the plant for eight to ten weeks.

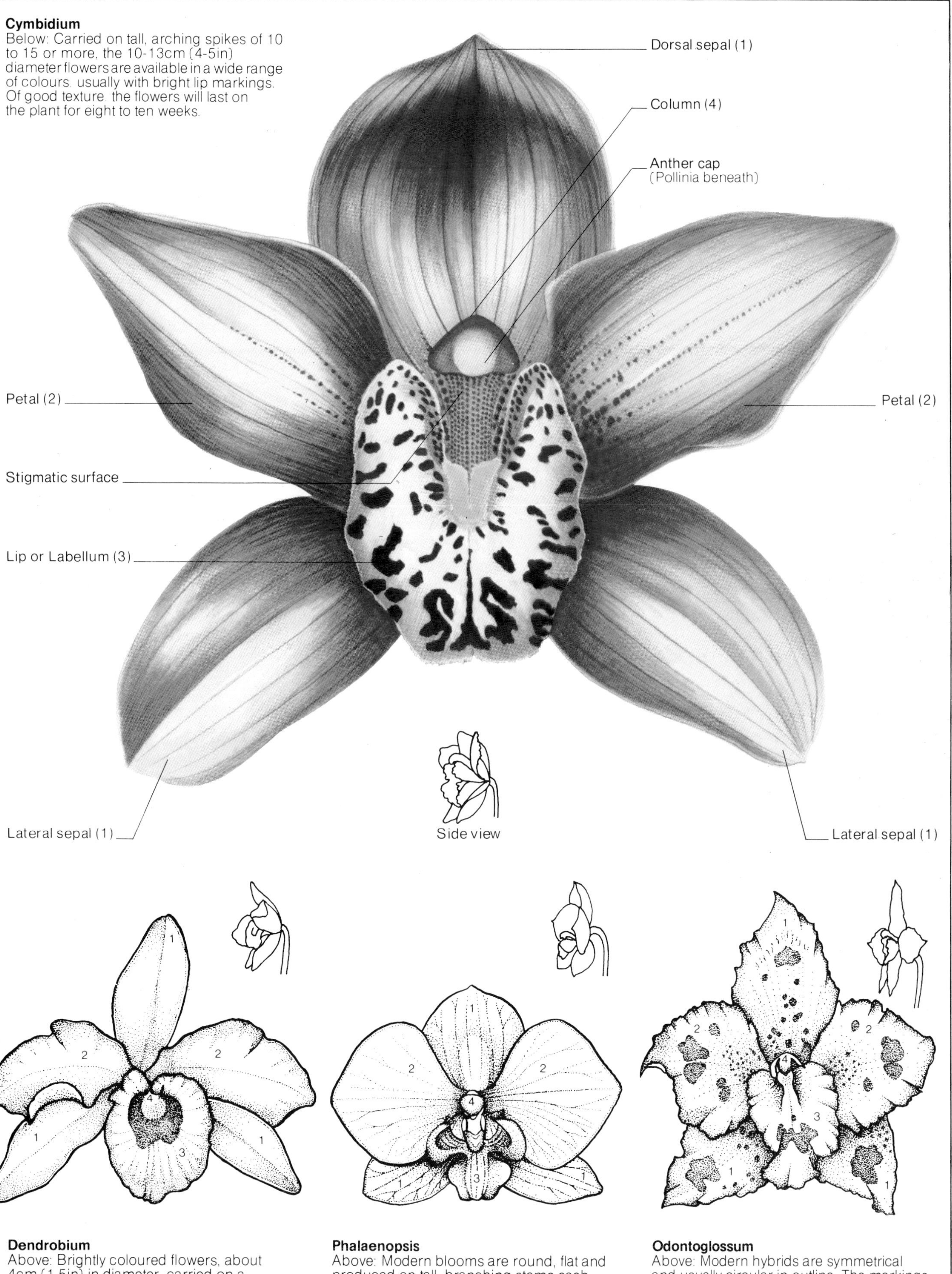

Dendrobium
Above: Brightly coloured flowers, about 4cm (1.5in) in diameter, carried on a variety of erect, arching or pendent spikes depending on type. The lateral petals are fused at the base, sometimes forming a short spur. The flowers will last on the plant for three to eight weeks.

Phalaenopsis
Above: Modern blooms are round, flat and produced on tall, branching stems each carrying 15 to 20 flowers. Colours are white, yellow or pink, often with spots and/or stripes. Deceptively fragile in appearance, the flowers will easily last for seven to eight weeks.

Odontoglossum
Above: Modern hybrids are symmetrical and usually circular in outline. The markings often contrast boldly with the base colour. Each flower spike carries 8 to 12 or more flowers, of attractive shape and held well clear of the foliage. The flowers will last for four to five weeks.

Pollination

The shape, colour or scent of a species orchid undoubtedly gives great pleasure to man, but this is purely incidental to its natural objective. The sole purpose of any ornamentation of an orchid flower is to attract a suitable pollinating agent, which in addition to the more 'normal' insects, such as flies, wasps and bees, includes such creatures as snails, bats, humming-birds and moths.

Cross-pollination

In order to improve vigour and variety in a species—an important survival factor where the 'law of the jungle' rules—it is desirable that the pollen of a flower is not used to fertilize that same flower (termed as *selfing*) but is transferred to a flower of the same species on a different plant. This process of *cross-pollination,* resulting in *cross-fertilization,* ensures continual redistribution of the various genes present in the entire population of the species; whereas self-pollination may lead to the accumulation of bad characteristics that usually occurs with inbreeding.

To achieve cross-pollination, the orchid flower has developed many intricate mechanisms to ensure that the pollen taken from one flower is not, in the majority of cases, deposited on the stigma of the same flower. This is particularly so where the flowers are pollinated by insects, and since orchids are predominantly plants of the tropics, where insect life is highly developed and abundant, we can see immediately why orchids—if left to their own devices — are efficient at reproduction.

Of course, insects do not visit flowers merely to transfer pollen from one flower to the next, but in a search for nectar or pollen on which to feed. Thus, in most cases, the provision of nectar is a vital part of the pollination mechanism. Colour is also significant in attracting specific pollinators and, at close range, the shape and markings of the lip and/or column play an important role in ensuring efficient pollination. But the initial attraction is probably one of scent, which to the human nose is not always sweet and is occasionally decidedly repugnant!

Purpose-built pollinators

Most orchids growing in natural environments are pollinated by one species of insect only and the entire structure of the flower is delicately balanced to match the visiting insect. Many orchids, for example,

store nectar within the walls of a hollow spur, which is an extension at the back of the lip, and only insects with a tongue, or proboscis, of a suitable length are able to reach this liquid. Significantly, it is these insects that have the correctly-shaped head to ensure pollination; as the insect pushes its proboscis down the spur it flips back the anther cap and the pollinia become attached in an upright position to the top of its head or body.

As the insect flies off in search of another flower, the pollinia play their part in the process. If the pollinia were to remain in an upright position they would merely come into contact with the anther cap or stamen of the next flower, but as the insect moves from flower to flower, possibly collecting further pollinia on the way, the pollinial stalk (*caudicle* or *stipe*) curls so that the pollinia pivot to a forward-facing position. When the insect alights on another flower the pollinia are brought into contact with the underside of the column and become attached to the sticky surface of the stigma. Where the orchid has laterally placed stigmas the pollinia do not pivot forward into a horizontal position but diverge slightly to each side. Again, this serves to bring them into precise contact with the stigmas of another flower.

Below: This flower produces a scent of aphid honeydew and fools the fly into laying its eggs inside the flower, at the same time removing the pollinia and effecting pollination. These flies normally feed on honeydew and lay their eggs near aphid colonies.

Pollinating insects appear to be naturally selected by the length of the orchids' spur; bees, with their comparatively short tongues, for example, are effective in pollinating short spurred orchids such as the British native *Orchis mascula;* whereas moths and butterflies, with their longer probosces, are the pollinating agents for the longer spurred orchids, which include most of the tropical angraecoids. Indeed, the pollinia of the latter have frequently been seen attached to the proboscis of visiting insects, particularly where the orchid has laterally placed stigmas. Not only would a bee's tongue be too short to reach into these longer spurs, but its head would be too broad to enter the opening in the flower centre.

The above are two perfect examples of flowers and pollinators that are balanced one to another. But the most famous and often cited example is the Madagascan orchid *Angraecum sesquipedale,* which has a spur of 30-35cm (10-12in) in length. Charles Darwin, in his book *On the Various Contrivances by which British and Foreign Orchids are Fertilized by Insects* (1862) concluded that only a very large and strong moth with a suitably long proboscis could effect pollination, but his theory was not proved until the discovery of just such an insect, *Xanthopan morgani praedicta,* in Madagascar many years later.

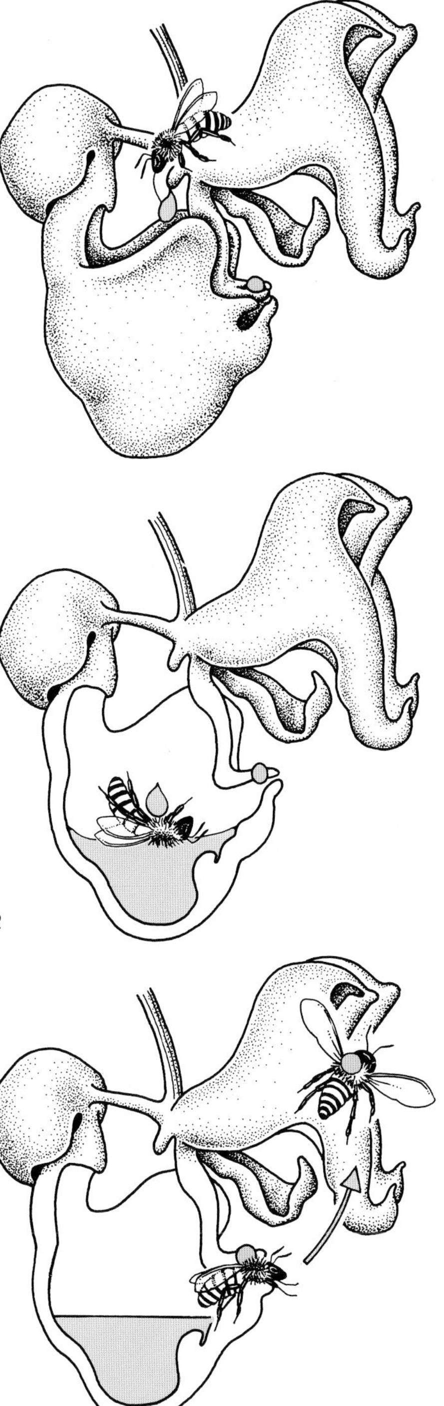

The tender trap

In many orchids, including paphiopedilums, cypripediums, coryanthes and stanhopeas, the lip has evolved into a pouch or slipper-like organ; again, the structure of the flower is aimed at efficient cross-pollination. A bee, probably initially attracted by scent, alights on the front edge of the pouch in search of nectar or occasionally, as in *Coryanthes macrantha,* to eat the interior brim of the pouch. Frequently, either through intoxication or accident, the poor unsuspecting bee tumbles in and, because of the angle of the pouch and its slippery interior surface, cannot make its exit through the pouch opening. Instead, assisted by hairs suitably placed on the surface of the pouch, it crawls up the back interior wall towards one of the small openings on either side of the column. These exits are a fairly tight fit and often considerable effort is required before the bee can escape. In doing so it rubs against the stamen, removing the pollinia onto its back. The bee then visits another flower where the 'tumbling in' process is repeated. This time, on crawling

Left: (1) Bees are attracted to the flower of *Coryanthes* by the fleshy lip which they gnaw with relish. (2) While investigating the flower the bee may be knocked into the 'bucket' by the droplet of liquid secreted by the lobes. (3) The exit for the bee is through the small opening in the lip. It has to push very hard to get through and while doing so collects the pollinia on its back.

up the back wall of the pouch, the bee's back comes into contact with the stigmatic surface, leaving the pollen behind. As it completes its escape it collects additional pollen, which will then be transferred to another flower.

Several points are important here. First, the design of the flower ensures that the bee passes under the stigmatic surface before reaching the pollen, thus making self-pollination extremely unlikely. Second, if a smaller insect visits the flower, possibly with pollinia from a different species on its back, it is able to pass with ease beneath the stigma and stamen, thus not interfering with the natural processes. Unfortunately, if a larger insect is unwise enough to enter the flower it cannot make its exit through the small side holes and dies miserably in the base of the pouch.

This is another example of an orchid flower which is in exact harmony with its pollinator.

Scent and colour

Scent has been mentioned as the probable initial attractant, and it certainly plays an important part in the pollination mechanism of many orchids. For example, where orchids are pollinated by moths the scent is virtually absent during daylight hours, but visit the greenhouse during the evening or night and it is a different story! Most of the angraecoids from tropical Africa, such as *Angraecum* and *Aerangis* species, fall within this category, and one can imagine the almost overpowering scent given off by a colony of these plants on a humid night.

Colour, too, plays its part. There would be little point in a dark or dull-coloured orchid giving off scent during the hours of darkness: the poor half-blind moth, attracted by the scent, would blunder round vainly in search of its source and might never find it. Nature is not so careless. Night-scented orchids are generally of glistening white and possess a well-defined shape. Thus the combination of scent, colour and shape ensures that the moths do not waste their time.

Not all scents that attract insects, however, are so sweet. Many tropical orchids, *Bulbophyllum fletcherianum* among them, emit a foetid smell of bad meat that attracts carrion flies. The British lizard orchid, *Himantoglossum hircinum,* is said to smell of goats and also attracts flies, several of which have been observed carrying pollinia on their heads. But there is little evidence that flies are the sole pollinators of any orchid species.

Mimicry

The common name applied to many orchids often alludes to the animal that part of the flower resembles. In the national flower of Panama, *Peristeria elata,* for example, the column bears a

Above: The brightly coloured area at the centre of this *Miltonia* flower acts as a map, guiding a visiting insect to the source of the nectar.

Below: The spider-like flowers of *Ophrys sphegodes* attract male spiders which remove the pollinia when 'mating'. Pseudocopulation with another flower ensures pollination.

Above and Right: Two examples of pseudocopulation. In both cases the flowers mimic the female insect, and by attempting to mate the male removes the pollinia.

striking resemblance to a dove and *Oncidium papilio* could easily be mistaken for a tropical butterfly with long antennae as the flower moves on its tall, wiry stem in the slightest breeze. Perhaps the most startling similarity, however, is provided by those orchids that resemble bees, wasps and spiders in order to attract corresponding pollinators. Striking examples of such mimicry can be found in the genus *Ophrys* of Europe, North Africa and the Middle East and in *Cryptostylis* of Victoria and New South Wales in Australia. Close studies of these flowers have revealed that the lip accurately mimics the female of a single kind of insect and that the flowers are visited only by the corresponding males. In some species a bee or wasp approaches the flower head first, while in others the insect thrusts its tail under the lip. These differences in behaviour have been correlated with variations in the shape and colour of the lip in relation to the female insect it resembles. It is evident from the movement of the insect that he has been fooled into thinking he has found a mate, and the process has come to be called *pseudocopulation.*

Recently in New South Wales a male wasp of the species *Lissopimpla excelsa* was observed and captured while visiting a flower of *Cryptostylis subulata* for pseudocopulation, and subsequently in the same location a second wasp was seen to remove the pollinia during his exertions. Obviously the performance would be repeated on another flower, thus achieving cross-pollination. In addition to several genera of Australian orchids pollinated in this manner, the phenomenon is known also in *Trichoceros parviflorus* from Ecuador and in *Oncidum henekenii* from the West Indies, and is suspected in many other orchids.

Significantly, orchids pollinated during pseudocopulation produce their flowers at a time when the male insect is active but before the female emerges from pupation several weeks later. Once the female is in circulation the competition for the male's attentions becomes too strong and visits to the flowers cease.

If all else fails, nature has found a way to effect self-pollination. Though this may not be desirable in terms of variability it is better than remaining unfertilized. In some species, such as the British bee orchid *Ophrys apifera,* the pollinial stalks of mature but unpollinated flowers shrink in such a way as to cause the pollinia to hang in front of the stigma. The slightest air movement will then take the pollinia into contact with the stigma and ensure pollination. In nearly all orchids the flower collapses shortly after pollination, presumably to prevent the pollinated flower remaining attractive and to ensure that the pollinator moves to the next flower.

It would be an interesting experiment to observe the reactions of these natural pollinating agents of specific species when confronted with a modern hybrid orchid of the same genus. If the actions of bumble bees in the cymbidium house during early spring are any indication, these insects would not be fooled for long!

Origins and Distribution

Tracing the origins of life—a subject that continues to intrigue most researchers—is based primarily on the chance discovery of fossil remains. However, the fossil record for all plant life is meagre and, unfortunately for orchid biologists, relatively few orchid fossils are known. Some researchers argue that this is not too surprising for several reasons: mainly that orchids occur predominantly in wet tropics, which are areas of rapid decay; and being primarily of epiphytic habit, orchids are precluded from the (usually aquatic) conditions most conducive to fossilization. Another school of thought believes that increased investigation will reveal a more comprehensive fossil record for orchids.

The origins of orchids

On currently available evidence most scientists consider that orchids originated approximately 100-120 million years ago, with Malaysia frequently cited as a 'birthplace'. Defined simply, evolution can be seen in terms of survival through adaptation. Although a large number of orchid species exist today, it is certain that many more perished along the way because they could not adapt to an epiphytic habit or could not survive competition as terrestrial plants. Indeed, several genera of orchids that have been identified only from fossil remains are now regarded as extinct.

The successful adaptation of orchids to their surroundings is best shown by their leaves. Where conditions are harsh or desert-like for part of the year, orchid leaves have developed into fleshy, almost succulent organs. They act as reservoirs for the plant, enabling it to survive long seasonal periods of drought. Without these succulent leaves, the orchid plant would surely perish. Many of the Australian tropical dendrobiums, for example, have characteristically fleshy leaves, and thus are able to thrive in the almost shadeless desert of northern Queensland. Other examples are the stout-leaved brassavolas from South America, and some vandas from Southeast Asia. Significantly, these orchids, having developed tough, pencil-shaped leaves in order to withstand long hours of hot sun, are usually without pseudobulbs; the plants can store sufficient moisture in their leaves.

By contrast, orchids growing in shadier environments need leaves with a large surface area in order to obtain sufficient light for photosynthesis. The genus *Lycaste,* for example, which sometimes grows on the underside of branches on deciduous trees overhanging rivers, produces large fan-like foliage that, in tune with the host tree, is deciduous and is discarded during the dry season. This type of orchid needs pseudobulbs for survival until the rains start again.

Above: In open habitats orchids usually grow terrestrially as adequate light is available for photosynthesis. The complex root system and storage organs grow beneath the soil.

Right: Epiphytes are most common in tropical rain forests where they often grow high in the canopy. The roots anchor the plant and some also absorb water from the atmosphere.

In subtropical areas of the world the dry season is usually a time of lower temperatures. Thus, dehydration of the orchid is seldom severe because the rate of transpiration falls in cooler conditions. But this 'check' to growth is vital because it is the mechanism that triggers off flower bud initiation, and most orchids produce their flowers immediately before the appearance of new growth that heralds the start of the rains.

Distribution

Orchids are distributed over almost the entire world; every continent—except Antarctica—has a large number of species represented often by enormous colonies but occasionally by only one or two plants. Only areas of extreme desert, at the summits and upper slopes of the highest, and thus coldest, mountains, the seas and the deepest lakes, are naturally devoid of orchids. By the ever increasing activities of man, a fifth non-orchid area must now be added—highly cultivated agricultural and horticultural land.

A look at the geographical spread of orchids will provide a few puzzles. Why, for instance, are odontoglossums found only in South America, usually at high elevations, and not in other areas of the world that enjoy virtually identical climates? A similar picture could be painted with many other orchids. Vandas, for example, are widely scattered over many parts of tropical Southeast Asia, mostly north of the equator, and not elsewhere in the world. This genus certainly grows well in other parts of the world, as witnessed by the highly successful com-

mercial nurseries in Hawaii and the West Indies, but it does not occur naturally in these areas.

One theory for such fragmented distribution is that the mountains on which high elevation orchids grow could be regarded as islands in a sea of lowland forest, making distribution of seed to another 'island' a chance affair that must rely on long distance means such as the wind. Therefore, it is extremely difficult for orchids growing on the Andes, for example, to colonize similar environments elsewhere in the world. Lowland species, by contrast, grow in vast areas of forest 'sea' where the widespread distribution of seed is a comparatively easy matter. Although this guarantees a stable population it works against diversity in a species; the varied and ever-changing niches on isolated mountains are more fertile in an evolutionary sense and are more likely to form the breeding grounds for new varieties.

Mysterious distribution

Many orchid genera, once thought to be widespread, have been found recently to have more restricted distributions. Habenarias are a case in point. This large genus of tuberous-rooted, terrestrial orchids has been found in Asia, South and Central Africa, America and Europe. However, greater knowledge and understanding of the plants has now limited *Habenaria* to tropical and subtropical areas, most of the temperate species having been transferred to other genera. A similar situation applies to *Angraecum*, a genus of monopodial, epiphytic orchids from tropical Africa, with a heavy concentration on the island of Madagascar. One .species, previously known as *Angraecum falcatum* came from Japan, a somewhat odd classification when one considers the distance separating this lone stray from the flock. Recently, however, this error has been corrected, and the plant in question is now known as *Neofinetia falcata.*

This tidying-up process by taxonomists —annoying though it might be to the horticulturist who has become used to the original name—suggests that individual genera of orchids are less widely distributed than was first thought. The reallocation process is still continuing, and could lead to a more complete understanding of why certain orchids are so restricted in their distribution.

Orchid Nomenclature

Throughout this book, and any other reputable publication on orchids, an internationally recognized form of naming is used as laid down by the International Orchid Commission in their *Handbook on Orchid Nomenclature and Registration.* Much of the somewhat complex information contained within that publication may not be of interest to most orchid growers, but points concerning typography will greatly assist anyone in their understanding of the text.

It will be noticed that some orchid names are *italicized* whilst other apparently similar names are in roman type; also that only some names start with a capital letter, and yet others are enclosed in single quotation marks. This system has resulted in the orchid family having a more orderly form of naming than any other plant family. It also means that whether an orchid grower is Chinese or Chilean, he will still have a full understanding of orchid names.

A binominal form of naming is used, consisting of a generic name and a specific epithet. The first name is the genus from which the orchid in question is derived; this name is always capitalized and *italicized* when used in reference to an orchid name, but not when used merely as a convenient reference to plants. The second name is the specific or hybrid epithet, and refers to a particular species or hybrid within the genus. Specific epithets are always *italicized* and entirely in lower case, whilst hybrid epithets start with a capital letter and are not *italicized.* For example: the genus is *Lycaste,* and the species is *skinneri;* thus *Lycaste skinneri* would be the only correct way of writing this name. But hybridize this with another *Lycaste* species and the resulting hybrid name will be, for instance, *Lycaste* Queen Elizabeth.

Within a species or hybrid group there will probably be many different clones (plants all grown from the same batch of seedlings), each of which may be given a clonal name or cultivar (cultivated variety) epithet; these are always enclosed in single quotation marks. Thus *Lycaste* Queen Elizabeth 'Gatton Park' and *Lycaste* Queen Elizabeth 'Wyld Court' will distinguish between two forms of the same hybrid: *Lycaste* Queen Elizabeth.

When referring to a plant in a non-generic sense, the word is written in the normal style, for example: 'those lycastes

Below: A species from South America, *Phragmipedium schlimii* 'Wilcox' (AM/AOS) is a collectors' item now rare enough to have received an award in the USA.

are growing well'. But if referring to a particular plant in any sense, the former rules still apply, for example: 'that *Lycaste skinneri* is growing well'.

Merit awards

Additionally many orchids have been granted awards by one or more of the judging authorities around the world. This is where the importance of the third, clonal name is apparent, as only vegetative propagations of that particular awarded clone, and not the hybrid group as a whole, may carry the appropriate title. Award names are normally abbreviated to just first letters of each word, and are in two parts; the first indicates the level of the award and the second part reveals the awarding authority. The highest award is the First Class Certificate (FCC) granted only to plants of exceptional quality. This is followed by the Award of Merit (AM) for particularly meritorious plants. Some judging authorities also have a third category, the Highly Commended Certificate (HCC), awarded to good quality orchids. Not all judging authorities use these awards, some instead have Gold, Silver and Bronze levels, but most have an award specifically for excellence in culture, which, of course, only applies to one particular period and is not carried forward into future years. This is usually shown as CCC—the Certificate of Cultural Commendation.

The longest established awarding authority is the Royal Horticultural Society (RHS), whilst the American Orchid Society (AOS) has awards dating back some 40 years. More recently the Australian Orchid Council (AOC), the German Orchid Society (Deutsche Orchideen-Gesellschaft [DOG]), the South African Orchid Council (SAOC) and many others have also been evaluating and awarding orchids.,

By using the above code, everyone interested in orchids may more fully understand the meaning of the various ways in which an orchid name is written, and also realize the significance and derivation of the award letters after the name. Thus *Lycaste* Queen Elizabeth 'Lady Colman' AM/RHS signifies that the clone of 'Lady Colman'—and not the hybrid group in general—received an Award of Merit from the Royal Horticultural Society.

Below: This hybrid *Cattleya* Pink Debutante (AM/RHS) was highly awarded for its outstanding quality of flower colour, size, shape and texture.

THE HISTORY OF ORCHIDS

The past is often as fascinating as the future; but whilst we are only able to forecast the future of orchids by gazing into a kind of botanical crystal ball, their history would appear to be comparatively well documented.

Early fascination

The earliest reports are from the period 370-285 BC, when the Greek philosopher *Theophrastus* referred to a group of plants called orchis, in his manuscript *Enquiry into Plants.* Thus the name orchid is probably derived from the terrestrial genus *Orchis*—as we now know this group of Mediterranean orchids. The Greek *orchis* means testis, and refers to the root of this genus and similar genera. These roots are in fact testiculate tubers occurring in pairs, and it is this part of the plant that for many hundreds of years was considered of value.

Medical theories of 2,000 years ago were based almost entirely on herbal remedies, many of which decreed that the treatment and cure of human ailments were best achieved by the use of plants or plant parts that resembled, in shape or colour, parts of the human anatomy. Therefore bloodroot, *Sanguinaria canadensis,* was considered efficient in curing anaemia and, by the same theory the testiculate tubers of *Orchis,* when crushed and eaten, were said to stimulate sexual activity. These beliefs continued well into the sixteenth and seventeenth centuries, by which time travel between Europe and the rest of the world was increasing, bringing in its wake a more enlightened approach to botany and the true properties of plants.

By the middle of the sixteenth century, some 13 different European orchids had been discovered; but long before this time, interest in orchids by the peoples of the Orient had been recorded. Legend would have us believe that the ancient Chinese Emperors as far back as 28 centuries BC described orchids in their writings. Accounts of early orchid cultivation in Japan are also available and in both countries—although the alleged aphrodisiac qualities were not discounted—these orchids were grown for their aesthetic beauty rather than other considerations. Superstition still played a large part in the choice of species, and the regarding of orchids as 'status symbols' originates from this area around the early 1700s. *Neofinetia falcata* was known as 'an orchid of wealth and nobility', a connotation for which many present growers of this delightful miniature species might yearn!

Much of this early research into tropical plants, including orchids, was carried out by physicians employed by trading companies. Churchmen and missionaries, sent to the newly colonized territories to 'spread the Gospel', were also fascinated by the flora of these warmer climates. Both groups—physicians and clergymen—would most likely have received at least a basic botanical education; and, possibly as much for their own pleasure as any other reason, many of them recorded by descriptive writing and drawing the plants indigenous to the region. Subsequently many of these works were published, although frequently only after a long interval, and they often formed the basis of much of our present knowledge of orchids. Obviously an infatuation with these kings and queens of the plant world is nothing new!

Above: In the 18th century, *Bletia verecunda* was the species that kindled interest in tropical orchids. Of Bahaman origin it was the first to flower under artificial conditions.

Right: As early as the 1500s, *Cypripedium acaule* was the first North American species to be recorded in literature. It is a terrestrial woodland plant often called the pink moccasin.

Experiments in cultivation

These valuable records had at least one catastrophic side-effect. As they were published and became distributed in the so-called civilized world of the period, ie Europe, these informative and often detailed reports stimulated interest in orchids, and before the end of the eighteenth century several attempts were made to cultivate tropical orchids in many northern European countries. It is reported that the plant we now know as *Brassavola nodosa* (although at that time most epiphytic orchids were classified as *Epidendrum,* thus *Epidendrum nodosum*) was the first tropical orchid to be cultivated in Europe, allegedly growing in Holland in the late seventeenth century. The Bahaman species *Bletia verecunda* was the first tropical orchid introduced into England, in 1731. But before this time, a plant believed to be the North American terrestrial species *Cypripedium acaule,* was described in 1640 by John Parkinson in his *Theatricum Botanicum.*

The *Bletia verecunda* was imported as a dried specimen, but the desiccated tubers that formed the rootstock were taken to the garden of a Sir Charles Wager. Here they were overwintered in a hothouse, mulched in a bed of tan-bark and sawdust, and during the next spring vegetative growth commenced, to be followed by flowers in the summer of 1732

CYPRIPEDIUM ACAULE.
L. PRANG & COMPANY, BOSTON.

—the first tropical orchid to flower in England.

More orchids followed, and by 1789 there were 15 exotic orchid species growing at the Royal Botanic Gardens, Kew. As much of the international trade of the early nineteenth century passed through the Port of Liverpool, it was logical that this city would become a centre of botanical interest—a position retained to this present day. The Liverpool Botanic Garden received the first species of the cattleya tribe known in cultivation; but although the plant flowered annually after its importation from Brazil in 1810, it was not described until nine years later, as *Epidendrum violaceum,* by Messrs Loddiges of Hackney, who had begun commercial orchid cultivation in 1812.

Above: John Lindley (1795-1865), the 'father of modern orchidology'.

Orchidomania

As with many major events in history, the most significant frequently occur by accident. So it was with the 'orchidomania' that was to sweep Europe, and subsequently the United States, during the next 100 years. A consignment of tropical plants was being despatched to England by a Mr William Swainson who, to protect them, packed round them some other tropical plants bearing strong 'stems' and tough foliage. At least some of this consignment reached a Mr William Cattley, of Barnet, a keen cultivator of tropical plants and one of the first amateur orchid growers. Cattley was obviously intrigued by this 'packing material' and succeeded in growing some of them, the first of which flowered in November 1818. The large flowers with their flamboyant trumpet-shaped lip created a sensation, as nothing similar had been seen before in cultivation.

Dr John Lindley, who became known as 'the father of modern orchidology', described the plant, naming the genus in honour of Cattley (*Cattleya*) and, as the lip was the most outstanding segment of the flower, the specific epithet *labiata* (from the Latin *labium*, meaning lip).

The first collections

The exact locations from whence *Cattleya labiata* was collected were not known, until its rediscovery on a mountain near Rio de Janeiro, in 1836. Even at that time, its discoverer, Dr Gardner, recorded that local farmers were burning the trees for charcoal, and thus destroying the orchids. Several other locations were discovered, and wealthy people, together with some commercial nurserymen, sent collectors into the forests to 'collect every available plant'. This action, together with increasing charcoal burning by local farmers, resulted in very serious depletion of all cattleyas in Brazil.

But everyone who saw the plants was fascinated by them, and those wealthy enough were determined to possess as many as were available. Orchid growing became a fashionable status symbol among the wealthy nobility, each stately home vying with others to possess the largest collection of orchids.

One of the first, and probably one of the finest and largest of all time, was started by the sixth Duke of Devonshire in 1833. A man of incredible wealth and extravagance, William George Spencer Cavendish lavished vast amounts of money on his new 'hobby'. Under the supervision of his head gardener, Joseph Paxton, a conservatory 91m (300ft) long, 18m (60ft high) and covering nearly an acre of garden was erected at Chatsworth House. By sending his own gardener, John Gibson, to collect orchids from Assam and elsewhere, and by sponsoring other collectors, within a decade the largest orchid collection in the world was amassed at Chatsworth.

Above: The Colombian epiphytic orchid *Cattleya warscewiczii* grows high up and exposed on branches of tall forest trees.

The orchid hunters

Elsewhere, the demand for all orchids increased, and to satisfy these whims a new breed of professional orchid hunter emerged. Many of the collectors had until this time been 'hobbyists', sending comparatively small consignments of orchids to Europe whilst simultaneously following their trade as merchants, or local agents for European-based companies. But as the mania to possess new orchids swept Europe, particularly England, these amateur collectors were ousted by the professionals who, as the financial gains increased, became both ruthless and cunning. Some of these would-be collectors started out into the jungles of the world with little more than great expectations—and were never heard of again.

Knowledge of the conditions likely to be encountered during a collecting trip was scant; in places the forest was almost inpenetrable, the local inhabitants frequently somewhat less than friendly towards intruders; tropical diseases, insects and often fierce animals had not been encountered before, and most early collectors were totally unprepared for the seasonal flooding. Thus the need was for physically strong men, with sufficient intelligence to organize the collecting and safe despatch of enormous quantities of orchids back to Europe.

One of the earliest English collectors was Joseph Banks, born in London in 1743, the son of a wealthy landowner. After a poor academic start at Harrow and Eton, his interest in plants was aroused and whilst still at school he started a herbarium, going on to Oxford, where he studied botany under a private tutor. Banks' first expedition to Newfoundland in 1766 became a disaster when most of the specimens he collected were thrown overboard during the return voyage, to prevent the ship sinking. Determined that subsequent journeys should not prove so futile, Banks spent £10,000 from his personal fortune in equipping the 1768 Royal Society expedition to the South Seas, an expedition of which he has been appointed Director at the age of 25 years. This journey was to last over three years, and although the areas visited

Above: Joseph Banks (1743-1820), explorer and naturalist.

—including what was then the unknown territory of Australia—yielded a rich reward in botanical specimens, it was not until 1780 that Banks brought back the first orchids of that region.

For his services to horticulture, Joseph Banks received a baronetcy in 1781. He remained active in horticulture, especially orchidology, helping to formulate the Royal Horticultural Society in 1804. He was also Director of Kew Gardens at its inception, under George III, in the middle 1770s, and was President of the Royal Society from 1778 until his death in 1820. A remarkable man, Sir Joseph Banks is commemorated in the specific epithet of many plants; subsequent collectors were not to surpass him either for the quality and organization of his many expeditions or for the rich variety of plants he introduced into cultivation.

Despite elaborate planning, several of these collectors perished in jungles around the world, often pushed beyond the levels of endurance by ruthless employers and/or the hopes of large financial reward.

The successful were immortalized in the names of the new orchids they discovered: *Miltonia warscewiczii* and *Cattleya warscewiczii* are just two of many species honouring their collector, Joseph Warscewicz, a Lithuanian of Polish descent, who made several expeditions into Central and South America during the period 1840 to 1850. Also from South America, Gustave Wallis collected *Epidendrum wallisii, Masdevallia wallisii* and many other species new to cultivation, before dying of fever and dysentry whilst collecting in Ecuador in 1878.

If Sir Joseph Banks and others collected orchids for botanical purposes, it became apparent to many commercial nurseries during the 1830s that there was a good chance of high profits in supplying the ever increasing demand for new orchid species. James Veitch and Son, nurserymen of Exeter, in south-west England, became one of the first commercial horticulturalists to employ collectors, sending Thomas Lobb to Java in 1843, India in 1848 and subsequently to the Philippines to collect orchids 'for the said James Veitch and Son, and for no other person.' Lobb was a discriminating collector, selecting only the best plants worthy of cultivation, among them two varieties of *Aerides multiflorum—lobbii* and *veitchii*—that commemorate both collector and sponsor.

Above: *Epidendrum wallisii* has strong honey and musk smelling flowers. It is a leafy and hirsute species with no pseudobulbs.

Unfortunately, subsequent collectors were somewhat less concerned with the future, and enormous tracts of jungle were felled in order to gain the orchid treasures growing on the tops of the trees. Regular consignments of 10,000 plants of a single species were being sent to England and elsewhere, and reports sent in by the collectors indicated that every plant had been cleared and the felled trees burned, resulting in the extinction of any orchid plants that remained.

As more collectors were sent into the jungles, and the competition to gather plants increased, deliberately misleading

Above: James Veitch (1792-1863) was the first nurseryman to use his own orchid collectors.

reports were published in order to confuse the opposition. Even botanical collectors, jealous of their reputations, were not immune from this practice. Exact locations were not revealed and, when preparing duplicate dried specimens for distribution to different scientific institutions, each set was labelled as coming from a different area. The resulting confusion among botanists is still being sorted out.

Sale by auction

Orchid plants arriving in England were sold by auction, usually in London or Liverpool, when large quantities of species, many unobtainable today, changed hands frequently for many pounds each. Any species considered 'new' would command a much higher price—occasionally up to several hundred pounds—the wealthy purchaser hoping to have his name perpetuated in botanical nomenclature.

If these sums appear vast by values of 100 years ago, it is reported that the cost of maintaining one collector in the field in 1870 was as high as £3,000 a year. It is also reported that in 1894 Messrs Sanders, a large commercial establishment founded at St Albans, England, 20 years previously, had 20 collectors in various jungles throughout the world, many of whom spent up to 10 years in the search for a new species.

The spread of interest

Whilst this orchid fever was raging in England, interest was also developing in other parts of Europe and the United States. The first epiphytic orchids to reach the States were sent in 1838 to a Mr John Boott, of Massachusetts, from his brother James, who resided in London. By the middle nineteenth century, many more exotic orchids had arrived, and several notable collections are reported, mainly in the New England area. In 1865, the large orchid collection of a Mr Edward Rand was presented to Harvard University, and housed at the Cambridge Botanic Gardens. It could not have been envisaged then that this gift would be the first of many similar ones that would establish Harvard in the pre-eminent position it still retains in the orchid world today.

Above: *Aerides multiflorum.* The generic name *Aerides* means 'air-plant'; they were thought to obtain nourishment from the air.

Poor survival

Until the 1840s, most tropical orchids being sent to Europe were lowland species which, if they survived the long sea journeys, stood a reasonable chance of adapting to the hot airless conditions supplied for them by their new owners. Only the wealthy few could afford to heat the structures in which orchids were expected to thrive. As these often had high, solid walls and admitted very little light or fresh air, the newly imported plants were subjected to extremely high temperatures and humidity. One admirer of orchids allegedly stated that although he loved orchids he could 'not abide the stewpans in which one has to view them'! But all this was to change with the arrival of species from higher elevations. At first these too were placed on hotbeds in high humidity, conditions which proved disastrous, and the few specimens that survived the long sea journey soon perished in these 'graveyards of orchids'.

Jean Linden, a Belgian commercial grower who frequently collected in South America and is jointly credited—together with Karl Hartweg—with the discovery of *Odontoglossum crispum,* was among the early collectors of these cooler growing orchids that bloomed in regions where the temperature frequently fell to freezing

Right: *Odontoglossum crispum* is a South American species that is very variable in the wild. It has been much used for breeding.

point each morning. Remarking on the difficulties involved, he comments: 'Once collected, the orchids have to be brought down to the port of embarkation by roads which cannot be imagined by any who have not traversed them. At this time no steamboat has yet crossed the ocean, and the poor plants had to endure the sea-voyage at the bottom of the hold of a rough sailing vessel, after having waited, sometimes during more than a month, for a chance of carriage to a port near their destination. Packed like herring in a barrel, they were subjected to heat and fermentation, and few of them arrived alive.'

Fortunately, as more detailed environmental information became available and cultural techniques improved, a greater number of these cooler growing species survived both the journey and the rigours of greenhouse life. The lower expenses involved in growing these orchids resulted in their being grown by a wider public, although not extensively until well into the twentieth century.

Orchids for everyone

Attempts to encourage the less wealthy to become interested in orchid growing were made by several leading horticulturists. Around 1850, an article in Paxton's *Magazine of Botany* urged that all available species from the higher altitudes of Mexico and elsewhere be procured, so that more amateurs of limited means had the opportunity to cultivate orchids.

In a similar vein, and at the encouragement of Dr John Lindley, who had been the founding editor of the *Gardeners' Chronicle* since 1841, Benjamin S. Williams began a series of articles for that journal entitled 'Orchids for the Millions'. These articles met with immediate success, and became the basis for Williams' *The Orchid-Grower's Manual* which, in turn, proved so popular that it was reprinted seven times by 1894 , the final, seventh edition being revised and enlarged by Henry Williams, after the death of his father in 1890. Even today this book is considered one of the orchid growers' 'bibles', and it is of interest to note that the Introduction begins: 'The cultivation of Orchidaceous plants is no longer exclusively the privilege of the few . . . .' Thus the Williams', father and son, can be credited with starting the efforts to popularize orchids.

Even so, the feeling that orchids were not 'plants', in the accepted sense of the word, remained. The catalogue of William Bull, a New Plant Merchant of Chelsea, London, states on its front cover: 'A List of New, Rare and Beautiful Plants *and* Orchids'. The index of this 1898 catalogue lists most plants by species' names, but all orchid species—an impressive list of over 100 genera—are lumped together under 'Orchids: pp. 23-37'. Although this invidious comparison was almost certainly unintentional, it did nothing to improve the reputation of orchids in the minds of the uninitiated. Significantly, the five genera most strongly represented in this catalogue are *Cattleya* (150 different species and hybrids), *Cypripedium* (now *Paphiopedilum*) (160), *Masdevallia* (150), *Odontoglossum* (160) and *Oncidium* (90). All these genera remain popular today—although many of the species and early hybrids available in 1898 are no longer in cultivation—to be joined by *Cymbidium* (then represented by 17 species) and *Phalaenopsis* (12 species), both of which are among the top four in cut-flower cultivation today.

But the trend towards popularizing orchids for the 'middle classes' continued, aided and abetted by some of the more far-sighted nurserymen, who could see that the days of the Grand Estate Collections were numbered. Fortunately, as the numbers of orchid growers increased the development of orchid hybrids became greater, thus taking the strain off the remaining species growing in the jungles.

The emergence of hybrids

The knowledge of how to fertilize orchids had eluded growers for many years, and although there are unsubstantiated reports of orchid hybrids in the 1830s, it was not until a physician at the Devon and Exeter Hospital, Dr John Harris, suggested the correct method to the grower at the Veitch nursery, John Dominy, that the first manmade orchid hybrids were raised. The first seedlings germinated were of the genus *Cattleya,* but a hybrid between *Calanthe furcata* and *Calanthe masuca* made by Dominy in 1853 was the first orchid hybrid to flower—at the Veitch nursery in 1856. Undoubtedly there were many natural hybrids before this time, a question which Dr John Lindley posed in the *Gardener's Chronicle* of January 2, 1859. However, this first manmade hybrid was named in honour of the hybridizer; thus *Calanthe* Dominyi started a trickle of orchid hybrids.

Thereafter producing seed capsules became a simple process, but successful germination was still proving difficult. In the wild, orchid seed germinates in close association (symbiosis) with a particular type of fungi (mycorrhizal fungi), and early orchid hybridizers attempted to simulate these conditions by sowing the minute, dust-like orchid seed onto the surface of the 'mother' plant. Some seed germinated but the majority was lost in the normal processes of cultivation,

Right: *Calanthe* Dominyi was the first orchid hybrid produced artificially. Solving the technical problems led to a rush of breeding.

Above: Hybridization techniques are continually improving and over 50,000 hybrids are now known. This *Sophrolaeliocattleya* is a recent example.

such as watering. Advances were made when French and German scientists proved that orchid seed would germinate in test-tubes on a chemical agar solution infected with the mycorrhizal fungus. But it was not until 1922, when a plant physiologist at Cornell University, USA, Dr Lewis Knudson, proved that the presence of fungi was not necessary, that the asymbiotic production of orchid seedlings became possible. The formulae, used continuously since that time to produce millions of orchid plants, became known as Knudson Formulae; they consist of various chemicals combined with cane-sugar or glucose, agar and water.

Knudson's research turned the trickle of orchid hybrids into a flood, and by the late 1930s *The Orchid Review* was publishing the names of several hundred new orchid hybrids each year. Luckily it was considered essential from the start that exact records be kept. From 1871 the *Gardener's Chronicle* published new hybrids, and in 1895 an Englishman living in California, Mr George Hansen, published *The Orchid Hybrids,* and included detailed information relevant to orchid hybrids known at that time. This was followed in 1909 by the *Orchid Stud Book,* published by Hurst and Rolfe, which has become a pattern for subsequent publications. By far the most comprehensive listing of orchid hybrids was begun in 1901 when Frederick K. Sander produced his first *Orchid Guide,* various editions of which appeared at increasingly short intervals as orchid hybridizing accelerated, until in 1946 all the hybrids were listed in *Sander's List of Orchid Hybrids.* This invaluable volume has subsequently been joined by three addenda, and the onerous task of registering and collating these hybrid names, which until 1961 was diligently undertaken by the Sander family, is now completed by the Royal Horticultural Society as the International Registrar of Orchid Hybrids.

Thus the orchid family has the most complete and detailed stud book of any botanical group, with the 50,000 or more hybrids existing at the present time listed in an orderly fashion and regulated in order that *all* the progeny of any two parents must bear the same group name.

WHERE TO GROW ORCHIDS

Excellent though *The Orchid Grower's Manual* undoubtedly is, it was written at a time when the idea of most people growing orchids in a small greenhouse situated in their backyard was unthinkable. However, times of relative peace and prosperity enable man's energies and ideas to be at least partially diverted to non-essential activities; thus the Victorian era from the middle nineteenth century onwards witnessed the beginnings of orchid growing in places other than the stately homes. As the wealth of the country began to filter slowly through to a greater number of people, the more skilled workers moved into managerial positions and the middle classes emerged.

This social revolution was reflected in the rows of Victorian 'pseudovillas' that still line many of the streets in the suburbs of British major cities. The more ornate the building, and the larger the garden that surrounded it, the greater the status of its owner/occupier. But to join the élite of these *nouveau-riche,* it was essential that a conservatory be attached to the villa. Following through the desire to emulate the nobility, what better plants to grow in these conservatories than the symbols of wealth and position—orchids.

Greenhouses

These early hobbyists—probably the first orchidists to actually *grow* their own plants—were genuinely encouraged by the writers and commercial growers of the day. In addition to writing numerous articles in horticultural journals extolling the virtues of orchids for everyone, B. S. Williams in his *Orchid Grower's Manual* begins the chapter on orchid houses: 'It is not absolutely necessary to build a house for the cultivation of Orchids'. Such advice still holds good despite the century that has elapsed since it was written. One thing that has changed, however, is the size of greenhouse recommended. In the 1890s the largest span-roof house 'should not be more than ten or eleven feet high in the centre, seventeen or eighteen feet wide, and about a hundred feet long', whilst an ideal size is suggested as 13.7-15.25m (45-50ft) long by 5-5.5m (17-18ft) wide and 3-3.7m (10-12ft) to the ridge! If these dimensions seem excessive by modern standards, they do embody at least one basic fact common to most greenhouse owners: when planning the size of your greenhouse, add at least 50 percent to the overall area upon which you eventually decide. Anyone who has owned and successfully used a greenhouse for a few years will immediately identify with this advice.

There are probably almost as many different designs of structure in which orchids may successfully be grown, as there are growers. Obviously many 'experts' will hold strong views on what they consider to be the ideal greenhouse

Above: This late Victorian greenhouse is still used today for orchid growing. The larger panes of glass and the angled roof line admit more light than earlier types.

Left: Early Victorian conservatories were rarely suitable for the successful cultivation of plants since they admitted little light or air.

for specific orchids, but it is a proven fact that most orchids will grow perfectly well in widely differing accommodation. There are, however, various alternatives that the potential greenhouse owner should consider, and several guidelines that may help in making the best possible decision.

Having suggested that orchids *will* grow in any greenhouse, there is a minimum recommended size of not less than 9.3m^2 (100sq ft) floor area; ie 2.4 x 3.7m (8 x 12ft) or, preferably 3 x 3m (10 x 10ft). Quite apart from the certainty that your orchid hobby will very quickly outgrow anything smaller in area, it is always more difficult to grow orchids—or any other plant—satisfactorily in, say, the 1.8 x 1.8m (6 x 6ft) size greenhouse frequently offered in the popular press.

Temperature fluctuation problems are increased greatly as the greenhouse size diminishes, and it will be almost impossible to contain the excessively high summer temperatures that characterize the typical small greenhouse. Additionally, the small volume retains less natural heat than its larger counterpart, which is important where artificial heating is necessary during the months of winter.

Another consideration is the plant growing area to path ratio: in our 1.8 x 1.8m up to 40 percent of the total floor area could be taken up by a centre path, essential for access in any greenhouse. Increase the width of the greenhouse to 2.4 m, or preferably 3m, and the percentage of path area is probably reduced to between 25 to 30 percent.

In deciding on the size of a new greenhouse, two things are most important: the most convenient size for the site allocated, bearing in mind the desirability of access to all sides of the structure (except in the case of a lean-to); and as large as can be afforded at the time. Also choose a model in which the manufacturer supplies lengthwise extensions available for future expansion.

As most greenhouses are highest along the central ridge, the centre position is the most convenient place to grow the taller plants. But how do you achieve this when most standard greenhouses available to the amateur have a path running longitudinally down the middle? The most satisfactory solution is to increase the greenhouse width to 3.7-4 .3m (12-14 ft), so that both the sides and middle of the area can be used for plant growing, with a narrow—but not less than 69cm (2ft 3in) path separating each area. This system cannot work, however, if the height to eaves is less than 1.5m (5ft) as this would leave insufficient headroom over the path.

However, this recommended width does not mean the overall structure must become vast. The length of the greenhouse need not be more than twice its width, indeed it is positively advantageous to have the shape as near square as possible. By increasing a greenhouse of 3.7 x 4.3m (16m^2; 112sq ft) to a structure of 4.3 x 4.3m (18.2m^2; 196sq ft), you will be using the available space to maximum capacity. The centre staging of approximately 1.8m in width will facilitate the growing of those tall plants, and solve the problem of housing the lengthy flower spikes of oncidiums and other genera. Doubling the size does not automatically double the heating costs, in fact they will be increased only by about 30 to 40 percent, thus reducing considerably the heat costs per plant.

Building your own greenhouse

There are, regrettably, only a very limited number of greenhouse manufacturers who offer square-shaped structures as standard. Some will be able to supply a greenhouse made specifically to the buyer's requirements, but these are usually manufacturers of higher quality models, which are considerably more expensive—even though the product will be of more sturdy construction and will give a lifetime's

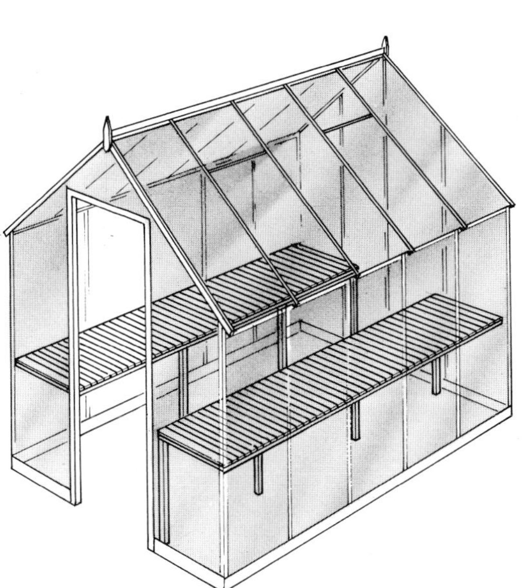

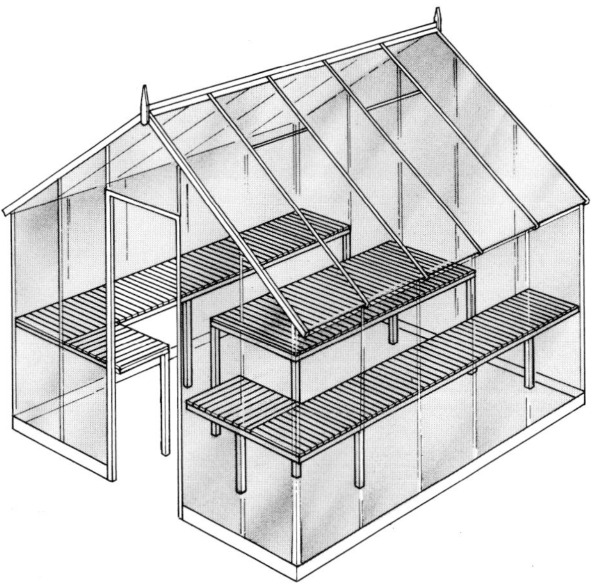

Left: The standard small greenhouse normally has staging either side of a central path. By slightly increasing the width of the house, it is possible to incorporate a centre staging. This will give you a larger growing area, allowing maximum use of the greenhouse height for the taller-growing orchids, such as vandas. Alternatively, you can use the space for an additional high-level shelf. The two paths also give easier access to all the staging areas, which is particularly useful for watering.

satisfactory use. The answer is probably to build the greenhouse yourself. This is not as difficult as it may seem, and certainly not beyond the capabilities of the average handyman; indeed many greenhouses being used by amateur and professional/commercial orchid growers were built by unskilled or semiskilled labour. Some greenhouse manufacturers will, in fact, supply all the parts necessary, and most larger timber merchants have available—or can produce to order—all the required shapes and lengths of timber.

So far we have spoken only of wooden constructions, a prejudice stemming from many years of successful orchid growing in this type of greenhouse. There have for some time been disagreements about which type is best, a situation carefully monitored by the manufacturers in their efforts to satisfy public demand. These efforts have resulted in the two styles coming more closely together, and the production of clips and springs for use in metal greenhouses in order to fix hooks and shelves and to hold the insulation material (usually polyethylene) in place during winter months.

In choosing materials, the advantages and disadvantages of the different metals or woods should be assessed in the individual situation. The only accepted generalization is that a low initial purchase price probably means higher maintenance costs. For most orchid lovers, valuable time spent on needless running chores could probably be spent more productively on growing the plants. Thus it makes sense to avoid any greenhouse where rust and corrosion are likely to be rapid; therefore aluminium framework is recommended where a metal greenhouse is preferred. Where a wooden construction is chosen, cedar has become the modern equivalent of teak, and has the advantage that little or no maintenance is required; whereas deal or other soft woods require regular painting to maintain the timber in reasonable condition.

Another subject that evokes considerable discussion is the amount of glass required. Until 1950 solid walls right up to the eaves, with merely a glass roof were frequently recommended for orchid houses. But as orchid plants have come to be grown by a multitude of people as part of their collection of plants, the somewhat overprecise requirements thought to be essential for orchid culture were compromised in order to satisfy the majority. It is now generally accepted that ample light from all directions is desirable when growing orchids, and most greenhouses have glazed walls down to the height of the staging. There is some argument in favour of a glass-to-ground structure, but the major disadvantage would be direct sun heat during summer months falling onto the plant pots and penetrating to the root system. However, certain genera, including *Cymbidium*, certainly grow well in a 'dutch-light' type of greenhouse,

which has sloping walls and large panes of glass; and glass-to-ground is essential where vertical staging begins at ground level.

Glazing materials

At present, several different glazing materials are available, ranging from polyethylene sheeting and fibre-glass to the conventional horticultural glass. Polyethylene sheeting is an excellent material, available in a wide range of sizes and thicknesses to satisfy every requirement, and some is available with a reinforcing galvanized wire-netting between two polyethylene skins which adds greatly to its strength. However, it is not a suitable material for a permanent greenhouse structure. Polyethylene is only translucent at the best of times, and exposure to the atmosphere with its great fluctuations in temperature will rapidly affect both the clarity and resilience of most of the 'plastic' materials that are often advertised as suitable for glazing.

Fibre-glass panels, also sold in a variety of sizes, are in their relative infancy as far as amateur orchid growers are concerned. But current developments in this area of glazing material should be beneficial as the newer types are claimed to be more resistant to weather. The advantages are low weight—thus a less sturdy greenhouse construction would suffice—diffuse light transmission and resistance to damage from hailstones or small tree branches. One word of warning: select only clear or white/yellow fibre-glass; apart from creating too much shade during dull winter months there is some thought that the light transmission through blue or green fibre-glass panels is not balanced correctly.

Another glazing material, so far little used, is an acrylic panel marketed as Plexiglas. This consists of double skin, clear acrylic sheets, each about 2.5mm (0.1in) thick, held apart and rigid by a network of 'ribs' of the same material. The finished product is about 1.3cm (0.5in) thick, flexible, yet tough, and available in a variety of sizes. The sealed air space between the two sheets results in excellent qualities of insulation and once the price becomes competitive with other glazing materials, Plexiglas should have much to recommend it.

Without doubt, glass is the best material with which to glaze the amateur's greenhouse. It is likely that plants arriving to join your collection will have been grown under glass in their previous 'home', thus one of the adjustments that a moved plant must necessarily make is minimized. Glass is impervious to weather, easy to clean and only becomes slightly brittle after many years' usage. Modern horticultural glass is now supplied in widths that permit the glazing bars to be widely spaced—up to 64cm (25in)—thus creating a building that will admit maximum light, especially important during winter. Variations include two types of plate glass, one of which is used extensively in Europe. This has a smooth surface on one side, while the outer surface is covered by small, regular, rippled protrusions which effectively diffuse the sun's rays, creating a gentle light within the greenhouse even during bright sunny days. The insulating qualities of this glass are far superior to conventional horticultural glass, keeping the greenhouse warmer in winter and—most important—cooler during summer.

A similar result could be obtained by using the more familiar 'wired' glass, in which a galvanized wire mesh is fixed between two layers of plate glass. This product is particularly useful in situations where people could be injured in the event of the glass breaking, as the central wire mesh adds greatly to its strength. This wired glass will, however, admit about the same amount of direct light as horticultural glass, thus shading will be needed during summer months. Despite two big disadvantages—initial cost and the additional weight—these two plate glass materials could be essential in certain locations.

Left. This half glass, half brick greenhouse is ideal for growing orchids. The box ventilators, paint-on shading and partially sunken walls all help to maintain even temperature inside.

Glazing materials	Advantages	Disadvantages	Comments
Horticultural glass	Strong, lightweight Good conductor		Most suitable for permanent structure
Rippled glass (Diffuse light)	Very strong	Heavy, Expensive	
Wired glass	Strong	Heavy, Expensive	Suitable for areas particularly at risk of being broken
Polyethylene sheeting	Inexpensive to buy	Short life—becomes opaque	Not suitable for permanent structure
Plexiglas	Lightweight Good conductor	Expensive	Becoming popular Good if you can afford it
Full glazing (Glass-to-ground greenhouse)	Increased light and heat to greenhouse in winter	Low insulative value Allows too much heat in summer Easily broken at ground level	Not suitable for most pot-grown plants
Half-glazing (part glass, part wood/brick greenhouse)	High insulation value and protection to pots Less fluctuation of temperature	May be difficult to construct 2-tier staging	Aesthetically pleasing Easier to Maintain optimum growing conditions for most plants

Above: All glazing materials have some faults, and by comparing the relative advantages and disadvantages of those available, you can decide on the best type for your situation.

Choosing a site

Often the choice of where to position the greenhouse is limited, and not helped by the ever diminishing size of gardens in modern homes. Before deciding, it would be wise to check with the local authority (City Council, County Council, etc) that planning consent is not required. Even when this consent is granted or automatic, there will almost certainly be regulations governing the minimum distance a greenhouse must be from a dwelling house. Thus it makes sense to be on the right side of the law before you start.

Even in a small garden, there are probably several possible locations, and all considerations should be taken into account. A greenhouse is seldom a thing of beauty so unless the view from your window is particularly gloomy, be careful that the new building does not dominate the scene. As with all horticulture, aesthetic considerations are of prime importance in choice of site and greenhouse. Whereas a modern setting with clean architectural lines may lend itself well to an aluminium or white painted greenhouse that same greenhouse in the garden of a half-timbered country cottage or Tudor-style house, would offend the eye. These rustic settings call for a teak or cedar wood construction that is allowed to take on a natural, weathered appearance and thus mellow into its surroundings.

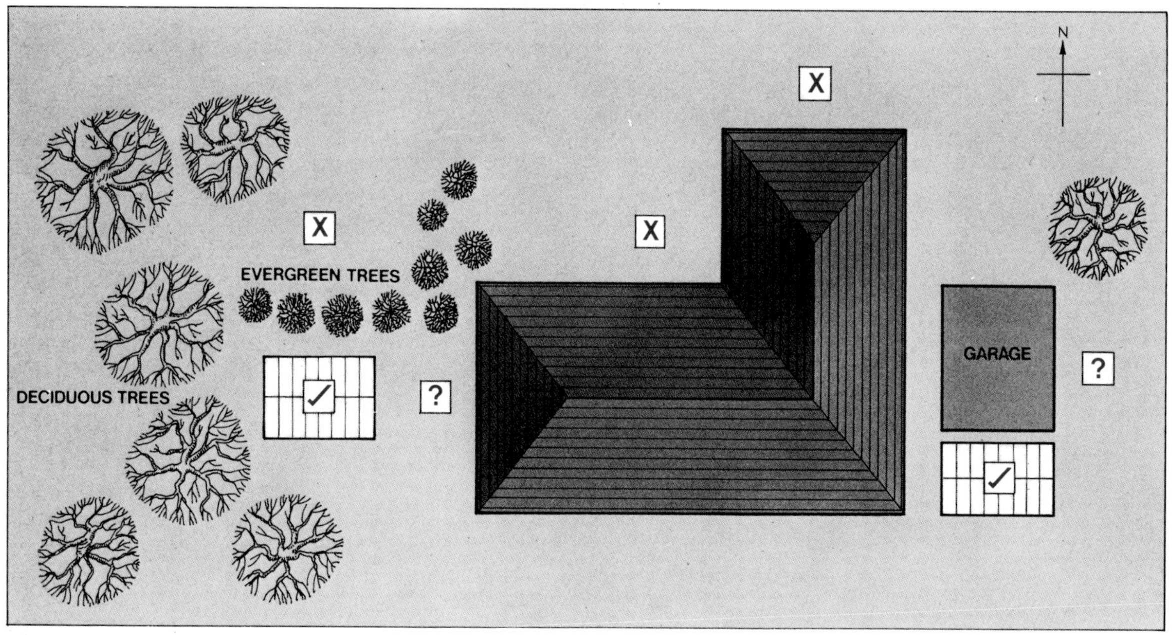

Left: Although no site is totally unsuitable for an orchid greenhouse, the ideal position will receive maximum light, especially in winter, be open to good air movement, yet be sheltered from prevailing winds.

☒ Areas of permanent shade should be avoided

? Sites too near buildings will lose winter light

☑ Open sites sheltered from prevailing winds are perfect.

The ideal site

Aesthetic considerations apart, the ideal site has several requirements. Winter light is probably the major limiting factor to successful growth; therefore, an open position not shaded by adjacent buildings or evergreen trees should be chosen. Deciduous trees will not obstruct much light during winter, and any shade offered by them when in leaf will probably be more than welcome. Again, maximum winter light in the greenhouse means lower heating bills, so your longest side should face south. If your garden is on a sloping site, then choose the highest available position for your greenhouse. Cold air always sinks, thus the bottom of any valley will always be several degrees cooler than halfway up the slope.

Another limiting factor on the greenhouse site will be the availability of mains (electric) services. Even if your initial requirements are modest, before long you may desire some degree of automation which could be dependent upon a supply of electricity. Few small greenhouses have facilities to store more than a few weeks supply of water, therefore the provision of water—preferably by underground, weatherproof piping—could be considered essential. Also if the greenhouse is near to the house or garage, it may be feasible to extend the domestic central heating system into the greenhouse. This would offer you the best possible supply of heat—hot water pipes or radiators—at low cost.

Orchid adaptability

If there is only one possible site for a greenhouse in your garden, then almost certainly this will suffice. Obviously the culture of any plant is more straightforward where the environment is perfect, but orchids are remarkably adaptable and, given even reasonable conditions, they will thrive. The author has grown orchids most successfully in a north-facing, three-quarter span greenhouse

Above: Given the right conditions, *Cypripedium reginae* will thrive in gardens.

Left: In many tropical areas, vandaceous orchids are grown commercially in large open beds.

Below: Hybrid miltonias grow well outside in warm climates. They also make good pot plants.

situated in a garden in the Thames Valley—a notoriously gloomy area during winter months. From late summer until middle spring, no greenhouse shading was necessary as the sun's rays touched only the very top of the greenhouse for about two months in mid-winter. Yet by adapting cultural methods and treating plants as individuals with specific likes and dislikes, it became possible to bring into flower a very mixed group of orchids, including the sun-loving vandas and dendrobiums.

Although obviously some sites are more advantageous than others, it is unlikely that any site is totally unsuitable for your greenhouse. Indeed, so adaptable have orchids proved during recent years, that they are fast becoming *the* houseplant, spending their entire lives beyond the seedling stage outside the confines of a greenhouse. Before discussing the various items of equipment and 'gadgets' that are available for today's greenhouse gardener, it is pertinent to consider areas other than the greenhouse where orchids can be grown successfully.

Orchids in the garden

Orchids will grow and flower in very diverse surroundings, and there are many suitable for growing in gardens, in both warm and cool climates.

Warm climates

If you are sufficiently fortunate to live in semitropical or warmer areas of the world, there are many exotic orchids that will lend themselves admirably to being treated as hardy garden plants. Possibly the most dramatic examples are the vandaceous intergeneric orchids that were transported from Southeast Asia (where the species occur naturally and where all the early hybridizing in vandaceous orchids took place during the 1920s and 1930s) to the West Indies and Hawaii. So successful are the culture and breeding of these vandas and allied genera in their new homes, that the commercial cut-flower industry and breeding of quality stud plants in these countries—particularly Hawaii—nearly rival those of Singapore and other Southeast Asian countries. Yet it probably originated as a result of the Fourth World Orchid Conference held in Singapore in 1963. Although some vandas had been growing in the West Indies for more than a century, it was not until visitors from these islands to the Singapore Conference realized that the two climates were not so different, and were inspired by the plants at the Conference Show, that the industry 'took off'. By studying the superb culture in Singapore and Bangkok, it became possible for people living in similar climatic zones elsewhere in the world to be equally successful—another example of the orchid's adaptability. Today there are commercial and amateur growers in these tropical areas using exotic orchids as bedding plants in the open garden!

Cool climates

Even those temperate areas of the world where frost conditions, often severe, are normal occurrences for at least six months of every year, have their own hardy orchid flora. These are genera of terrestrial, tuberous-rooted orchids, which are completely deciduous during the cold weather. Such orchids grow rapidly with the onset of spring, and generally flower from late spring to mid-summer. Despite the hardiness of these orchids and the quiet charm of their comparatively small flowers, do not be fooled into thinking they will make ideal plants for the woodland garden. All orchid species throughout the civilized world are now protected plants, and it is illegal to remove any part of the plants from their natural environment. Quite apart from this legal consideration aimed at the conservation of dwindling natural resources, the mycorrhizal fungal associations that exist with many, if not all, of the temperate terrestrial orchids will almost certainly prevent the re-establishment of the plant once it is disturbed from its natural habitat.

Certain genera, however, available from commercial suppliers, have proved good garden plants in the northern hemisphere. Whether these plants—notably cypripediums—are nursery raised or collected under licence is uncertain, but for those gardeners willing to provide the fairly precise conditions needed for their successful culture, the genus *Cypripedium* can offer some spectacularly different flowers for the garden. This genus of hardy and half-hardy orchids should not be confused with the popular commercial cut-flower *Paphiopedilum* that at various times in its history has been included under *Cypripedium* (the 'Cyps' of the older gardeners and nurserymen).

The true cypripediums thrive in humus-rich, retentive soil. Often a coniferous leaf-soil has proved satisfactory, but whichever type of soil is used, it should never become waterlogged or allowed to dry out. Ordinary garden soil should be improved by the addition of peat moss and decayed leaves, forked in to a depth of at least 25-30cm (10-12in). The dormant tubers should be planted about 5cm (2in) deep in this prepared mixture, and any fibrous roots spread out horizontally. A position in partial shade towards the back of a shrub or conifer border would be ideal for most species, although *Cypripedium cordigerum* from India, or *Cyp. reginae*—the state flower of Minnesota—will thrive in full sun provided the soil and root system are kept cool and moist, ie similar conditions to those recommended for clematis.

Although most cypripediums like a slightly acid soil, the European species *Cyp. calceolus* requires a calcareous mixture, which may be achieved by the addition of limestone chips in the top 7.5-10cm (3-4in) of soil. Two species that have proved more tolerant of slightly less-than-perfect conditions are *Cyp. pubescens* and *Cyp. parviflorum*, both widespread in Canada and the United States. Newcomers to growing terrestrial orchids outside in temperate areas are recommended to gain experience with these two 'slipper' species, before progressing to the remaining 12 or 15 *Cypripedium* species, which could prove more difficult.

Cold frames

A link between the open garden and heated greenhouse could be provided by a cold frame or greenhouse in which there is no provision of artificial heat. These locations are particularly useful for growing plants that are not 100 percent hardy, most of which appreciate the protection from winter rains although they can tolerate subzero temperatures. Loosely grouped under 'alpines', these are plants that in their natural habitats enjoy a cold, dry resting period each winter. Several orchids come into this category, notably species from high elevations approaching the snow line in their countries of origin. None is more spectacularly successful for cold-frame culture than the genus *Pleione*, orchids which range from the Himalayas across Burma, Thailand, China and into Taiwan. Of dwarf habit and forming clusters of circular or flagon-shaped pseudobulbs, the long pleated, solitary leaf is deciduous and, in most species, the comparatively large flowers—not unlike small cattleya blooms—appear concurrently with the new growth each spring.

They thrive in shallow pans or similar containers, and should be repotted into a compost that is very free draining, yet retentive, each year as growth commences during late winter. The discarded one-year-old compost from paphiopedilums has proved a perfect growing medium for pleiones, as the shredded pine bark/charcoal mixture is slightly decomposed and has become a little acidic. Although these beautiful orchids are now gaining in popularity, they have been largely ignored by the professional/commercial orchid élite, who often sneeringly refer to them as 'windowsill orchids'.

Orchids indoors

The more enlightened commercial growers have at long last recognized that many orchids will grow very happily on the windowsill, and are encouraging the development started by amateur gardeners in mainland Europe, especially Germany and Scandinavia, and the United States.

Right: Orchids grown in a trough or basket will effectively decorate a sun lounge. Moisture-retentive material within the basket will provide sufficient humidity.

Below: In warmer climates many orchids can be grown outside in the shelter of a porch. Providing they receive sufficient light, they will give a beautiful display.

The 'explosion' in the building of high-rise apartment blocks since the 1950s has meant that many plant lovers are no longer able to cultivate a garden. Instead, they have diverted their efforts and resources into growing plants inside their homes— something that can be achieved without the burden of additional heating costs. During the past 20 years, the increase in the number of 'house plants' produced and sold by an ever-expanding industry has been astronomical. Of the millions of plants produced annually, only a very few are orchids. Yet few plants can rival the orchid for longevity, and the flowers—which in the right conditions could appear more often than once a year— often last 8 to 10 weeks on the plant and a further few weeks as cut flowers.

Windowsill orchids

Depending upon the aspect of the windowsill, there is an orchid to suit every location. In general terms, the plants will thrive best on an east or west-facing windowsill during the spring-to-autumn period, moving to one with a southern aspect (or northern aspect in the southern hemisphere) for the duller days of winter. A narrow windowsill can be widened by the addition of a suitable piece of timber, fixed in front of the window by wall brackets. If you are able to increase the sill to a minimum depth of about 30-38cm (12-15in), there are polypropylene gravel trays available from most hardware and garden stores that will conveniently fit the area. Approximately 2.5cm (1in) of water-retentive aggregate, such as Lytag or perlite, should be placed in the bottom of the gravel tray, and the plant pots placed on top. To maintain reasonable humidity, this gravel tray should be kept perpetually moist, *but not waterlogged.*

With only sufficient space for perhaps 20 to 25 plants, windowsill growers should be especially selective in the type of orchid they acquire. In the average home, maintained at comfortable temperatures, cool-growing orchids are unlikely to flower well. Instead, a windowsill offers the opportunity to grow the warmth-loving genera that would not flourish in the cool greenhouse. But select only those plants of compact growth habit and a tidy root system. Two genera that immediately come to mind are *Paphiopedilum* and *Phalaenopsis,* with a probable third in *Cattleya*—particularly the modern bigeneric hybrids with *Sophronitis* and *Laelia,* that give a smaller growing plant with a larger flower-to-plant ratio.

Sun lounges and garden rooms

As your hobby develops and the windowsills around the house become full of orchids, it is possible to move into a sun-lounge or even a glazed porch area. Although some additional heating will almost certainly be necessary, not much is required as warmth will be 'borrowed' from the house. Many sun lounges or garden rooms will already by equipped with a radiator, but ensure that the time-switch (where fitted) does not turn off the boiler during the middle of the night as this is obviously the critical time for warmth where plants are concerned. If this situation exists, a thermostatically controlled fan heater could be left running to maintain nocturnal temperatures at a preset level.

Although it may be aesthetically pleasing to have orchid plants dotted around a summer house, sun lounge or garden room, on tables or placed on shelves, this is impractical from a cultural standpoint. Unless plants are grouped into some limited area, it becomes difficult to water and/or spray them. After a hot summer's day, when a light overhead spray during the early evening is beneficial to the orchids, it will be impossible to 'freshen-up' the plants without damping any furnishings that may be present! Far better to restrict the orchids to a prescribed area where their cultural requirements can best be supplied. The all-important microclimate around the plants will also be more easily established where a number of orchids are grown together in close proximity. This does not preclude the temporary removal of an orchid in flower into the living room for decorative purposes. But if any plant remains indoors for longer than a few days, it would be beneficial to arrange some form of humidity supply—similar to that described for windowsill cultivation.

The cultural requirements of orchids grown in a sun lounge or similar area are not dissimilar to those of greenhouse culture (see pages 64-85).

Orchids under artificial light

For owners of homes where it is impossible or undesirable to have a greenhouse or indoor area supplied with natural light, orchids are once more proving their adaptability by growing and flowering completely under artificial light. Far from this being a handicap to culture, results are often superior to 'normal', as the grower is able to control both the intensity and duration of the light. Here again there is no hard and fast rule regarding day length, and different growers have been equally successful with varying regimes. By arranging for the lights to be on for 12 hours and off for six, it is possible to simulate 10 days in each normal week. But despite the excellent culture achieved

by some growers using this system, there is little evidence to suggest that the plants are fooled by this adjustment to the number and length of days, or that the results in flowering obtained are any better than those from plants grown under more conventional conditions.

What does seem possible with culture under lights is the virtual elimination of the dull, short winter's day. By maintaining the day length at 16 hours, with perhaps only slight seasonal adjustments, the plants respond by growing vigorously almost throughout the year. The more regular supply of light and warmth also means that the orchids can be watered and fertilized at summer levels, with the inevitable result of steady, year-round growth.

In most homes there are at least two or three areas that could be converted fairly easily into a 'growing room' suitable for orchids. Any recess or alcove, such as that formed by a staircase, would be ideal. Rather than hide all your 'rubbish' in the loft, you can put this area to good use at very little expense. Similarly, your basement or cellar, with its excellent insulative qualities, could be transformed into an Aladdin's cave by the addition of a modest collection of orchids.

The size of your indoor growing area will be dictated by the dimensions of the alcove or window recess, although most lofts and cellars will be larger than the space required. In these situations it will therefore be necessary to build a suitable 'room' in order to confine the orchid-growing activities to a predetermined area. As artificial heating will almost certainly be needed, the restricted space will also be less costly to maintain at correct temperatures.

Basic rules for under-lights growing apply to all three areas, but where these differ for one or more of the locations, this will obviously be mentioned.

Rule one is safety! To grow plants under artificial lights you need two ingredients that do not mix: water and electricity. Therefore, unless you are qualified, have an electrician install the wiring, ensuring that he knows that water will never be far away once the plants have moved in.

Water

Water will, of course, remain a problem when growing plants indoors, and it is essential to provide thorough and adequate facilities to drain off the surplus water. This will be most difficult in the loft, but it should be possible to arrange a drainage pipe out of the trough that forms the floor of your growing area. This drainage pipe could be linked with the bathroom overflow pipe, since although it *must* be available, it will not carry much water under normal operating conditions. Drainage in a cellar is usually installed when the house is built but, if not, a small soakaway will suffice.

If running only a small installation in an alcove or window recess off one of the living rooms, the base or floor area must be made waterproof. This can be achieved by building a wall from timber (10 x 7.5cm; 4 x 3in is suitable) round the perimeter of the floor area, and then lining the entire floor space with plastic

Above and Left: A garden room built on to the house makes a perfect winter home for orchids, which, in warmer areas, can stand outside during the growing season.

Right: Flourescent tubes arranged on an adjustable board will provide sufficient light to grow many orchids successfully in attic or cellar. Fans are essential to provide adequate ventilation.

sheeting to form a trough. When fitting the sluice, ensure that the surplus water can either drain safely through an outside wall or be drained into a suitable container which can then be emptied.

Another major cultural difference with indoor growing as opposed to culture in the greenhouse, is the amount of watering necessary. Generally speaking, lofts or cellars, with their more constant temperatures and comparative lack of ventilation, will maintain higher average (relative) humidity than most greenhouses. This means that the compost in the pots will remain moist for a longer period after watering. Indeed, many growers only water the pots occasionally, relying instead on a fairly heavy misting once or twice each day, depending upon day-to-day conditions.

To protect the fabric and furnishings of the house from the excess of moisture produced by spraying, the walls and roof of the growing areas should be lined. In a window recess, use polyethylene, as this will allow the natural light to reach the plants, and also reflect any artificial light used back onto the growing area. An alcove away from a window, or the area within either loft or cellar, should be lined with silver foil or painted white in order to make the interior surfaces reflective. Where the area concerned is comparatively small, such as the window recess or alcove, the front of the unit should be left open to prevent a build-up of excessive humidity around the plants.

Light

Many types of commercial light fittings are available, and most makes of fluorescent tube have proved satisfactory. Select a length of tube suited to the dimensions of your growing area, then attach the light fixtures to a stout piece of plywood or similar material, setting the fluorescent tubes approximately 7.5cm (3in) apart. This density of tubes will provide a light output of 2,000 foot candles about 5cm (2in) from the tubes, where plants with a high light requirement should be placed. Orchids satisfied with lower light conditions, eg paphiopedilums and—to a lesser extent—phalaenopsis, could be set at a slightly lower level (achieved by standing the light-loving plants on top of an inverted pot), or placed towards the perimeter of your shelves, where inevitably the intensity of light is lower.

Plants with similar light requirements should be grouped together, and the lights then suspended at the appropriate height above the plants. This is more easily achieved if the boards to which the light fixtures are attached are suspended on chains from the ceiling. By altering the length of the chains, the correct level will be achieved.

It is impossible to give hard and fast rules on subjects related to culture, as no two situations are identical. The important point to watch is that the light, water, temperature, nutriment and air movement are as near correctly balanced as possible. With certain reservations, when the temperature and light density are higher than normal, more food and water can with safety be applied to the orchids, which will respond by maintaining growth for most of the year.

ORCHIDS FOR INDOOR CULTIVATION

Windowsill	Growing case	Attic or Cellar
Brassolaeliocattleya Norman's Bay	Brassia verrucosa	Ada aurantiaca
Cattleya aurantiaca	Brassolaeliocattleya Norman's Bay	Aerides fieldingii
Cattleya bowringiana	Cattleya aurantiaca	Bifrenaria harrisoniae
Coelogyne cristata	Cattleya Bow Bells	Brassia verrucosa
Cymbidium devonianum	Dendrobium phalaenopsis	Calanthe vestita
Cymbidium Peter Pan	Epidendrum cochliatum	Cattleya Bow Bells
Cymbidium Touchstone	Paphiopedilum callosum	Chysis bractescens
Dendrobium nobile	Paphiopedilum fairieanum	Dendrobium phalaenopsis
Epidendrum cochliatum	Paphiopedilum Honey Gorse	Dendrochilum glumaceum
Laelia anceps	Paphiopedilum Silvara	Gomesa crispa
Maxillaria luteo-alba	Paphiopedilum Small World	Lycaste aromatica
Maxillaria tenuifolia	Phalaenopsis equestris	Masdevallia coccinea
Miltonia clowesii	Phalaenopsis lueddemanniana	Miltonia endresii
Odontoglossum grande	Phalaenopsis Party Dress	Odontoglossum crispum
Paphiopedilum callosum	Phalaenopsis sanderiana	Paphiopedilum Small World
Paphiopedilum fairieanum	Phalaenopsis Temple Cloud	Phalaenopsis equestris
Paphiopedilum Honey Gorse	Phalaenopsis Zada	Rhynchostylis gigantea
Paphiopedilum Silvara		Trichopilia suavis
Pleione formosana		Vanda coerulea
Vanda cristata		Zygopetalum intermedium

Above: Paphiopedilums and phalaenopsis are good subjects for permanent culture in a growing case.

Temperature

However, this increased temperature and light system must be kept within reason. Cool-growing orchids, such as cymbidiums, odontoglossums and most coelogynes, may make good vegetative growth under warmer conditions, but almost certainly will not flower. Likewise, the warm-growing types will not appreciate daytime temperatures of much above 24-27°C (75-81°F). The temperatures recommended for each genus or group of orchids when growing in a greenhouse apply equally to plants grown under artificial light conditions, the only major difference being that under lights, orchids enjoy almost perpetual summer.

Ventilation

In the early days of growing under lights—especially where the area was lined with polyethylene—many orchids grew too fast, with the result that leaves became soft and floppy, and were usually pale green in colour. This soft growth, especially in what was virtually a polyethylene tent, fell prone to numerous diseases, particularly botrytis and general rotting problems. It was considered that air movement would solve the latter fault, thus it became standard practice to install circulation fans. In the event, this vigorous air movement that caused leaves to almost snap in the breeze, also cured the unbalanced growth and dispersed excess

humidity. Circulation fans, running continuously, have proved to be more essential in a restricted environment, ie in a comparatively small area under lights, than in conventional greenhouse culture.

Although it may not be possible to ventilate in the true sense of the word whenever possible, fresh air should be admitted daily into the loft or cellar, either through a conveniently positioned window or by making a small vent hole through to the outside.

Supplementary heating
Provision should also be made in the loft or cellar for some form of heating, which may be necessary during winter nights. The domestic central heating boiler is often located in a basement or cellar, in which case it may even be necessary to lower the temperature at night by opening the window or ventilator. In unheated cellars or in lofts, a thermostatically controlled fan-heater is probably the best supplier of warmth, as the fan can be left running continuously to circulate the air, with the heating element only switching in when the thermostat calls for heat.

Above: This attractive Wardian growing case, with its automatic heating and lighting, doubles as a useful piece of furniture.

Where the orchids are growing in a recess or alcove off the living area, it is unlikely that supplementary heating will be needed. Although the floor size of the chosen recess may not be large, this need not restrict your orchid-growing activities. In the window recess of a New York apartment, over 400 orchids were once grown in an area only 91cm (3ft) deep, 106cm (3.5ft) wide and 2.4 m (8ft) high! These orchids were not all miniature types or 'botanicals', but included paphiopedilums, phalaenopsis, oncidiums, cattleyas and even vandas. The owner-designed-and-built unit contained five shelves, the light fittings for one shelf being fixed to the underside of the shelf immediately above it. Apart from space an obvious advantage of this type of unit is that each shelf may be given a different light intensity. However, the problems of growing plants in any restricted area are intensified where space is really limited, and it was found necessary to install two small fans on each shelf of the unit. It is also essential to ensure that the light fittings below each shelf are perfectly insulated from the water above—best achieved by fixing a lead sheet between the light fittings and the shelf to which these are screwed.

Growing cases
Modern homes and open-plan offices lend themselves very well to room dividers, which often take the form of a shelf unit or bamboo lattice panel. A more original method of defining boundaries within a large area could be achieved by the use of a growing case. These miniature indoor greenhouses—the modern counterpart to last century's Wardian case—are available in a great variety of sizes to suit any location. A typical case would be about 2m (6.5ft) high, 1.5-1.8m (5-6ft) long and approximately 61cm (2ft) wide. They are constructed either in traditional materials, using a wooden framework for the plate glass sides, or with stainless steel or aluminium frames to suit a modern setting. These cases usually stand on short legs, a waterproof tray being set into the base in order to prevent carpets being ruined by water. Several inches of moisture-retentive material should be placed in the bottom of this tray, and the orchids stood on this material. Other plants could be attached to a suitably positioned 'tree' mounted within the case to give a natural effect, and a few small foliage plants would complete the picture.

A heating cable is usually installed beneath the gravel tray, and lights recessed into the top panel of the case. As both heating and lighting are controlled automatically, it is possible to leave the orchids for many days without harm coming to them. Humidity within the case remains high, and ventilators are provided both in the base and the roof, thus creating a chimney effect which ensures good air movement. This type of growing may not satisfy the compulsive gardener, but it does enable orchid lovers with very limited time to have an aesthetically pleasing, albeit restricted collection. A growing case is also the perfect answer for flat dwellers, or handicapped people who may not be able to go into the garden. Most of the locations suggested as suitable areas for growing orchids will require similar cultural techniques. The same basic principles, adapted to suit each location, apply whether orchids are being grown on the windowsill or in the greenhouse. Success can be obtained under most conditions, and the next chapter should help prospective growers avoid some of the pitfalls.

BASIC EQUIPMENT AND TECHNIQUES

To make full and economic use of your greenhouse, it will be necessary to arrange the layout carefully so that all the different kinds of orchids in your collection receive the best possible environment. But there is more to layout than just the height of the staging, and whether or not shelves will be needed. Position of the heat source, and the various methods of heating available, number and position of ventilators, practical and efficient ways of supplying shade during summer months: these are just some of the questions to answer if the grower is to obtain maximum satisfaction from a greenhouse.

Equipment for a greenhouse falls into two different categories: basic necessities without which it will be difficult (though not impossible) to grow plants successfully, and extra equipment, or labour-saving gadgetry, that may either be installed when the greenhouse is erected, or introduced as the collection develops or circumstances change.

Heating systems

Heating a greenhouse is one of those topics that often evokes definite views, which are frequently based less on scientific knowledge of what is needed in terms of heat input, than on personal preferences. As always, it is best to consider the various options, and then decide which method is most suited to the particular situation.

The first priority required of a heating system is adequate heat output to maintain the desired temperature even when the outside temperature is below freezing point. At these times many heating systems will be unable to keep the greenhouse sufficiently warm, but providing such lapses are neither too severe nor occur too frequently, little harm will come to the plants.

Convenient methods of measuring heat include British Thermal Units, calories (4.2 BTUs per calorie) or watts (3.4 BTUs per watt), but to use three systems here will be needlessly complicated. Heat always flows from a high to a lower temperature, thus the warm air in a greenhouse will flow through the glass, brickwork and floor to the outside. The rate of flow depends upon the areas of each surface, the insulation properties of the various component materials and the difference in temperature. As it is generally accepted that the flow of heat through glass is twice the rate of flow through brickwork, it is immediately obvious that a glass-to-ground greenhouse will be more costly to heat than one with at least some brick walls.

If, for example, your greenhouse is the conventional 3.7 x 2.4m (12 x 8ft) size, with solid walls to 76cm (29in) in height, and the average required temperature 'lift' is 11°C (20°F) above that outside, the approximate heat input needed to replace the lost heat would be 7,000 BTUs per hour. This could be supplied by 2kw of electricity, so a 2.5-3kw fan-heater is required in order to have some margin of safety. Alternatively, about 10.3m (34ft) of 10cm (4in) hot water pipe heated to 55.5°C (100°F) hotter than the required air temperature would suffice. A portable oil-burning greenhouse heater would use approximately 300ml (0.5pt) of paraffin (kerosene) per hour to achieve a similar result.

Thermostatic control

A second priority is that the heating system must be thermostatically controlled in order to achieve maximum economy—there is little point in supplying artificial heat once there is sufficient sun heat or radiation to maintain the desired temperature. Also during the night when there is unlikely to be any manual control of the heating system, a thermostat will do the job. Any system that cannot be controlled automatically, will probably prove more costly to run despite the apparent lower costs per unit.

Although they are not cheap to install, thermostatically controlled valves are the most efficient method of controlling the flow of hot water, where this system is adopted. Likewise with electric heating systems. Do not be satisfied with the type of thermostat that is commonly used in

Left: This greenhouse is heated by hot water circulating in a system of cast iron pipes beneath the staging. The boiler is controlled by a thermostat positioned just above head height in the centre of the greenhouse.

Above: By building a greenhouse on the roof of a garden room or conservatory, it is possible to grow almost any orchid successfully, particularly the sun-loving types, such as vandas.

domestic central heating systems, or worse still the very small thermostats that are frequently built in to electric fan-heaters. The degree of tolerance with these types of small thermostats, especially after several years use, may be as great as + or − 3°C (5°F), an unnecessarily high margin of error. It would be preferable—and certainly more economical—to incorporate into the system a rod-type thermostat that has much finer settings.

Thermostats are generally positioned at between two-thirds and three-quarters of the greenhouse height, i.e. approximately 1.8m (6ft) high in the average 2.4m (8ft) height-to-ridge house. The position should be such that there is a good flow of air around the thermostat, which should not be directly affected either by the warm air rising from the heating system or the direct rays of the sun. To counteract this latter tendency, some rod-type thermostats are encased in a perforated sleeve through which a gentle flow of air is circulated. In this way the thermostat becomes more sensitive to the air temperature within the greenhouse, and the heating system is more responsive.

To ensure that preselected temperatures are maintained throughout the night and day, a reliable thermometer should be used. If this is the manually reset minimum/maximum type, both the lowest and highest temperatures over a given period of time will be recorded. In this way the grower will easily discover whether or not the overnight temperature dropped below the preselected minimum. This thermometer should be hung at the approximate height of the plants, as it is in this area that the correct temperature is most critical. Even in the average smaller greenhouse of, say, 2.3-2.4m (7.5-8ft) high at the ridge, recent experiments have shown that, since cool air sinks and hot air rises, the temperature difference between floor level and the top third of the greenhouse can be as much as 5.5-6.5°C (10-12°F), and the installation of air circulating fans can only reduce this temperature gradient by about half.

Natural convection

Several growers have used natural convection to advantage, and by installing tiered staging have been able to grow plants preferring cool conditions, such as cymbidiums and odontoglossums, together with their warmth-loving cousins, the cattleyas and phalaenopsis. One internationally known and successful grower from the United States built his greenhouse at an angle of 45° on the roof of a south-facing garage. The staging consisted of narrow-stepped shelves from floor level up to the roof, with access by a central staircase. Plants from the high mountains of the Andes were housed on the lower shelves whilst the heat and sun-loving vandas occupied the uppermost areas. In this approximately 4.5-5.5m (15-18ft) high greenhouse, conditions ranged from a cool and shady 10°C (50°F) to a much brighter and less humid 21°C (70°F).

Hot-water systems

Given the choice, most growers would select a heating method using hot water circulated through a system of pipes. Although modern thinking decrees that 5cm (2in) pipes have a greater surface area and thus higher heat output than a single 10cm (4in) pipe, there is much in favour of the older 10cm pipe for the amateur. These larger pipes can be used in a location where electricity is not available, the water circulating around the pipes by natural convection, whereas a system using 5cm piping will need a water-circulating pump incorporated into the flow pipe. A second advantage is the reservoir of hot water stored within the pipes (obviously much greater in a larger pipe), thereby maintaining temperatures for a longer period of time after a boiler

Heating and Staging

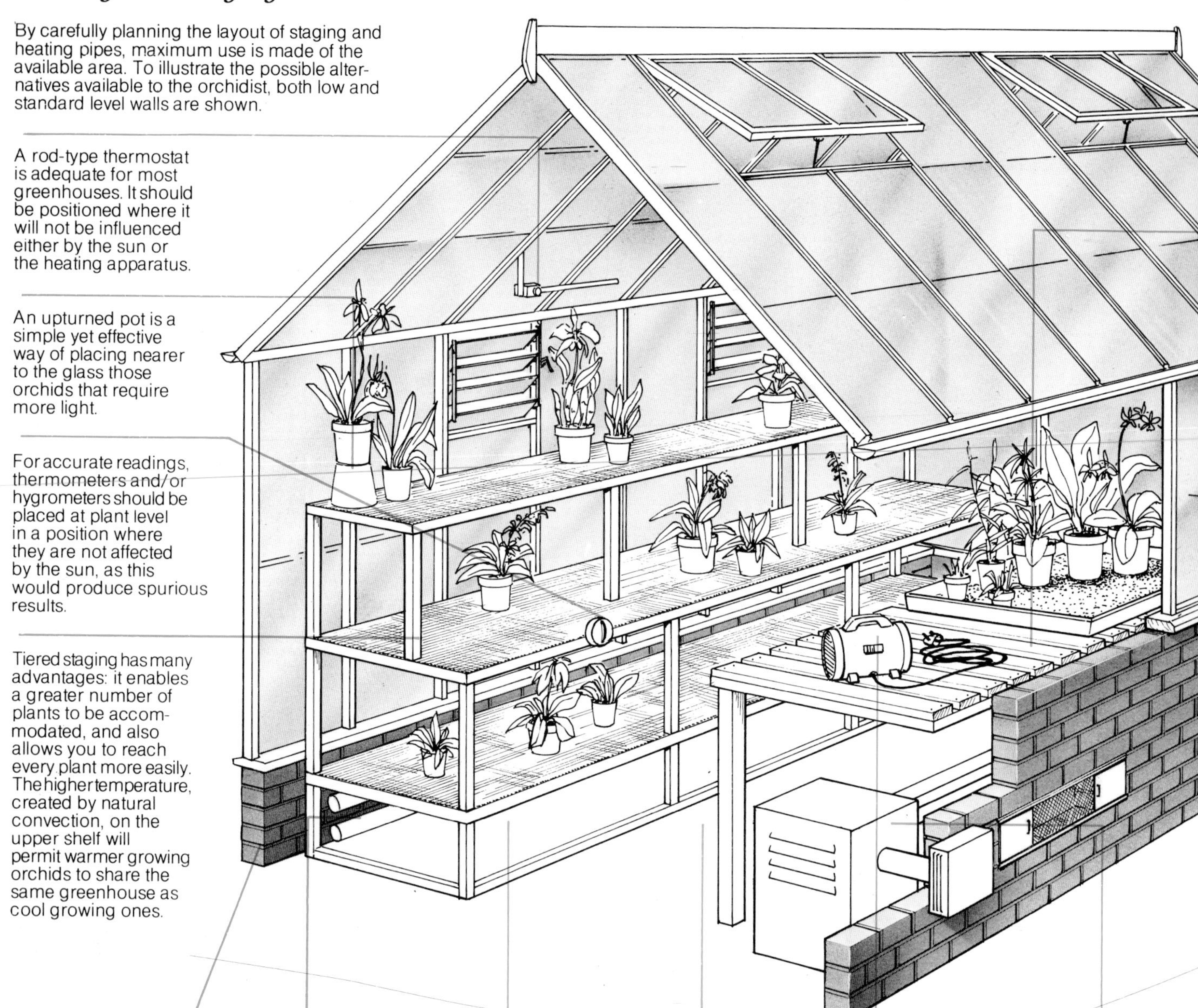

By carefully planning the layout of staging and heating pipes, maximum use is made of the available area. To illustrate the possible alternatives available to the orchidist, both low and standard level walls are shown.

A rod-type thermostat is adequate for most greenhouses. It should be positioned where it will not be influenced either by the sun or the heating apparatus.

An upturned pot is a simple yet effective way of placing nearer to the glass those orchids that require more light.

For accurate readings, thermometers and/or hygrometers should be placed at plant level in a position where they are not affected by the sun, as this would produce spurious results.

Tiered staging has many advantages: it enables a greater number of plants to be accommodated, and also allows you to reach every plant more easily. The higher temperature, created by natural convection, on the upper shelf will permit warmer growing orchids to share the same greenhouse as cool growing ones.

Lower walls on at least one side will allow more light into the greenhouse. This is an advantage where some form of multitiered staging is in use, and will also benefit cymbidiums and the sun-loving vandaceous orchids.

Hot water pipes have an advantage over most other heating systems because they stay warm during temporary breakdowns. A large overall surface area of pipe will permit the boiler (water) temperature to be set lower, thus creating the gentle heat supply so desirous to good culture.

Water 'troughs' below the staging and/or at floor level should be filled with Lytag (perlite) or a similar water-retentive material, which, if kept moist, will help to maintain the correct relative humidity.

Although pathways should be sufficiently wide to allow room to work, they should not occupy too much of the greenhouse area. A hard, easily cleaned surface is preferable.

Useful for topping up the temperature when the boiler is not in use, fan heaters have the added advantage of providing a portable supply of either heat or moving air.

Boiler capacity should be sufficient to maintain required temperatures even during very cold weather. By placing the boiler inside the greenhouse, the boiler surface heat can be utilized. But in this position it is essential to use some form of external flue.

breakdown. Against these advantages must be measured the more rapid response of the small bore system, together with relative ease of greenhouse installation.

The water within the pipes may be heated by a variety of energy sources. Four fuels are generally available in most countries: oil, gas, electricity and solid fuel. Gas or oil-fired boilers can be completely automatically controlled and, apart from regular servicing by experienced engineers, are virtually maintenance free. As a fuel in the UK and the US, natural gas has the advantage of being readily available and favourably priced, but many rural areas are not supplied with gas and have thus found oil or propane gas good substitutes. Solid fuel boilers are now better designed than previously, when cleaning at least two to three times each day coupled with adding extra fuel, made heating a greenhouse an onerous chore! A more sophisticated boiler, 'automatically' loaded with a modern solid fuel, has reduced this chore to once each day but can never eliminate daily attention. However, this type of boiler is independent of an electricity supply and, therefore, will maintain greenhouse temperatures during power failures. Electric immersion heaters may also be used but, although installation costs are low, the 6kw needed to maintain 10°C (50°F) in a 6 x 3.5m (20 x 12ft) greenhouse will mean high electricity costs!

Electric heating

An alternative method of electric heating that has been popular in the past for the smaller greenhouse, is tubular-heating. This system consists of metal tubes of various lengths, containing an electrically heated element rated at approximately 60watts per 30cm (1ft). Although this form of heating is relatively inexpensive to install and can be fully controlled by means of a thermostat, the surface temperature of the tubes becomes very high. This means that the areas near the heaters are frequently above the present temperature, whilst other areas within the greenhouse are too cool. Some form of air movement would certainly reduce this differential, but because of the localized

Right: Tiered staging is easy to construct. The three shelves offer varying degrees of light and temperature, permitting the cultivation of a high density of plants.

If it is not possible to have a potting shed, a portable potting bench can usually be accommodated in the greenhouse. This layout has the advantage of bringing plants and working area into close proximity, but a high degree of cleanliness should be observed.

Below Right: In this greenhouse, designed and built by an amateur orchidist, the high level shelf, curving path and hanging space for orchids mounted on rafts, have created both interest and extra space in this conventional 3m (10ft) wide greenhouse.

heat output tubular heaters have lost favour in recent years. As with all forms of direct heating that rely on an external power supply, the grower is at the mercy of breakdowns and other problems beyond his control, and without the reservoir of heat contained in a hot water pipe system, temperatures within the greenhouse drop very rapidly in the event of any interruption to the supply of heat.

Gas or oil-fired heaters

Gas or oil used as fuels in direct burners within the greenhouse need very careful handling. Close attention must be paid to the cleanliness and correct adjustment of the burner or wick, as a slight malfunction of the burner will result in the incomplete combustion of the gas or oil (usually paraffin or kerosene) with the subsequent build-up of fumes. But even a correctly operating greenhouse heater of this type will be harmful to plants unless adequate ventilation is supplied. A flame uses oxygen during burning, and the 'fumes' produced are, in fact, a build-up of carbon dioxide. Therefore, a supply of air to the burner is essential (some portable modern burners have a pipe leading to the outside for this purpose), but it is also necessary to have a small ventilator open near the floor of the greenhouse in order to allow the heavier carbon dioxide to escape. Gas and oil-fired convector heaters with a flue to extract the burnt gases are now available, and are preferable to the fully portable but flueless greenhouse heaters. These may have worked satisfactorily in the past when greenhouses were less airtight, but greenhouses are now lined with polyurethane and have thus become virtually sealed units.

Hot air

The greenhouse may also be heated by circulating warm air either by means of a simple fan-heater or through a system of polyethylene tubes. With this latter method, a boiler (fueled by any of the energy sources previously mentioned) is used to heat a network of 'radiators'. Air is drawn through and over these heated surfaces, and then blown down one or more polyethylene tubes which have small holes at irregular intervals. Using this method, the warm air is very rapidly circulated around the entire greenhouse area, with the added bonus of a buoyant atmosphere created by the moving air.

A less satisfactory result is obtained by using a fan-heater, as any plant directly in the current of hot air will experience some degree of dehydration. It is preferable to direct the hot air down the centre path or under the staging, ensuring that all plants in front of the heater are at least 2m away. Despite this potential hazard, electric fan-heaters have many points in their favour for use in small greenhouses. They are not too expensive initially, can be installed without expert attention (a 'power-point' or outlet is adequate for the supply of electricity), are thermostatically controlled, thus only produce heat when the temperature drops below the preselected level (especially sensitive if fitted with a rod-type thermostat), and the fan may be used independently during warmer weather to help maintain a better atmosphere within the house.

Staging

Staging is the term used to describe the tabling, or stage, on which plants are frequently stood. The amount and type of staging used depend upon the type of orchids being grown and the design of the greenhouse, ranging from its absence to a form of tiered shelving, with or without a moisture bench beneath. Cool-growing orchids, such as cymbidiums and laelias, grow more successfully on an open-mesh staging where there is a good circulation of fresh air around the pot and plant.

Moisture staging

With some orchids, such as odontoglossums, it is advisable to install a moisture staging several inches below the shelves on which the plants stand.

This moisture staging consists of a solid base, such as sheets of corrugated iron, asbestos or similarly durable material covered with a moisture retentive substance. Many years ago the clinker from the solid fuel boilers was used, giving not only a retentive material, but also one that was disliked by slugs. Now that clinker is a product of the past, the modern equivalents are expanded lightweight aggregate, such as Lytag (perlite), crushed volcanic rock, pumice, or pea-gravel. Surplus water draining from the pots after each watering, or water that is applied directly to the moisture staging, ensures that the material remains moist. This moisture slowly evaporates, particularly in warm conditions, resulting in the desired humid atmosphere.

Another purpose of a solid staging, with or without the moisture retentive material, is to act as a 'baffle' to the heat rising from the hot water pipes. It is therefore more important to have this moisture staging in warm houses than in those where the temperature is allowed to drop to 10-12°C (50-52°F). In greenhouses built on a heavy or naturally wet soil, it will not be necessary to cover the solid staging as reasonably high humidity will be maintained.

In the cool house, cymbidiums prefer the more airy and slightly drier atmosphere of a greenhouse without a moisture staging, but in situations where it is then difficult to retain sufficient humidity, a layer of Lytag or similar material should be spread on the greenhouse floor beneath the staging. Alternatively, odontoglossums and many other genera are happiest where the air is moist and buoyant, and thus will benefit from the humid air rising off the moisture staging. Similarly, the warmer-growing paphiopedilums and phalaenopsis like humid conditions; whilst vandas, most angraecoids and some cattleyas grow best in conditions of good air circulation and less constant humidity.

Ensuring drainage and stability

When a plant pot is standing on a flat surface, a watertight seal may be made between pot and bench during watering, with the result that the all-important drainage becomes ineffective. Also where slatted staging is used, the smaller sizes of pot can very easily be knocked over. Both of these potential problems will be prevented if the slatted or mesh staging is covered with a material such as the extruded polyurethane network (Netlon) sold as a windbreak. This means that the base of even the smallest plant pot is in partial contact with many surfaces, and as a result drainage cannot be impaired and stability is ensured.

This emphasis on fresh air being circulated not only around the plants but also the pots, may seem strange to the non-orchid grower. But remember that most orchids being grown in greenhouses are of epiphytic origin, and even the terrestrials have comparatively thick roots. Almost without exception, orchid roots will suffer if air is excluded from the compost, and even orchids cannot live for more than a year or two without roots! Thus if an abundance of air moves around the entire plant, the orchid will thrive and produce even better flowers.

For this reason, orchids have not proved too successful on a capillary bench where the supply of water to the plant is constant. The continuously wet conditions in the lower part of the pot tend to rot away roots in that area. Also the very open composts used by most growers do not lend themselves to capillary attraction.

Above: Circulation of air by means of an electric fan will greatly reduce the chance of hot or cold air pockets forming in parts of the greenhouse.

Above: Tiered staging enables you to see every plant clearly, and it is easy to see which are in need of water. Watering can be simplified with the help of a system that pumps water from the storage tank to a trigger-operated watering lance.

Experimental staging

Experiments are currently being carried out, on a small commercial scale, into the feasibility of growing orchids by hydroculture. With this method, the staging is a shallow trough containing approximately 2.5cm (1in) of water, in which the basket or mesh-pot grown plants are stood. The water is continuously circulating, and on its journey is both oxygenated and adjusted to a predetermined chemical formula. Although a wide range of foliage and flowering plants are now grown successfully by this method, there are no great expectations that orchids—with their peculiar epiphytic root systems—will eventually be grown in this manner.

Ventilation

That orchids need an abundance of fresh air is not a new concept, and it was realized over a century ago that epiphytic plants need air as much as any other commodity in order to thrive. Yet as recently as 1964, it was stated in a book on orchid culture—when referring to the warm house—that 'the air must be admitted only with the greatest care and in small quantities'. Whilst it is true that it would be unwise to open the ventilators into a cold prevailing wind, it is equally true to state that fresh air should be admitted liberally on every possible occasion. To achieve this, an efficient system of ventilators is required. The smaller the greenhouse, the more critical are the size, position and operation of the ventilating system. Regrettably, it is in this type of greenhouse that manufacturers almost seem to forget ventilation, relying on a gullible purchaser to modify the ventilators later.

The average standard greenhouse of, say, 9.3m^2 (100ft^2) floor area, is often fitted with just two roof ventilators plus one at staging height in each side wall. In almost all circumstances, these are not only of inadequate size, but are also wrongly positioned! To achieve good air flow through the greenhouse, it is necessary to be able to admit air at floor level (or at least from below staging level). There are several ways of doing this, but only two basic methods.

Box ventilators

Most plant houses have solid walls up to staging height—approximately 84cm (33in) from floor level—giving ample opportunity to fit some form of box ventilator. It is normal to install these when building the brick base, as the standard size of these ventilators is 61cm (24in) long x 15cm (6in) high. Box ventilators are fitted either with a door which hinges open and shut by a system of internally operated ropes and pulleys, or with two manually adjustable sliding doors which are fitted to the outside of the greenhouse wall. Where unheated frames are built as 'lean-tos' on the greenhouse base wall, the ventilator doors should be fitted to the inside wall. During very cold weather, the box ventilators opening into the cold frames can be left open—thus giving an element of frost protection to the plants growing within the frames. As with all ventilators, at least one is needed on each side wall, in order to avoid opening any ventilator into the wind.

With wooden base greenhouses low-level ventilators can be fitted easily at any time: simply cut a hole to the required size as low as possible in the base wall, and fit a covering door, slightly larger than the hole, to slide on runners over the aperture when ventilation is not needed.

Ventilation and Shading

Ventilation and shading are the main methods by which the temperature inside the greenhouse can be prevented from rising too high during hot weather. Preferably, both should be completely flexible and adjustable, and it is possible to have most systems automatically controlled.

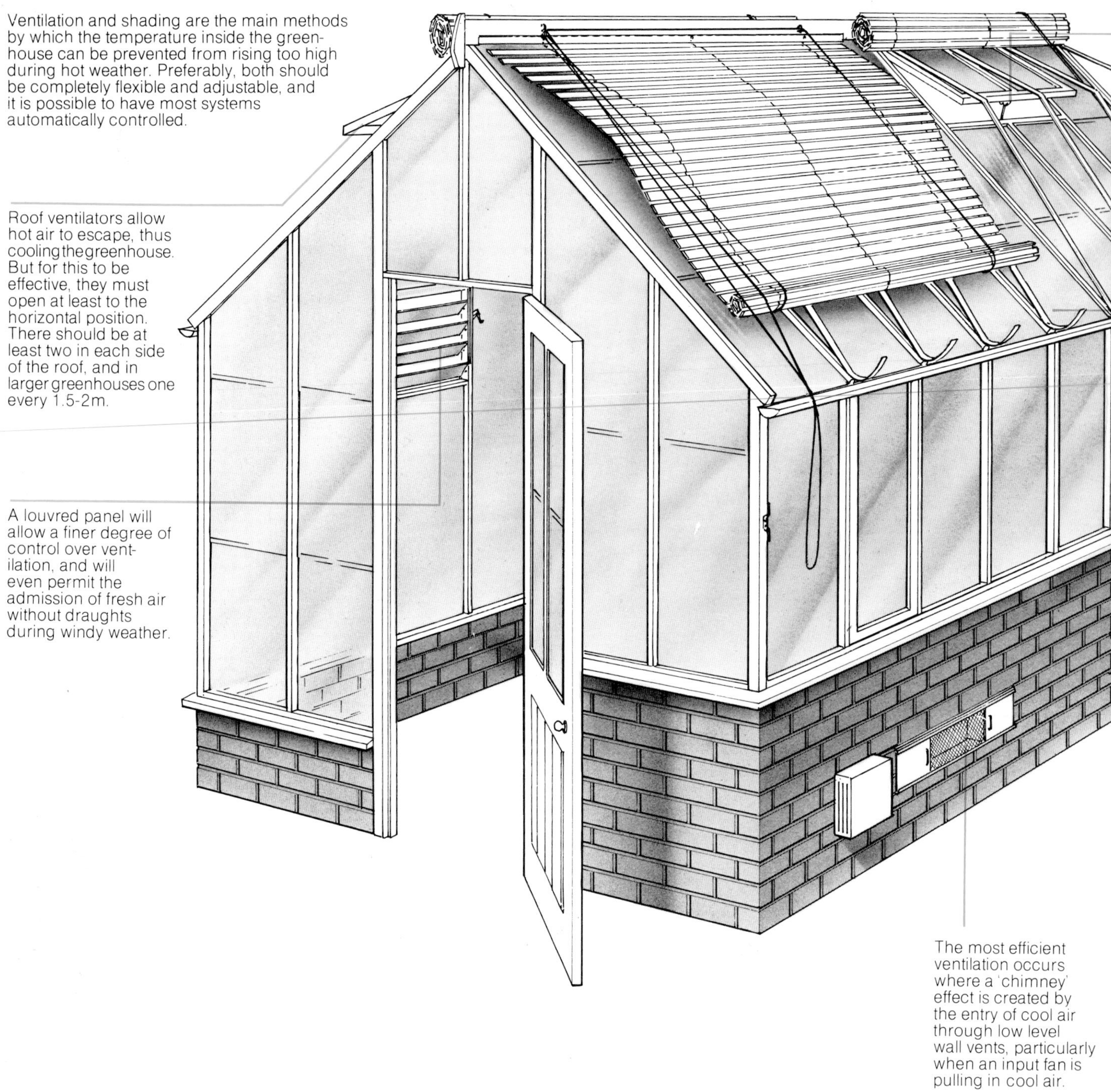

Roof ventilators allow hot air to escape, thus cooling the greenhouse. But for this to be effective, they must open at least to the horizontal position. There should be at least two in each side of the roof, and in larger greenhouses one every 1.5-2m.

A louvred panel will allow a finer degree of control over ventilation, and will even permit the admission of fresh air without draughts during windy weather.

The most efficient ventilation occurs where a 'chimney' effect is created by the entry of cool air through low level wall vents, particularly when an input fan is pulling in cool air.

Louvred panel ventilators

With glass-to-ground greenhouses, a different technique of ventilation is needed. Box ventilators would obviously be impractical in a glass wall, and instead a 'louvred panel' can be fitted in place of one or more of the panes of glass. The simple metal framework and specially toughened glass used in the construction of these louvres are obtained from most hardware stores, timber yards, builders' or horticultural merchants. When operated, the framework holding the pieces of glass turns on a centre pivot from vertical to horizontal. Depending upon the ventilation required, the louvre will remain in any position from completely open to nearly closed and, when absolutely closed, will remain locked in this position. Louvres give finer control of the amount of air admitted, and may even be opened slightly on the windward side of the greenhouse without harming the plants.

Roof ventilators

Greenhouses of yesteryear were frequently fitted with roof ventilators running the entire length of each side of the ridge. Undoubtedly this gave almost perfect control of the ventilation as one—or occasionally both—ventilator could be opened very slightly, even during inclement weather. Economics of modern times dictate that this type of ventilator is no longer a viable proposition, but even relatively small greenhouses should have at least three roof ventilators, two on the north-facing or leeward roof and one on the opposite side.

In larger greenhouses there should be at least one roof vent every 1.5m (5ft), alternating from north to south, as anything less will encourage the formation or 'still' areas within the greenhouse. Tests have shown that until a roof ventilator is approaching the horizontal position, very little hot air will escape; therefore, it is important to ensure that all ventilators in the roof are able to open beyond this critical stage.

Unsuitable ventilators

About the only place where plants growing on the staging do not need a ventilator is at staging level, yet most standard greenhouses—both glass-to-ground and plant houses—have ventilators fitted in this position. If these ventilators are open, the local humidity around the orchids will become far too low, and where this condition is prolonged the plants may become dehydrated, with the inevitable result of reduced growth. Therefore, any side ventilators are best permanently secured in the closed position!

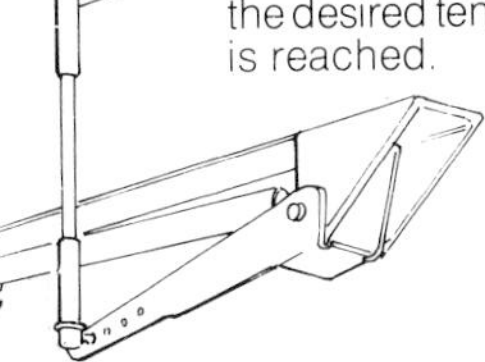

An inexpensive device for automatically operating roof ventilators will remove one headache for the hobbyist orchid grower. Independent of electricity, these autovents can be preset to function when the desired temperature is reached.

Slatted roller blinds should be held clear of the glass on metal runners. This allows the roof vents to open correctly, and also creates a blanket of cool air between the glass and blind, so helping to maintain the correct greenhouse temperature.

Below: The cavity created by the wall vents should be covered with a fine mesh—perforated zinc is best—to exclude pests, such as bees or mice, which would wreak havoc inside the greenhouse.

Above: The filtered light provided by slatted blinds is ideal for a wide range of orchids. Used in conjunction with tiered staging, masdevallias can be grown in the extra shade created by the summer foliage of lycastes.

Right: Louvred panel ventilators are especially useful during cool weather, as they admit only small amounts of fresh air without draughts.

Extractor (exhaust) fans

In warmer climates, many greenhouses are ventilated, or cooled, by means of a large extractor fan fitted in one end of the greenhouse and louvred or open panels in the other. The fan is controlled by a thermostat, and comes into operation when the greenhouse temperature exceeds a preset level.

One of the drawbacks of this system is the rapid reduction in the atmospheric moisture. Moving air—especially *warm* moving air—takes moisture from any source, including plants. Even plants growing in a marsh will flag on a very hot windy day, and although, if temporary, this dehydration will not harm the plant, it must be compensated for (usually at night when temperatures cool naturally).

Warm air is capable of holding more moisture than cool air, and thus the oft-used term 'humidity' should more correctly be called 'relative humidity', the amount of moisture in the air being expressed as a percentage. For example, if the relative humidity of the air is 100 percent at 10°C (50°F) in the evening, during the day at a temperature of 26.7°C (80°F), the same *amount* of moisture may represent only 35 percent of the moisture the air is capable of holding at that temperature; therefore, the *relative* humidity is 35 percent, and plants will lose water to the atmosphere.

Where low relative humidity is a chronic problem it is advisable to install a 'wet-pad' in front of the louvred panel. (Fuller details of this method are given on page 84.)

It is possible to use a modified extraction system for ventilation in smaller greenhouses, and many amateur growers successfully use this as their sole method. A louvred panel, as already described, fitted to one end of the greenhouse, coupled with an extract/intake fan—preferably not less than 41cm (16in) in width—placed diagonally opposite, will prove adequate. The advantage of using a two-way fan is that moist night air, which is particularly advantageous during hot weather, may be drawn into the greenhouse.

Shading

One of the purposes of ventilation is to control excessively high temperatures, but to achieve the desired results it is usually necessary to also have some form of shading on the greenhouse during the hottest months, except when certain colours of orchids are in flower, particularly yellows and greens, as high light intensity may tarnish the blooms. The purpose of shading is not to reduce the light but to limit high temperatures. The best way to do this is to prevent the heat of the sun reaching the glass in the first instance, as once the outside of the glass becomes hot, this heat will pass through to the cooler interior of the greenhouse until the temperatures inside and outside the greenhouse are similar, the reverse problem to our heat retention during winter.

It will immediately be obvious that any form of interior shading—and several types are available specifically for this purpose—will be far less effective in controlling high temperatures than all forms of shading applied to the outside of the greenhouse. Indeed, in the small house, interior shading is almost wholly ineffective, and should therefore be avoided.

Painting

There are many methods of shading a greenhouse from the outside, and in many ways the depth of one's pocket is the limiting factor. The simplest method is to apply a coat or coats of 'paint' directly to the glass, either with a brush or through a coarse spray. Originally the material used was made from quick-lime and called a lime-wash, but over the years many proprietary brands have appeared.

Amongst others there is a green powder that must be mixed with hot water and applied immediately. This adheres to the glass very well, which is an advantage during summer storms, but less desirable in the autumn when it defies all but the most vigorous attempts at removal. A newer substance, white and—it is claimed—resistant to the heaviest rains, yet removable with a dry cloth when desired, has been used by many growers with moderate success. A point to remember when using paint shading to limit excessive temperature is that dark surfaces absorb and white surfaces reflect heat: a factor used to good advantage by people living in areas with extremes of temperature. It should also be remembered that to obtain good coverage, the glass should be clean and dry before the paint is applied.

Roller blinds

An equally proven but more effective method of shading is provided by lath roller blinds. These blinds are constructed from approximately 25mm x 4 .5mm (1in x 0.2in) laths cut to the required length, and joined by simple clips. Cedar wood should preferably be used, and the clips manufactured from copper to give durability; less expensive materials are occasionally used. The clips fix the laths approximately 13mm (0.5in) apart, thus the sun moving over the greenhouse casts shadow and light alternately. The blinds can either be manually operated and open horizontally along the greenhouse, or raised and lowered vertically on the greenhouse roof using a system of ropes and pulleys. The advantage of blinds over paint is mainly one of adaptability: on dull, sunless days the blinds can be rolled back—or up—so that the plants have the benefit of all available light. Similarly, the blinds may be removed each evening. The disadvantage is, of course, one of cost, but once the blinds are made—which is not difficult as all the components are readily available—they should last for many years. If the blind is designed to cover the entire roof, provision to open the roof ventilators by 'cut-out' sections in the blind should be made.

Shading clear of the glass

Both paint and roller blinds have one major fault; they are, to a greater or lesser extent, in direct contact with the glass and thus some of the heat will be transmitted into the greenhouse. Ideally, the shading material should be some 15-23cm (6-9in) above the glass in order to allow a good circulation of air which will assist in the reduction of temperature. This could be achieved by rolling the horizontal blinds on two or three runners fixed horizontally across the glazing bars, or preferably by keeping the vertical blinds on a metal framework well clear of the glass. This is not an inexpensive method but is highly effective.

Using this method of blinds with ropes and pulleys, it is possible to raise and lower the blinds automatically by means of a photoelectric cell. It is also possible in larger, commercial greenhouses to operate

Above: There are many brands of greenhouse shading that may be painted on to the exterior of the glass. As light colours reflect the sun's rays, white shading is more effective at reducing the temperature of the glass, and thus the internal greenhouse temperature.

Above: Greenhouse shading provided by slatted roller blinds, held well above the glass on metal runners, and controlled either by photoelectric cells that will activate the winding gear when the light intensity drops, or time switches (right) that will operate the blinds at a predetermined time.

internal blinds both by thermostat and photoelectric cell, with the shading being brought into position when either the light becomes too strong or the temperature too high. And perhaps the ultimate in automatic shading is provided by a form of glass that becomes translucent as the light intensity increases! Some may feel that this is taking one's hobby to extremes, and the provision of such lavish equipment is certainly not necessary in order to grow orchids successfully. But there are many useful gadgets that will be of great help in taking the chores out of greenhouse gardening.

SUPPLEMENTARY EQUIPMENT AND TECHNIQUES

The provision of extra equipment or 'gadgets' in an amateur's greenhouse is open to debate. It could be argued that a hobbyist chose to grow orchids as a means of relaxation, a way of returning to a more basic activity—the growing of plants—in an increasingly automated world. If this is the case, then 'automating' the greenhouse would obviously hinder this process.

Yet despite the large scale installation of time-saving equipment in both industry and commerce, most people seem to have less time than previously in which to indulge their hobbies. Thus, if by taking care of some of the daily routine chores, labour-saving gadgetry enables someone, otherwise unable, to grow orchids, then this is beneficial to the popularity of orchids and to potential orchid growers.

There are several small pieces of equipment available that will take the 'muscle' out of greenhouse culture, and the resulting decrease in required effort will enable partially disabled people or those who are no longer in their first flush of youth, to grow orchids successfully. Also of significance are the various aids which cut down the cost of growing orchids, and as the supply of winter heat is the largest single item of continual expense, any method of conserving heat is well worth considering.

Insulation

Although this subject does not specifically fall into the category of gadgets or even equipment, there are few orchid houses situated in the cooler, temperate areas of the world that do not have at least some degree of insulation. It is generally accepted that by raising the minimum night temperature by 2.7°C (5°F), ie from 10°-12.7°C (50°-55°F), the cost of heating is doubled. However, even a simple but efficient form of double glazing will save anything from 4°-5.5°C (8°-10°F), making it possible to reduce the heat input, and thus the cost, yet maintain existing minimum temperatures. Alternatively, the greenhouse can be transformed from a cool to an intermediate growing area without increasing the heating costs.

Double glazing

The major area of any greenhouse is obviously the glass, which is also the material with the greatest heat loss. Much of this loss can be prevented simply by lining the roof and walls of the greenhouse *completely* with a polyethylene skin. As with all double glazing systems, it is not the two surfaces—be they glass, polyethylene or acrylic—that prevent the heat from passing through to the outside, but the air trapped between them. As moving air has little insulative value, it is important that the air remains still. This can be achieved by ensuring that the seal between the ridge bar and the polyethylene is as air tight as possible. In a wooden greenhouse it is comparatively easy to fix the polyethylene lining by means of 25mm (1in) wooden laths nailed along the ridge bar, stretching the polyethylene tightly down the roof before fixing to the glazing bars, again by using wooden laths. With metal-framed greenhouses it is more difficult, despite the availability of patent clips designed to assist the fixing of a lining. But help is at hand: some greenhouses are now produced with an inner channel on the glazing bars into which the polyethylene is fixed by means of a rubber grummet — a point well worth looking for when purchasing a new greenhouse. All folds and creases in the lining material should be straightened out before fixing, as any that remain will become a source of condensation, which drips onto the plants below.

From the eaves, the polyethylene should be continued down the side walls until below the staging level or, with a glass-to-ground greenhouse, completely to floor level. As polyethylene is easily obtainable in widths up to 4 m (13ft), it should be possible to line the roof and side walls of small greenhouses with only one piece; but where a joint is necessary, for instance when lining to floor level, a generous overlap should be allowed. The gap between outer glass and inner lining material should be at least 38-50mm (1.5-2in) as a smaller air space has a lower insulation factor, and there is a possible danger of the two surfaces touching and thus eliminating any insulatory effect. So that fresh air may be admitted on all favourable occasions, roof ventilators and those below the staging should be lined separately, cutting out the relevant areas in the main lining. Any outer doors—often neglected when a greenhouse is lined—should be similarly treated, or better still, a polyethylene curtain or 'second door' made to act as a windbreak when the outer door is opened.

Materials available

Some growers use a very thin grade of polyethylene which has to be replaced annually, or at the most every two years, whilst others prefer a thicker grade that is sufficiently tough to last five to eight years before deteriorating. Both methods have their advantages but where the greenhouse is relatively small, with not more 14m² (150sq ft) floor area, for example, and the quantity of plants to be moved is not too great, it is probably best to install the lining each autumn and to remove it late in the following spring. The principal advantages with this method are that the greenhouse is thoroughly cleaned at least twice a year, and this provides the opportunity to handle the orchids, which is the ideal way to spot and deal with potential trouble before it develops into anything too serious. Thus the installation and removal of a lining material provide at least two annual stimuli for necessary action.

Above: To eliminate the condensation that could occur during cold weather, the polyethylene lining should be stretched tightly. In a wooden greenhouse, 2.5cm (1in) laths are ideal for holding the lining permanently in position.

In larger greenhouses, or where specific designs make lining a tedious and time-consuming job, it is preferable to use a more permanent material. A heavier grade of polyethylene has the advantage of being fairly tough and thus less likely to tear during installation or subsequent use. It will also retain its 'elasticity' for

several years, making it possible to wash off the accumulated dust and algae at regular intervals. A similar but superior material that will last almost indefinitely is acrylic sheeting, available from most hardware stores and builders' suppliers. This flat, clear material may be cut with either a sharp knife or a fine-toothed saw, to fit the required shape and size, and is held in place by laths or battens screwed to the glazing bars. Acrylic material is far tougher than polyethylene, and will take most normal wear without deteriorating. It will also remain clear—polyethylene discolours and becomes translucent after a few years—and is easily cleaned.

The ultimate in glasshouse insulation is provided by specially constructed double-skin glass units, hermetically sealed for life-long efficiency. However, not only are the units themselves extremely costly, but the greenhouse structure would need to be strengthened considerably in order to withstand the additional weight. This method of insulation, super-efficient though it undoubtedly is, can therefore be disregarded by most greenhouse owners.

The one problem frequently encountered with polyethylene-lined greenhouses is excessive condensation, particularly during prolonged cold weather when it is not possible to ventilate. Where the lining has been installed in such a way that folds and creases are almost non-existent, and the pitch of the roof is reasonably steep—35° or more, for example—this condensation will run down the polyethylene to the staging or floor without harming the plants. But where the greenhouse design renders this impossible, it is worth considering fixing the polyethylene as an *outer* skin; with this method internal condensation is minimal.

Installation of an outer polyethylene 'tent' is straightforward. Firstly, fix one end of the polyethylene to the outside of the wall or floor plate (whichever is applicable), then unroll the polyethylene over the top of the greenhouse and fix to the corresponding position on the opposite side. The ends can be dealt with separately. Apart from the lack of condensation, this method has several other advantages: the outer surface of a greenhouse is considerably less cluttered than the internal one, where various fitments have to be 'negotiated' by the lining, and, of course, the plants are not disturbed. Furthermore, the tent is very easily removed when warmer weather returns. Where this method has been successfully used for several years, negligible problems have been caused even by gale-force winds. The only drawback would seem to be the removal of the motivation to thoroughly clean the greenhouse interior.

When using a portable flueless oil or gas heater in a greenhouse that has been lined completely, it is imperative to make provision for adequate ventilation. A supply of air to the burner, coupled with a low-level vent through which the fumes may escape, is even more important where the lining renders the greenhouse almost a sealed unit.

Other areas of heat loss

Having taken great care to ensure a perfect lining within the greenhouse, it should not be forgotten that the glass will also need periodic attention, especially after winter gales. Before lining greenhouses became popular, even the smallest crack in the glass was immediately obvious. Even if all seems well, a regular inspection of the roof glass may prevent serious damage.

Many growers tend to forget that heat is also escaping—albeit at a slower rate—through the base walls and floor. In the conventional greenhouse that has some form of path and, usually, an earth floor covered with shingle or similar material, it is difficult, if not impossible, to provide effective insulation. But as the amounts of heat loss involved are not great, it is one of the least important areas to insulate.

In fact, it is only realistic where a greenhouse has been built on a concrete raft that incorporates a polyethylene damp-proof course about 25mm (1in) below the surface. A 13 or 19mm (0.5-0.75in) thick sheet of polystyrene positioned immediately below the damp-proof course should prevent some of the heat loss down through the floor. However, most growers prefer some form of earth floor through which excess water may drain, yet from which some humidity will rise.

Loss of heat through the basewalls of a greenhouse is another area often overlooked. Any solid wall will absorb heat from the inside of the greenhouse and pass it through to the cooler outside. Obviously, if the walls are constructed from 13mm (0.5in) thick match-boarding, there will be a greater heat loss than through a 23cm (9in) solid brick wall, but all non-insulated walls are a potential source of unnecessary expense. This expense could be reduced by fixing sheets of 13mm (0.5in) thick polystyrene to the inside surface of the greenhouse walls, or by constructing an interior false wall, after which the resulting cavity is fitted with any modern insulating material. A similar solution may be reached with an existing 35.5cm (14in) cavity wall, where the processes used for dwelling house insulation would be suitable. If building a new greenhouse, a 23cm (9in) building block is now on the market. This has a built-in 15.2cm (6in) deep cavity which, if filled with suitable material, will provide excellent insulation.

Above: An outer skin of polyethylene is easier to install and remove than an internal lining, and largely eliminates condensation.

Establishing air circulation

These efforts to retain warmth within the greenhouse have, if functioning correctly, reduced the amount of natural air movement that was often synonymous with many of the draughty greenhouses of the 1950s. The post-war demand for greenhouses that were suitable for the average working man sometimes resulted in a rash of badly constructed greenhouses that within a few months were in need of major reinforcement. Plants will not thrive if placed in a draughty position, yet conversely most plants like moving air around them. By studying the natural habitats of orchids, it has become increasingly clear that fresh air is nearly always in evidence—frequently in such quantity that their foliage and flowers are perpetually moving.

In temperate areas of the world, for many weeks or even months of the year, weather conditions make it impractical to open the ventilators. When these conditions prevail, growers are often advised to keep the greenhouse 'quiet' by barely maintaining the minimum temperature and only watering the plants sufficiently to prevent dehydration. This is fine for short periods, but any length of time under these conditions will certainly limit the plants' growth rate. Yet if surplus water is allowed to remain on the surface of either the plants or the greenhouse floor and staging when temperatures fall to their minimum or below, the atmosphere becomes dank and there is a real danger of fungal infection. Moving air would reduce this risk, but even if it were possible to open the ventilators it is

Above: In a small greenhouse, an oscillating fan used to circulate the air is ideal for maintaining a buoyant atmosphere.

Right: A small fan fixed at plant level will provide localized air movement for those orchids intolerant of stale conditions.

unlikely that the air within the greenhouse would move sufficiently to improve the situation significantly. It is now generally accepted that the modern greenhouse is incomplete without one or two fans that frequently run continuously. Various types are available to suit specific requirements.

The best method of moving the air within the greenhouse is to use an oscillating fan, which turns automatically back and forth through an angle of 180°. Most have three speed settings that may be adjusted to suit both the total greenhouse area and the prevailing conditions, and will give a buoyant atmosphere together with a more even temperature throughout the house. If more vigorous air movement is required by some plants—many high altitude South American genera such as *Odontoglossum* and *Masdevallia* seem to thrive in a 'gale'—these can be placed nearest to the fan where obviously the air movement is more brisk. Alternatively, a secondary smaller fan could be placed adjacent to this particular group of plants, thus giving localized 'mountain' conditions for those that cannot tolerate any degree of stagnation.

The advantages of vigorously moving air are not, however, limited to the winter months when the heating system is operating and the ventilators have to remain closed. In warmer climates and during summer in temperate areas, it is often necessary to shade too heavily in order to prevent sun-scorch on the foliage. But in the wild, and in cultivation in tropical or equatorial regions, many orchids are exposed to almost full summer sun without burning. Here the air moving over the surface of the leaf takes off excess heat, and, of course, there is no layer of glass to accentuate the sun's heat. Therefore, a brisk movement of air over the plants within a greenhouse will reduce the risk of sun-scorch, with the result that more of the all important light can be admitted to the plants. Maintaining a buoyant atmosphere during the hottest of summer days is not easy. The air movement over the plants may not be sufficient and an additional fan positioned near a low-level ventilator would be of great help. By pulling in fresh, cool air from near ground level on the shadier (north or east) side of the greenhouse, it is even possible with only light shading to maintain temperatures a few degrees below the temperature outside.

Maintaining a moist atmosphere

The maintenance of vigorous air movement, particularly where the ventilators are much in use, may result in a slight loss of humidity.

If water is sprayed around and beneath the plants and over the entire floor area, the percentage of moisture in the air will increase, thereby reducing the amount of water the plant needs to absorb through its root system. There are various methods of supplying this requirement, from the basic to a completely automated system which is equally suited to the amateur's small greenhouse as to large commercial nurseries.

Undoubtedly a hosepipe is still the most reliable method of creating humidity within the confines of a greenhouse. By

and large, this system does not break down, does not rely on a supply of electricity or the reliability of switches and controls. But its major weakness is the assumption that someone is available with the necessary time and enthusiasm to carry this out at least once daily, and frequently more often. It may be easy merely to saturate the floor of the greenhouse periodically, but there may be times when this is not possible.

In fact, the maintenance of atmospheric humidity when you are away for any length of time is probably one area where some degree of automation is called for. The simplest method is to remove a shallow layer of the soil from beneath the staging, and line the area with polyethylene, thus creating a broad but shallow trough which can then be filled with shingle or, preferably, Lytag (or perlite). Fill the trough with water, not higher than 2.5-5cm (1-2in) below the level of the aggregate, and maintain the water level either by a drip-feed from a suitably placed header tank, or by topping-up by hand every three or four days. This method will not give a perfect result, but will prevent the atmosphere in the greenhouse from becoming excessively arid.

Another simple and more effective method, again independent of power supply, is provided by a length of flat, 3-section perforated hose fixed to the underside of the ridge board. This type of hose is normally used to provide a fine, drenching mist to seedbeds in the open garden, or similar areas needing careful but thorough irrigation. Fix the hose with the holes downwards along the entire length of the ridge board, and turn on the tap just enough to obtain a steady drip through the perforations. If higher relative humidity is required, extra holes could be made in the hose. Although this method may sound unreliable, it has worked satisfactorily in at least one amateur grower's greenhouse for several years, even for a week to 10 days during his absence. One modification has been the installation of a short polyethylene curtain on either side of the hose, to prevent the water dripping onto plants nearest the centre path.

Both these methods, although reliable, have their limitations, as the quantity of moisture within the greenhouse will

Left: Interchangeable nozzles for standard watering lances are ideal for spraying orchids mounted on rafts or with aerial roots. Using this method, high level shelves can be reached effortlessly.

Above: Spray nozzles fixed into a pipeline below the staging can be either hand controlled or fully automatic. The jet is adjustable from a coarse spray to fine mist, and will cover an area of approximately 1.5m².

remain constant regardless of temperature and other factors. Thus, during very hot daytime conditions, the relative humidity may fall to less than 40 percent; conversely when night temperatures become low and the humidity is naturally higher, saturation point of 100 percent relative humidity may result.

The only alternative to using a hosepipe is is install some form of spray nozzle controlled through an electrically operated valve and humidistat, which is able to sense the quantity of moisture in the atmosphere (much as a thermostat senses temperature). If the relative humidity falls below the desired preset level, the humidistat opens the valve, which in turn operates the spray nozzles until the humidity reaches the correct level, when the humidistat closes the valve. Alternatively, the system may be controlled by a time-clock, which opens the valve for, say, five minutes every hour; again, however, there is the risk of excessive humidity during cool conditions, and possibly inadequate atmospheric moisture—despite the adjustable spraying interval—on hot days.

Many different spray nozzles are available, from inexpensive plastic to a solid brass system in which the spray can be finely adjusted from coarse droplets to a fine mist. Similarly, the plumbing can be plastic hose using screwclips to seal the joints. But once again you get what you pay for! The water within a mains connected spray line is under mains pressure, and thus when the sprays are not operating all joints must be capable of withstanding this pressure. In practice, there will be a weak spot, and within a few weeks the hoseline will split completely. For almost total reliability, use 15mm (0.5in) copper piping and compression fittings for all the joints. These fittings eliminate the need to use solder, as they can be tightened with a spanner.

By suspending the pipework below the staging, and having a spray nozzle about every 1.2m (4 ft) on either side of a central path, you can cover the whole greenhouse area. Although a fully automated humidity system may seem an unnecessary extravagance, it will give many years of reliable service and take at least one worry out of orchid growing when you are temporarily absent.

Labour-free watering

The automated humidity system will also provide labour-free watering of your plants. A pipeline, complete with the required number of spray nozzles, can be suspended from the glazing bars over the plants, and connected to the water supply through a humidistat or time-clock controlled valve or, preferably, direct to the tap for manual control.

The main disadvantage of this system for the amateur growing a very mixed collection, is that several orchids will always be flowering, and the blooms will not appreciate being saturated at regular intervals. But where a large number of similar plants are growing together in the same-sized pots, this system works extremely well. Similar criteria apply where a system of individual water pipes to each pot, radiating from a central supply line, is adopted. All automated watering depends upon every plant having the same water requirement, and all plant pots drying out at the same rate, which is obviously not applicable to most mixed orchid collections.

So how can the owner of such a collection take the effort and time out of watering? Fortunately, a reasonably priced method is available, and involves using a watering lance and a small, submersible electric water pump. Watering lances have a trigger control on the handle, and interchangeable heads from straight jet to fine spray. The submersible pump need not be large—one similar to that used for small garden fountains would suffice—providing it has a maximum 'head' of not less than the height of your greenhouse. Anything less will not be sufficiently powerful to reach those plants on the high shelves. A suitable length of hosepipe connects the pump outlet to the watering lance, and by placing the pump in the nearest water tank, and connecting the lead to a convenient power point, an effortless and fully portable watering method has been installed, at little cost. One word of warning, however: do not leave the pump switched on for long periods without opening the valve on the watering lance, or back pressure may burn out the pump. More sophisticated—and hence considerably more expensive—electric water pumps have an on/off solenoid valve controlled by the water pressure, which turns off the pump when the lance valve is closed.

Despite the apparently complicated gadgetry involved with watering aids, it is very easy to install a basic pump/watering lance system that is more than adequate for even quite large collections.

For those who prefer the good old-fashioned watering can, there is again a choice. Discard any that have a short or wide spout; it is impossible to reach plants at the back of the staging with this type of can, and the wide spout will mean poor control of the water flow, with the inevitable washing-out of many smaller plants. Better quality watering cans have long slim outlets, and in addition to coarse and fine roses, an extension spout, even slimmer than the main one and usually curved downwards at the end, will enable those awkwardly placed plants to be watered with ease, without washing half the compost out of the pot.

Below: An inexpensive electric water pump similar to those used in small garden fountains, connected through a length of hose from the tank to a watering lance, will be sufficiently powerful for most greenhouses.

Controlling pests

Pest control is another field in which gadgets have long been in use. In the early nineteenth century, growers used manually operated bellows on a 'horticultural vaporizer' in order to pump the insecticide (even at this time nicotine was recognized as an effective killer of most pests) into the greenhouse. Various forms of fumigating apparatus, often complicated, appeared at frequent intervals, and although most have now passed into history, at least one—Richard's Patent Fumigator—first available in 1925, is still in regular and frequent use in the UK today. It consists of a simple perforated metal cone, open at both ends, with a shallow saucer placed on top. The required amount of insecticide or fungicide is poured into the saucer, after which a small spirit lamp inside the metal cone is lit. This heats the chemical, which then vaporizes into the atmosphere to the detriment of the offending pest.

A modern version of this fumigator has been available for some years, but requires a supply of electricity. These vaporizing lamps, generally using crystals of the

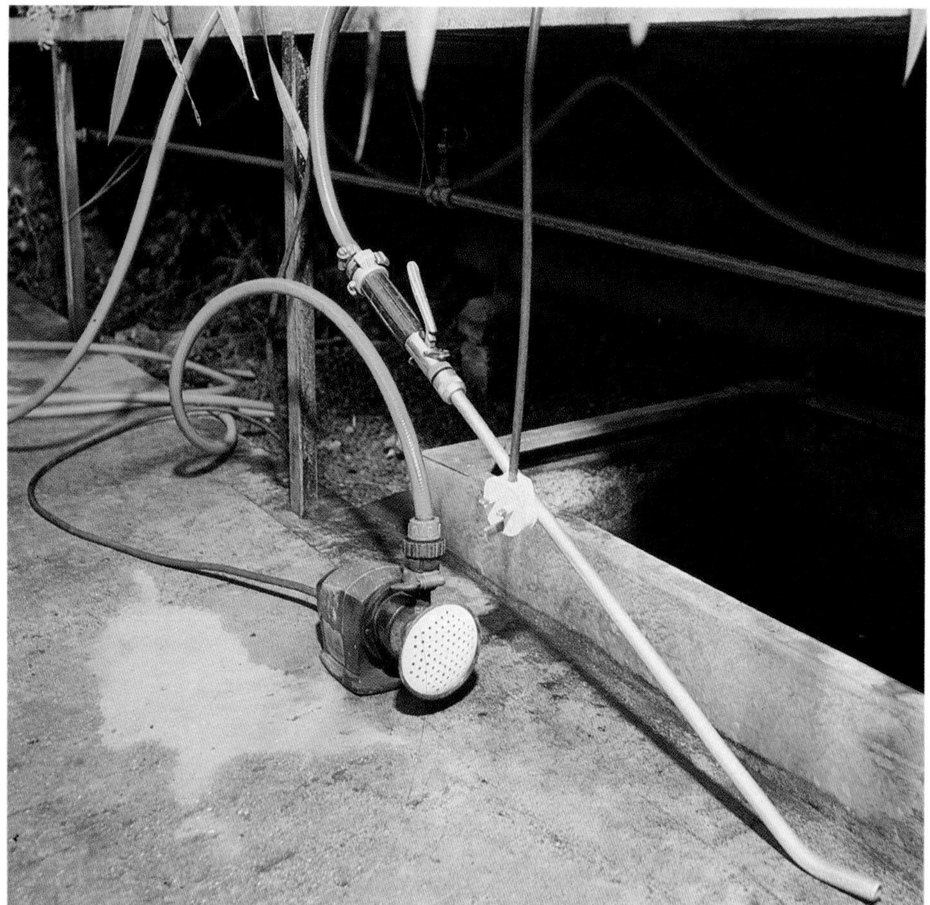

chemicals that control most pests and diseases, are comprised of a cup-shaped metal unit into which a heat-resistant glass beaker containing the relevant chemical is placed. A thermostatically controlled heating element in the unit melts (where appropriate) and vaporizes the chemical into the atmosphere. The main advantages of this electric fumigator over the older but equally effective spirit lamp model, are cleanliness in operation and thermostatically controlled supply of heat to the fumigant.

Another electric fumigator, used for the rapid dispersal of insecticidal or fungicidal smoke within the greenhouse, has been available for several years. Designed on the lines of a hand-held hair dryer, a cartridge of chemically impregnated cardboard is placed in the nozzle of the unit, and hot air blown through the cartridge vaporizes the chemical into a smoke, which is then blown round the greenhouse.

Many pesticides are also available in liquid or powder form, the latter often in puffer packs ready for immediate use. Liquids should be diluted with the appropriate amount of water and, sometimes, soft soap (to act as a 'spreader'), and applied with a simple syringe or pressure sprayer.

Obviously when handling or using potentially dangerous chemicals, you must observe certain precautions for your own and your plants' safety. These, together with other general guidelines for the successful culture of your orchids, will be discussed in following pages.

Above and Below: Fumigation is best carried out on warm evenings so that the greenhouse can remain closed all night and allow the insecticide to take effect. But ventilate the greenhouse well the next morning. Electrically operated fumigators (above) can be used to control most insect pests and fungal diseases, but take care that plants are not directly above the unit during operation. Below: By blowing hot air through an impregnated cardboard cartridge, this hand-held fumigator fills the greenhouse with insecticidal smoke.

HOW TO GROW ORCHIDS

Advice on the culture of any plant is always extremely difficult to offer: there are so many contributing factors to be taken into account, and no two growers will put the same interpretation on results. There are no hard and fast rules by which to abide, and no scientific or mathematical formulae that will ensure successful culture. Instead, various suggestions based on practical experience can be made in the hope that understanding an orchid's basic requirements will at least point the unsure grower in the right direction.

Successful cultivation of any group of plants depends upon the correct balance of the various aspects of culture, and is as important with orchids as any hardy garden plant. Before starting to grow a plant, a knowledge of its natural environment is helpful. For example, the area and altitude at which a particular species grows, and thus the temperature it enjoys; how far it is subjected to seasonal droughts (interpreted in cultivation by 'resting' the plant) or monsoon periods; or whether it revels in full sunshine, or requires at least partial shade. When dealing with a group of plants so widely distributed as orchids, coming as they do from almost every conceivable location or ecological niche, a knowledge of this natural environment is even more critical.

Temperature categories

It would be impossible to replicate exactly these presumably ideal conditions for every different species or genus growing in most amateurs' orchid collections. Almost all orchids are extremely resilient, and have proved very adaptable to 'foreign' conditions.

Basically, orchids can be divided into three main temperature categories: warm, ie needing a minimum night temperature of 15.5°C (60°F), intermediate, slightly cooler at 13°C (55°F), and cool, where the minimum night temperature may be allowed to fall to around 10°C (50°F). Obviously, different orchids prefer different temperatures, and it will be found that many artificial microclimates exist within the confines of any greenhouse. Areas nearest the heating pipes will naturally be slightly warmer and less moist than those not directly affected by heating apparatus, even when an air-circulating fan is in operation. Conversely, any plants positioned near the door must be tolerant of the slightly lower temperatures that will inevitably occur at frequent intervals.

Making the most of your greenhouse

The majority of amateur growers have but one greenhouse in which to grow their frequently mixed collections, and usually this greenhouse is heated only to maintain a minimum temperature of 10 to 12°C (50°-54°F). In this case only orchids in the 'cool' category are generally recommended. Yet warmer areas do exist within such greenhouses, and by finding these and incorporating a high-level shelf, it is possible to grow a much wider range of genera. Many of the South American Laeliinae, such as *Cattleya, Brassavola* and *Laelia,* would appreciate the slightly warmer and less humid conditions obtainable on a shelf. Their leathery leaves and stout pseudobulbs would also benefit from the extra light and, providing the temperature does not fall below 12°C (54°F), these normally intermediate species will produce their flamboyant blooms in a cool house.

From this it could be deduced that greenhouses should be divided vertically to obtain the various temperature differentials, and certainly more effective use could be made of the natural convection within most greenhouses. But *physical* horizontal divisions would not only prevent heat from rising, and thus defeat the advantages of convection, but would also prove impractical. Therefore, if you need an area for growing warmth-loving orchids within a cool house, it will be necessary to curtain off the warmest part of the greenhouse, thereby retaining more of the heat within this confined space. This area could be either a permanent structure, in which case the curtain should be similar in construction to the greenhouse, or a short-term winter home for less cold-tolerant orchids, when a polyethylene curtain would suffice. In either case, a means of access and provision for ventila-

Left: Although a few of the species will thrive in the cool greenhouse, most paphiopedilums require intermediate temperatures. Because of this, and their compact growth and long-lasting flowers, they make ideal pot plants for the home.

Right: A modern version of the Wardian case, heated by an air-warming cable, will provide a small area for growing warmth-loving orchids in a cool greenhouse.

Below: Dendrobiums such as this species, *D. victoriae reginae*, are best grown in a warm greenhouse, though a cool resting period may be needed to produce the flowers.

tion must be provided. To further boost the temperature within this area, a secondary supply of heat could be introduced by means of a small electric fan heater, or a length of space-heating cable (as used in many propagating cases).

Orchids for the warm or intermediate house

The warmest part of any greenhouse is the top third, yet very few orchid growers utilize this area except to 'rest' certain (mainly deciduous) orchids during the winter months. Small greenhouses of less than 3m (10ft) in width, are unlikely to have sufficient headroom for a high-level shelf over part of the central path, although it is seldom impossible to arrange some form of two-tier staging, especially where the standard bench height of 84 cm (2ft 9in) can be lowered to accommodate a second layer of plants above it. Temperatures at this higher level will remain 3 to 4 °C (5-8°F) above the floor-level temperature, thus enabling some intermediate house orchids to be successfully grown in what is ostensibly a cool house. A similar situation pertains in a greenhouse normally maintained at intermediate temperatures—certain warm-growing orchids will thrive on the high-level shelves.

There are two main drawbacks to growing plants on these high shelves, both of which are accentuated during the summer months. As a result of their position near to the glass, any plants growing on these shelves will receive a great deal more light than those at the lower level. Furthermore, as temperatures are higher the relative humidity in the upper areas will be lower, therefore those plants growing on high-level shelves or staging will dry out rapidly and consequently may need watering more frequently. Although this area may sound an inhospitable home for plants, many orchids positively enjoy the conditions, particularly during late summer and autumn when it is important to ripen the maturing growths and pseudobulbs.

Dendrobiums

Dendrobiums are not the easiest of orchids to flower really well, but if the developing pseudobulb is fully ripened during late summer by exposure to full light and air—a high shelf near the roof ventilators providing these conditions perfectly—there is a greater chance of successfully bringing these beautiful orchids into flower. The fleshy leaved species, such as *D. lingueforme* and *D. teretifolium*, which come mainly from Australia where they grow exposed to almost full sun in what are regularly drought conditions, are especially well suited to 'life at the top'; indeed these dendrobiums are unlikely to flower under northern temperate conditions unless they receive all available light, especially during the winter months.

Paphiopedilums and Phalaenopsis

A wider range of temperatures will enable the grower to satisfy that natural urge to diversify, and areas where a minimum 15.5°C (60°F) can be maintained will be perfect for the warmer-growing paphiopedilums and phalaenopsis. Both genera require fairly shady and humid conditions during the summer months—as will the majority of the warm-growing angraecoids from the African continent.

Suitable partners for these three groups, but more sun-loving and thus candidates for the high shelf, are many of the vandaceous orchids from Southeast Asia. Plants in this group have either strap-leaved or terete (pencil-shaped) foliage, with several intermediate types. Hybridizers have created other intermediate types by crossing terete with strap-leaved vandas, producing semiterete and quarter-terete forms; but the higher the percentage of terete 'blood', the more light the orchid will demand in order to flower. Indeed, terete vandas are not good subjects for small greenhouses in northern temperate zones. Not only do they require strong light all the time—a commodity that is sadly lacking during winter months—but the majority also have a climbing habit with the leaves spaced well apart on a tall stem. Many aerial roots, so necessary to climbing orchids in their natural environment, are also produced, making conventional pot culture impossible.

Oncidiums

Not all light-loving, warm-growing orchids have such embarrassing habits. Oncidiums are normally thought of as cool-growing companions to their cousins the odontoglossums, but there are several species and an increasing number of hybrids that make ideal subjects for a shelf in the warm house. (However, only a small group of oncidiums [equitant oncidiums] will thrive in these conditions; most species should be grown in the cool house.)

These have thick, almost terete or 'squared' leaves not more than 8-10cm (3-4 in) long, which grow closely together to form a tuft of foliage. The comparatively sparse root system is intolerant of wet conditions, as the fine roots like to dry out rapidly after watering. This environment can be supplied by using very small pots, just large enough to accommodate the plant, and ensuring that the compost is both free draining and durable, in order to avoid frequent repotting. A very open compost, such as a chunky, large-grade bark, will mean daily watering during hotter weather, particularly as these miniature-growing orchids like good light conditions and not too much humidity.

However, there is nothing miniature about the sprays of brightly coloured flowers produced by these particular oncidiums, derived mostly from the species *Oncidium desertorum, pulchellum* and *variegatum*—a reward well worth the extra effort required to grow these orchids. In the wild these plants enjoy strong light, little rainfall and occasionally almost desert conditions; they come from several of the West Indian islands.

Orchids for the cool house

The provision of high temperatures will not ensure success with all orchids.

ORCHIDS FOR DIFFERENT TEMPERATURES

Warm Growing	Intermediate Growing	Cool Growing
Aerides fieldingii	Bifrenaria harrisoniae	Ada aurantiaca
Angraecum sesquipedale	Brassia verrucosa	Coelogyne cristata
Angraecum veitchii	Brassolaeliocattleya Norman's Bay	Cymbidium devonianum
Ansellia africana	Cattleya Bow Bells	Cattleya aurantiaca
Calanthe vestita	Cattleya bowringiana	Cymbidium Pearl Balkis
Chysis bractescens	Dendrochilum glumaceum	Cymbidium Peter Pan
Dendrobium phalaenopsis	Epidendrum cochliatum	Cymbidium Vieux Rose
Phalaenopsis aphrodite	Epidendrum ibaguense	Dendrobium nobile
Phalaenopsis equestris	Gomesa crispa	Dendrochilum glumaceum
Phalaenopsis lueddemanniana	Lycaste aromatica	Gomesa crispa
Phalaenopsis Party Dress	Maxillaria luteo-alba	Laelia anceps
Phalaenopsis sanderiana	Miltonia clowesii	Masdevallia coccinea
Phalaenopsis Temple Cloud	Paphiopedilum callosum	Masdevallia simula
Phalaenopsis Zada	Paphiopedilum fairieanum	Maxillaria tenuifolia
Potinaria Sunrise	Stanhopea wardii	Odontioda Memtor
Rhynchostylis gigantea	Trichopilia suavis	Odontoglossum crispum
Sobralia macrantha	Vanda coerulea	Odontoglossum grande
Thunia marshalliana	Vuylstekeara Cambria	Pleione formosana
Vanda sanderana	Wilsonaria Lyoth	Vuylstekeara Cambria
Vanda tricolor suavis	Zygopetalum intermedium	Zygopetalum intermedium

Left: Cymbidiums are ideal for the greenhouse in which winter night temperatures are maintained to 10°C. But they also need cool summer nights to flower successfully.

Right: The compact growth and tall flower spikes of *Odontocidium* Thwaitesii make it a popular orchid for the cool greenhouse.

Although many of those classified as cool-growing will grow in warm temperatures, they will almost certainly not flower without a low night temperature—preferably down to or below 10°C (50°F)—during mid-summer, which is needed to initiate flower buds. In tropical and subtropical areas of the world, where nocturnal temperatures seldom drop sufficiently, it is almost impossible to grow such genera as *Cymbidium*, *Odontoglossum*, most *Masdevallia* and many cool-growing species derived from high altitudes.

Knowledge of the altitude as well as the country of origin of many species is the pointer to successful cultivation of the hybrids derived from these species. One example may be seen in Thailand, where the traditional area for commercial orchid growing is around the capital, Bangkok, once a coastal city. Cattleyas, the warmer-growing *Dendrobium phalaenopsis* hybrids and superlatively vanda hybrids and intergenerics grow in abundance on every verandah and front garden. The constant heat and high humidity are ideal for these orchids, but impossible for the cooler-growing genera so widely known in temperate zones. Yet on a visit to Chiang Mai, a hill town some 800km (500 miles) north of Bangkok, cymbidium hybrids were observed growing well and flowering abundantly. Although daytime temperatures of 30-32°C (86-99°F) are common in Chiang Mai, at night the temperature often falls to 11-13°C (52-55°F) and bud initiation is therefore possible.

Amateur growers of cymbidiums who are experiencing problems with the production of ample flowers may like to apply the 'Thai' solution to their own situation. Where cymbidiums are grown in a greenhouse without other orchids, the problem of obtaining good flower production—every mature cymbidium pseudobulb is capable of producing at least two spikes—does not exist, as the entire cultural regime cán be directed toward the cymbidiums' requirements. But, as in the majority of amateurs' collections, where cymbidiums are just one of 20 or 30 genera, the provision of light, warmth and ventilation must be dictated by the requirements of the majority.

Orchids outside

To obtain as low as possible summer night temperatures (especially desired by cymbidiums), it is advantageous to create a 'summer quarters' area outside the greenhouse where the cymbidiums will live happily from summer to early autumn.

Indeed, in temperate areas that do not suffer from frosts during the winter, many commercial cymbidium growers house their plants all year round in 'shade houses'. These consist of a tubular metal framework covered by Sarlon cloth, a fine mesh material that provides both the necessary shade in summer and protects the blooms from heavy rain during the cooler winter months. Shade houses also provide partial protection from strong winds. This will not only prevent any possible physical damage to young or semimature growths, but will also assist in the maintenance of a humid atmosphere around the plants, and reduce rapid drying out of the compost.

Alternatively, some growers place their cool-growing orchids on benches in the dappled shade provided by, for example, a large apple tree. However, many fruit trees, unless regularly sprayed, become infested with red spider mite and aphids during the summer and autumn months, and great care must be taken to ensure that the orchids do not become similarly affected. This is particularly important immediately before the orchids are returned to the greenhouse where, in the artificially extended 'summer' provided by the additional warmth, a few stray insects or even eggs could rapidly result in potentially dangerous colonies.

An added bonus of moving at least part of the collection outside for the summer months is the extra—albeit temporary—space created in the greenhouse. The temptation to fill this space with additional orchids should be resisted, unless autumnal accommodation problems can be solved in another way! Instead, use this extra area to space out the orchids remaining in the greenhouse. In this way they will be able to take full advantage of the all-important light and air during the growing season; and, being in full view, will also receive the correct amounts of water and food. However conscientious the grower, crowded conditions are not conducive to perfect culture. During late summer, it is desirable to clean the greenhouse thoroughly before the onset of winter weather, and to ensure that the structure is in good repair—two tasks that are carried out more easily in a partially empty greenhouse.

Orchid resting periods

So far we have dealt solely with the conditions that are desirable for the growth of orchids, but of almost equal importance to the successful flowering of a well grown plant is that part of culture known as 'resting'. The question of when and how to rest an orchid causes much confusion among amateur growers, and even more experienced growers cannot offer precise guidelines on the subject. In most cases, resting a plant is merely co-operating with the orchid's natural desire to slow down its rate of growth during winter months. This is usually less critical with hybrid orchids than with species which, in their natural environment, would adapt their growth pattern in order to survive a seasonal period of drought. In extreme cases, all foliage is shed in order to reduce the plant's moisture requirement, and severe shrivelling of the pseudobulbs is occasionally evident.

Requirements of deciduous orchids

In areas where this seasonal drought is severe, it is normal for average temperatures to be lower than those during the wet season, thus extreme desiccation of the orchid is uncommon. But it is not only the orchid that adapts to the changing season: the tree on which it grows, having provided shelter from the hot sun, also becomes deciduous, thereby exposing the mature pseudobulbs and growths to all available light. Not all orchids receive this treatment in the wild, as some grow in evergreen forests or in areas with little seasonal fluctuation in temperature, but careful observation of each individual orchid will greatly assist in deciding the degree of rest required.

With orchids that naturally become completely deciduous during winter and early spring—most pleiones, calanthes, *nobile*-type dendrobiums and catasetums, for example—the supply of water should be gradually reduced as the foliage begins to turn yellow during early autumn. Simultaneously, the amount of light and air given to the plant should be increased. This can be achieved by reducing the shading or by moving the orchid to a brighter position in the greenhouse. Where possible, it would also be advantageous to reduce the temperature slightly.

Another indication that the orchid is approaching a natural period of rest is a reduction or even a complete stop in root activity. When this occurs the velamen (the greenish-white outer layer of absorbent cells) grows partially or completely over the normally bright green root tips. This is the plant's way of saying that winter is approaching, and the velamen covers the very tender root tip as a form of protection from both the elements and possible physical damage.

Above: The bluish venation of the leaves indicates that this plant is in need of water. But do not saturate the compost when the plant is at rest, as the roots may be killed.

Below: The end of the resting period is heralded by the appearance of a new shoot at the base of the previous year s pseudobulb.

Above and Right: Many cattleyas produce their flower buds in autumn just before their resting period. Late winter sunshine encourages the buds to develop within the sheath (right), and in a few weeks they will grow through the top to produce a flamboyant display.

With negligible root activity and partial or complete loss of leaves, the moisture requirement of the plant is very small. Unless severe shrivelling of the pseudobulbs is noticed, all watering should be withheld until new growth is apparent with the onset of brighter, warmer conditions the following spring. An occasional overhead spray will prevent excessive desiccation of the plant during its resting period, but this light spray should be applied infrequently, for example, during the occasional spells of brighter winter weather.

Requirements of evergreen orchids

Not only deciduous orchids require a rest; evergreen types also undergo a period of reduced activity, usually coinciding with the duller days of winter. With an orchid that discards its foliage—providing this is for natural reasons—and thus loses little water, the moisture requirement is obviously minimal. However, with orchids that retain their foliage for several seasons, the grower must be more critically observant; taking careful note of the root tip activity. The foliage also offers subtle guidelines: if the leaves become lank, or in extreme cases slightly desiccated, the plant has been left too long without water. But just before this stage, the leaves of many genera take on a bluish tint, an indication that water should be applied before dehydration of the tissue causes permanent damage.

Duration of rest

The duration of rest may vary from a few weeks to several months, but the plant will indicate when normal culture should be resumed by recommencing growth. In sympodial orchids, a new shoot will start to grow from the base of the current

pseudobulb, and this resurgence of activity will frequently coincide with the development of the overwintered flower buds that have remained wholly or partially dormant during the resting period. Spring-flowering cattleyas that produced a flower sheath the previous autumn will send up their flower buds within the sheath; in dendrobiums, the nodes of the pseudobulbs will start to swell and produce flower buds. When this occurs some moisture will be required, but do not try to hurry the orchid into growth by applying too much water before the new shoot is growing vigorously.

As with all arbitrary rules, there are exceptions. The tropical species from the Philippines, *Dendrochilum glumaceum,* which produces its long sprays of sweetly scented, creamy white flowers in early spring, completes its new growths by midsummer, and then has a lengthy period of very reduced activity until early winter, when the new shoots—from the centre of which the flower spikes emerge—start into growth. The angraecums, aerangis and other members of the subtribe Sarcanthinae, when grown in northern temperate areas, undergo a short rest period during late summer. As these African species are evergreen monopodial orchids, this lessening of activity is indicated by the root tips, which stop growing for approximately three to four weeks. During this period, water should not be withheld completely as these orchids are without pseudobulbs and cannot store much moisture. But this reduction in water, coupled with almost full exposure to light and an abundance of fresh air, appears to stimulate the production of flower spikes, which appear from the leaf axils simultaneously with the resurgence of root activity.

Survival of terrestrial orchids

Whereas tropical orchids enter a period of rest in order to survive a dry season that is unfavourable for growth, the problem facing terrestrial European and northern hemisphere orchids is not one of drought, but freezing temperatures. As with other temperate perennial plants, these hardy orchids protect themselves from the severe cold of winter by dying down to the surface of the soil. Many of these orchids possess a tuberous or thickened root system underground that stores the food manufactured by the plant during one growing season. With the return of warmer weather the following spring, this food is used to produce a new shoot, which in time will manufacture its own tubers to replace the by now exhausted ones from the previous season. Potatoes and dahlias have similar patterns of growth and survival, except that they are not frost hardy.

However, the problems of growing these hardy terrestrial orchids need not concern us, as apart from their essential mycorrhizal fungus associations, which make garden culture difficult, nearly all temperate orchids are protected plants, and therefore it is illegal to collect them.

Composts and Potting

As with all other aspects of plant culture, selection of the correct medium in which to grow an orchid is an important part of its environment. Successful cultivation depends upon each part of this environment being as near the ideal as possible, therefore it is necessary to ascertain what an orchid needs from the compost around its roots.

Basic requirements of a compost

Most orchids grown commercially or in amateurs' collections are derived from the tropics. Many are epiphytes, their roots growing exposed to the atmosphere, and even the terrestrial orchids, which live on the ground, do not send their roots down into the soil in the manner of most ground-dwelling plants. Instead, they spread out horizontally in the aerated upper layer of humus on the forest floor, and therefore the most important constituent of the medium around the orchid roots is air.

In tropical areas, where rainfall—although often seasonal—is usually very heavy, orchids are not commonly found in places that remain waterlogged. Despite the frequent, often daily, falls of rain, both epiphytic orchids and those growing in the loose surface of the ground do not remain wet for long once the rain has stopped. A second prerequisite of the compost, therefore, will be perfect drainage—a quality that will almost certainly be present if there is an abundance of air.

Yet orchid roots also require reasonably firm anchorage as they like to be in close contact with the surface on or in which they are growing. Anyone who has grown vandas or phalaenopsis will have experienced the adventitious roots that adhere very firmly to any solid surface within reach. Even the finer roots of oncidiums and odontoglossums, for instance, will become attached to the inner surface of the pot or to the drainage material, particularly potsherd or polystyrene. In most cases the root adheres so firmly that it will break when removed.

Despite these requirements, orchids appreciate a reasonably retentive compost, except for a few species that revel in mainly dry conditions. If the compost dries out too quickly, within hours after each watering, most orchids are unable to absorb sufficient moisture for steady growth. Where this situation persists, the plant grows on a stop-go basis, which results at the end of the growing season in smaller growths and/or pseudobulbs that are unlikely to flower satisfactorily.

Coupled with a retentive compost is a supply of nutrient to the plant. Less emphasis than previously is now placed on

Right: Orchids will grow well in pots, pans, baskets or on rafts, and a mixed collection will make a varied and attractive display in greenhouse or sun lounge.

the compost's ability to release nutrient to the plant over a long period, better results being obtained by regularly adding feed to the watering schedule. Obviously the compost should be reasonably water-retentive, otherwise the nutrient will not remain in the pot.

The perfect compost will be free-draining yet retentive, and provide good physical support to the orchid. If this sounds contradictory, remember that similar qualities are sought by the grower of hardy plants in the selection of the most suitable soil. But above all, an abundance of air in the compost is essential, as very few plants will thrive where the medium around their roots is airless. In the open ground the texture of the soil is improved by incorporating extra humus or by applying lime. Such processes allow more air to enter the soil, with the result that better growth is achieved. Orchids, however, require far more air around their roots than most other plants.

A brief review of composts over the past two centuries may reveal how present-day mixtures have evolved.

Evolution of composts

When tropical orchids were first introduced into Europe during the first half of the eighteenth century, very little was known about their cultural requirements. Mistakenly thinking that all orchids needed an abundance of heat and moisture, early growers placed their newly imported plants in a mixture of rotted wood and leaves, then plunged the pots in beds of sawdust placed over the heating pipes or the brick flues of coal fires. Although the excessively high temperatures and humidity did little to encourage the orchids to thrive, it was the almost completely airless conditions—particularly around the roots—that were primarily responsible for the hundreds of thousands of orchids that perished, mainly in England, during the first 100 years of importation.

Success was not achieved until the middle nineteenth century, when it was realized that light and air were important to the orchid's well-being. By this time a peat-based compost was being used, with reasonably satisfactory results, but 'hard potting' was still practised, and hence very little air remained in the compost. As suitable peat became scarce, growers—by now armed with a greater knowledge of the orchid's natural environments—searched for an alternative material. Fibrous roots of ferns, *Polypodium vulgare* in Europe, and *Osmunda gracilis* and *O. regalis* in the United States, when finely chopped and mixed with sphagnum moss, provided the alternative that was to remain the standard compost for over half a century, and which is still used by some growers today.

Modern composts

Apart from diminishing resources, with the inevitable large increase in cost, osmunda/sphagnum compost has several big drawbacks. It decomposes rapidly when subjected to modern inorganic fertilizers, and preparation of the mixture, which involves cleaning the osmunda, gathering and cleaning the sphagnum moss, then cutting it into approximately 2.5cm (1in) lengths, is very time-consuming. Additionally, it may take many months or even seasons to become proficient at potting with this compost, whereas anyone can successfully pot an orchid when using a modern potting material. Thus, although a peat-based compost is still favoured by some growers, one based on shredded pine bark or redwood bark is now widely used. It is difficult to be precise about the various constituents of composts, but the following two mixtures have proved satisfactory with a wide range of genera in many parts of the world.

Bark-based compost
10 parts medium grade pine bark
5 parts fine grade pine bark
1½ parts perlag
¼ part granulated 0.6cm (0.25in) charcoal

Peat-based compost
2 parts sphagnum moss peat
1 part horticultural sand
1 part perlite

Charcoal
Perlag
Fine grade pine bark
Medium grade pine bark
Polystyrene chunks for pot drainage

Above: Bark-based compost

Above: Peat-based compost

Composts and Potting

Added to this should be approximately 85g (3oz) of Dolomite lime per 36 litres (1 bushel) of mixture to reduce the acidity of the compost (bringing the pH up to around 5.5-6.0). Some genera, notably paphiopedilums, require a slightly more alkaline compost, with a pH up to 6.5. Medium-grade bark is generally about the size of a finger nail, with an average particle size of around 1.3cm (0.5in), whilst fine-grade is approximately one third of this size. Perlag and perlite are both thermally processed volcanic rock, highly absorbent and light in weight. Neither breaks down under bacterial action nor do they absorb or release measurable amounts of nutrient. Both are widely used in horticulture. The possible advantages of perlag over perlite are superior strength and greater absorption. This results in a more evenly moist compost throughout the pot, regardless of size, and hence less frequent watering.

One word of warning: although it is possible to aerate a peat-based compost by the addition of shredded bark, do not be tempted to increase the density of a bark mixture by adding peat. The finer particles of peat will be washed through the upper layers of a bark compost by the action of normal watering, until the lower half of the pot becomes clogged with wet peat and drainage is seriously impaired.

If a closer bark compost is needed, for instance when potting young seedlings, increase the quantity of fine bark whilst simultaneously reducing the medium bark content until the two ratios are reversed (10 parts fine: 5 parts medium).

In some parts of the world, alternative materials are used with great success. It is obviously more economical to use locally available materials—one South African orchidist living near a fruit cannery used to grow cattleyas on peach stones. The rough outer surface of a peach stone would hold only a limited amount of moisture, but would be an ideal material to which the roots of epiphytic orchids could adhere. Also in Africa, and presumably Asia, rice husks are used to aerate composts in place of grit or sand. But the greatest economy is practised by many growers of vandaceous plants in Southeast Asia: the orchids—*Vanda, Arachnis, Renanthera* and other monopodial genera—are tied into teak baskets without *any* medium around their roots, which, in the very humid conditions, rapidly grow round and through the baskets. Repotting merely involves fixing the small initial basket into a larger basket.

Orchids in baskets

Growing orchids in wooden baskets is not confined to the Far East. Once the theory of fresh air around an orchid's

Below: Many epiphytic orchids, such as the Madagascan species, *Angraecum sesquipedale*, are ideal subjects for growing in baskets. Baskets can be purchased ready made, or be assembled from offcuts of timber: teak is the traditional wood used, but cedar and pine are also suitable.

Right: While smaller-growing orchids can be successfully cultivated in pots, larger plants may fair better in wooden baskets.

roots became accepted practice, growers in nineteenth century Europe and the United States adopted baskets for the successful culture of many genera, even the terrestrial paphiopedilums (or cypripediums as they were then called).

Baskets are best made from strips of approximately 1.3 x 1.3cm (0.5 x 0.5in) teak (cedar being a modern alternative); the size of the basket can easily be varied by altering the length of the strip. Small holes are drilled through both ends of each strip, and a strong wire threaded through the holes. The sides of the basket need not exceed 7.5cm (3in) in depth, thus using three or four strips of wood with an equal space between each strip. Similar strips are tacked across the base, again leaving a space between each piece.

There is no doubt that some very fine orchids were grown in these containers. The fibre/moss compost of the day, coupled with an abundance of cheap labour needed to maintain many of the large collections, was admirably suited to basket culture. But as modern peat or bark-based composts came into use and with skilled horticultural workers both scarce and relatively expensive, it became impractical to use baskets unless essential. Some genera, for instance *Stanhopea* and *Coryanthes,* produce pendulous flower spikes that would languish in the compost if grown in pots. Indeed, stanhopeas could not be brought into bloom in Europe until, in about 1820, one was accidentally dropped, breaking the pot and thereby exposing the frustrated flower spikes!

However, modern composts do not lend themselves easily to being used in basket culture, and it will be necessary either to line the basket before use, or to reduce the size of the spaces between the slots in the basket's sides and base by inserting additional pieces of wood. If lining the basket is preferred, use either fresh sphagnum moss or strips and offcuts of polypropylene mesh.

Below: Positioning a sympodial orchid diagonally in the basket makes maximum use of the growing area and allows the plant to remain undisturbed for two or three years. The long rhizomes of some cattleyas make pot culture difficult and bulbophyllums are happier growing in baskets.

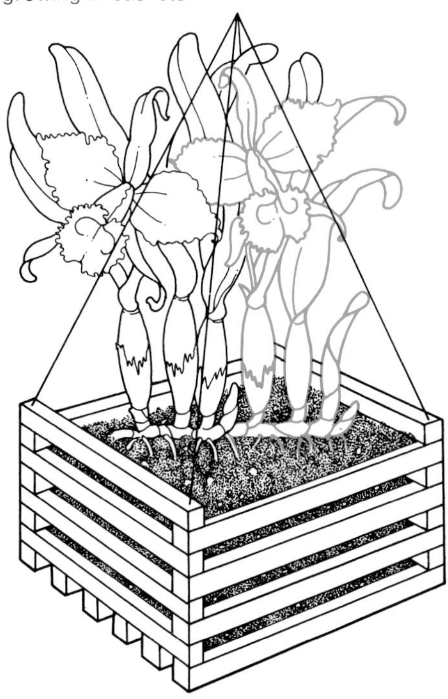

Once the basket is prepared, position the orchid so that there is ample space for the next two years' growth; for this reason diagonal placing is often preferred. Then merely fill the basket with compost, ensuring that the spaces under the rhizome and between the roots are firmly packed, but not compressed, as this will assist in steadying the orchid until the new roots become active.

Top heavy orchids may need to be secured initially with fishing line, from one side of the basket, around the rhizome, and across to the other side of the basket. When finished, the orchid plant should not sway in the breeze, and the rhizome should lie just on the surface of the compost, with all available space in front of the leading pseudobulb(s) or new growth(s).

Orchids in pots

During the early part of this century a special orchid pot was developed, with large holes around the sides and in the base. In those days, clay flower pots were made by hand, and it was not difficult to obtain pots of almost any design or size. These pots were unglazed, leaving a rough, permeable surface through which, it is said, the plant's roots could 'breathe'. So firmly did the orchid roots adhere to this rough surface that the only practical way to repot the plant was to smash the pot, a perfectly acceptable method where labour and materials are both available and inexpensive.

The demise of the local pottery — a trend fortunately now reversed — in the 1930s, coupled again with a changing compost, meant that by the middle of this century most pot plants, including orchids, were being grown in factory produced, semi-glazed clay pots with just a small drainage hole in the centre of the base.

With the advent of plastics, clay pots became increasingly scarce. However, the major disadvantage of conventional plastic pots is that they become brittle and useless after a few years. They have now been superseded by pots made of polypropylene, which has many advantages over both clay and plastic. Polypropylene pots are light, flexible, seldom break or crack in storage or when dropped, and are readily available in a great variety of sizes and shapes, including square pots. There is even a mesh or basket pot for those orchids requiring drier conditions around their roots, and another with very large drainage holes through which pendulous spikes of coryanthes, stanhopeas and, for instance, *Cymbidium devonianum,* can easily emerge. Polypropylene is not a permeable material, there is no evaporation of moisture through the pot sides and thus no accumulation of

Left: There is a pot to suit every orchid. Available in polypropylene or clay they come in all shapes and sizes. Mesh pots make good substitutes for wooden baskets.

Composts and Potting

salts on the inner surface of the pot. It also has good insulation qualities, thus the roots are less subject to the fluctuations in temperature that frequently occur where clay pots are used.

Mesh pots, also made from polypropylene, are suitable for some vandas, phalaenopsis, and several of the smaller cool-growing species that prefer a reasonably fine retentive compost, but produce pendulous or horizontal flower spikes, thus making both basket and conventional pot culture impractical. *Masdevallia bella* is a typical example. The standard potting procedure is followed when using mesh pots but 'crocking' the pot bottom with drainage material is not necessary.

Orchids on trees or rafts

Adaptable as orchids generally are, there are some species that, because of either their straggling, strictly epiphytic habit of growth or their insistence on having their roots fully exposed to the atmosphere, are not comfortable when pot culture is attempted. These orchids may be contained in a variety of ways: by tying them to blocks of tree-fern fibre or pieces of cork bark, or even by arranging a small 'tree' within the greenhouse to which all such orchids could be attached.

In the tropics this method can easily be practised in the open garden where spraying or watering several times daily, if necessary, will not interfere with the growth of neighbouring plants. However, this may be difficult under glass, so all plants mounted on blocks should be grouped in one place.

Many of the monopodial angraecoid orchids, from mainland Africa or Madagascar, are particularly well suited to mounting on rafts of tree fern or cork bark—none more so than *Cyrtorchis arcuata,* a beautifully scented, white-flowered species from East Africa. This orchid, when grown in a pot or pan, seems to produce its roots horizontally, and any attempt at training these roots towards their intended home merely results in their breaking. However, if you grow this species as a true epiphyte—which it is in the wild—the roots will very rapidly cling to the surface of the raft provided.

Mounting these plants is simplicity itself. First, select a piece of tree fern, the dimensions of which match the size of the plant. Although it would be wasteful of space to use a large raft for a compact, slow-growing species, conversely you should not need to reraft the orchid for at least two or three years, so allow room for future growth. Both tree-fern fibre blocks and rafts and cork bark pieces are readily available in a wide variety of sizes

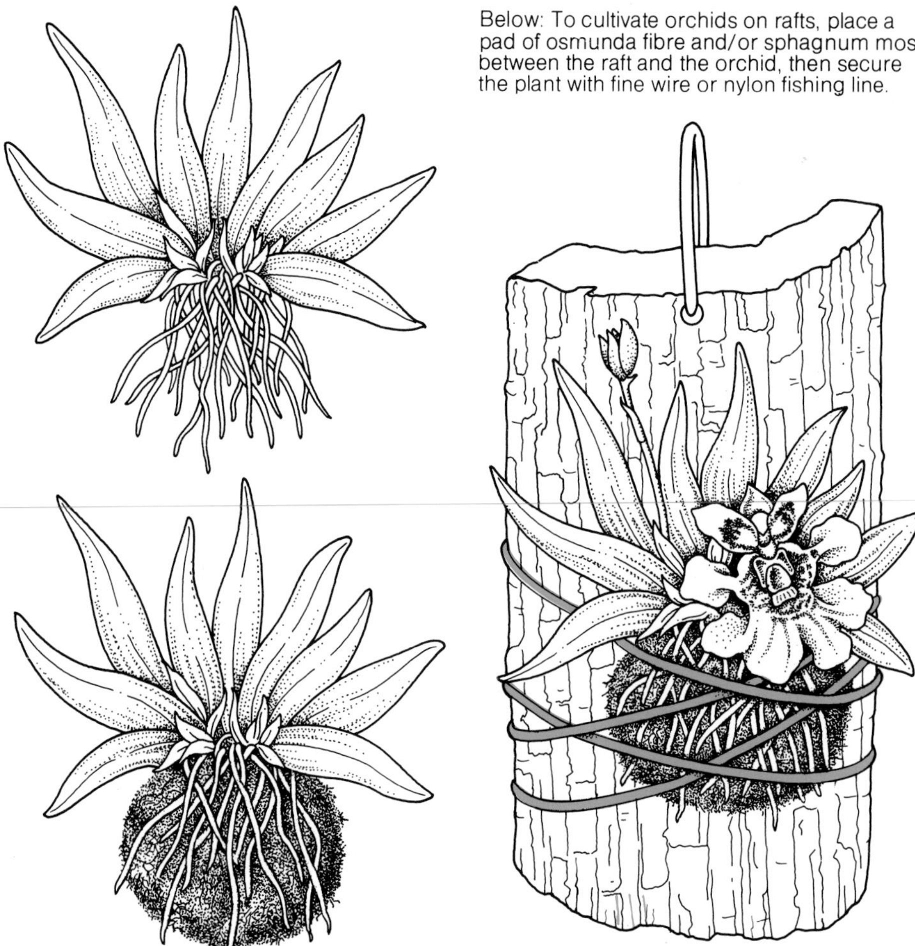

Below: To cultivate orchids on rafts, place a pad of osmunda fibre and/or sphagnum moss between the raft and the orchid, then secure the plant with fine wire or nylon fishing line.

Right: Many orchids—especially those with long, aerial roots—will thrive on rafts of bark suspended from the greenhouse roof.

Above and Below: A tree branch 'planted' in the greenhouse makes a good home for orchids with long, climbing rhizomes. The pendulous flower spikes of *Coelogyne massangeana* (below) are displayed to full advantage when the plant is grown in this way.

and shapes, making correct selection easy. Having chosen a suitable raft, merely fasten the orchid on top with fishing line or plastic-covered wire. Some growers place a pad of osmunda fibre and/or spagnum moss between the orchid and the raft, as this helps to retain some moisture around the plant until the new roots emerge.

Sympodial pseudobulbous orchids are also suitable candidates for growing on rafts. Some have a lengthy rhizome between each pseudobulb, while others possess a rhizome that grows upwards at an angle of approximately 45°, thus the orchid rapidly 'climbs out' of a normal pot. These orchids are fastened to a suitable raft in a similar manner to that described for monopodials, ensuring that the leading growth or pseudobulb is facing inwards—pointing *towards* the potential host. This will encourage the new roots, as they emerge from the base of the growth, to head straight for the raft.

However aesthetically pleasing it is to grow plants in this 'natural' manner in the greenhouse, there are certain disadvantages. The main one is maintaining sufficient moisture around the plant for steady growth. This will entail spraying at least once daily, which will be difficult when the plants are taken into the house whilst in flower. A compromise solution for these undisciplinable orchids is to plant them in baskets. The monopodials will still have a hard surface to which their roots may adhere, yet there will be some compost around them. For those orchids with elongated rhizomes, most baskets will squeeze into a long diamond shape to allow extra forward space when required.

Repotting Orchids

The most advantageous time to repot an orchid is when the new growth is approximately 5cm (2in) high, just before the new roots emerge. In most cases this will be during early spring and will coincide with the orchid's resurgence of activity as the day length increases. Plants may also be repotted in early autumn, when the heat of the summer has diminished, but there is still time for the orchid's root system to re-establish before the onset of winter. It is obviously not possible to repot every orchid at these times, and in practice any period except midsummer—when plants need their entire root system intact in order to grow well—and midwinter—when most orchids are at least partially dormant—has proved satisfactory.

How to repot

Orchids scheduled for repotting should be allowed to dry out slightly beforehand, as this will loosen the compost around the roots. To remove an orchid from its pot prior to repotting, place one hand over the top of the pot with the orchid plant between the fingers. Invert the pot and then sharply tap the top on the edge of the potting bench or table. If the plant is reluctant to leave the pot, some gentle persuasion may be needed. Here another advantage of polypropylene pots becomes evident; being pliable, they can be squeezed, thus encouraging the plant's removal. As the plant is removed, much of the old compost will fall away. Unless you are potting-on seedlings or young plants to slightly larger pots, all old compost should be removed, thus exposing the root system for scrutiny. On an old plant,

Composts and Potting

or one that has not been repotted for several years, part of the root system will be dead. Cut these decaying roots back to healthy tissue, and shorten any overlong roots that could easily by broken during potting.

Place the orchid in a pot just large enough to accommodate its root system and allow for approximately two years growth. Orchids prefer to be slightly underpotted rather than be planted in too large a pot. For forward growing orchids, such as cattleyas, odontoglossums and lycastes, the oldest pseudobulb should be placed against one side of the pot, with all available space in front of the new growth. Other types which usually grow on all sides—paphiopedilums and masdevallias are but two examples—should be placed in the centre of the pot, as should monopodial orchids.

Holding the orchid so that the base of the growth is approximately 2.5cm (1in) below the pot edge, place a handful of drainage material into the pot, working it through the root system until about 1.3 to 2.5cm (0.5-1in) of material covers the bottom of the pot. Polystyrene or large-grade perlag are preferred for this purpose, but pea-grit or large-grade pine or redwood bark may also be used. Then fill the pot with the chosen compost—which should be moist—tapping the pot on the bench and steadily working the compost under the rhizome and between the roots.

Gentle pressure round the surface of the compost will steady the orchid in its new pot, although tall pseudobulbs may need staking until the new root system is underway. Any orchid scheduled for propagation is obviously best divided during a repotting session.

Potting-on

This procedure is sometimes used when

Above: When growing orchids with pendulous flower spikes in pots, watch for the emergence of the young spike. In *Cymbidium devonianum*, the spike grows downwards from the base of the pseudobulbs and may bury itself in the compost. Planting the orchid high up in the pots—slightly above the level of the rim—(Above right) allows the spike to grow freely down over the side of the pot.

Right: This plant is well overdue for repotting—the new roots should be in compost. The new growths can be cut from the parent plant and potted up in fresh compost.

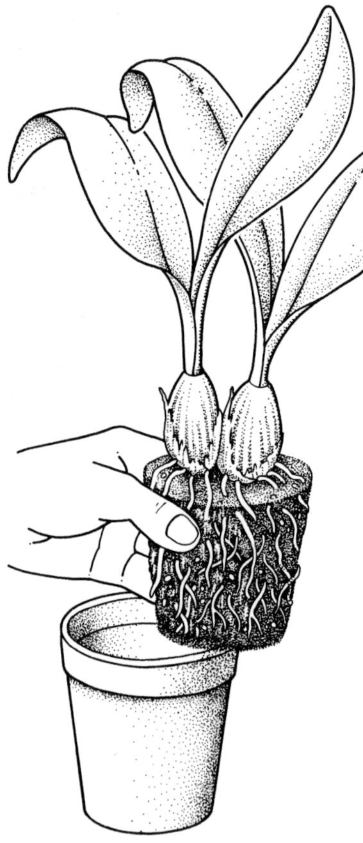

Above: To remove the plant from its pot, invert the pot, holding the orchid between your fingers, and tap the pot rim sharply on the bench.

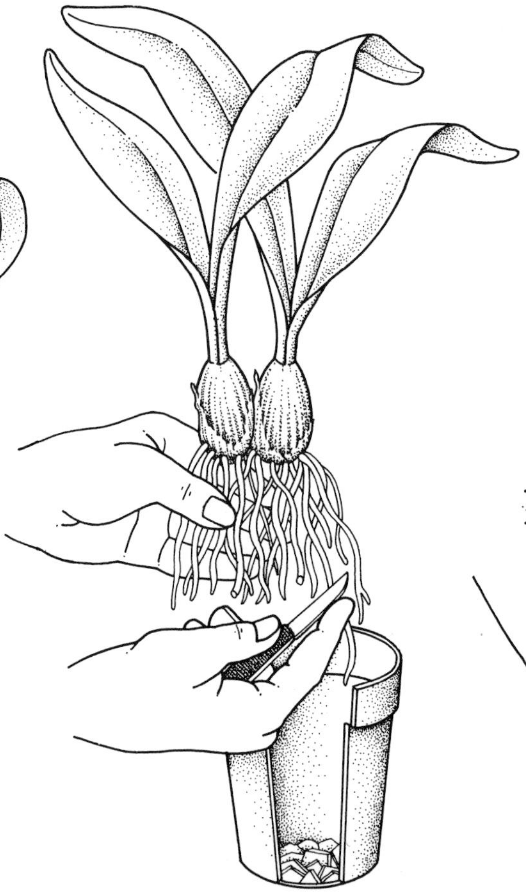

Above: Remove all the old compost, cut away dead roots and trim back any overlong roots that might be damaged during repotting.

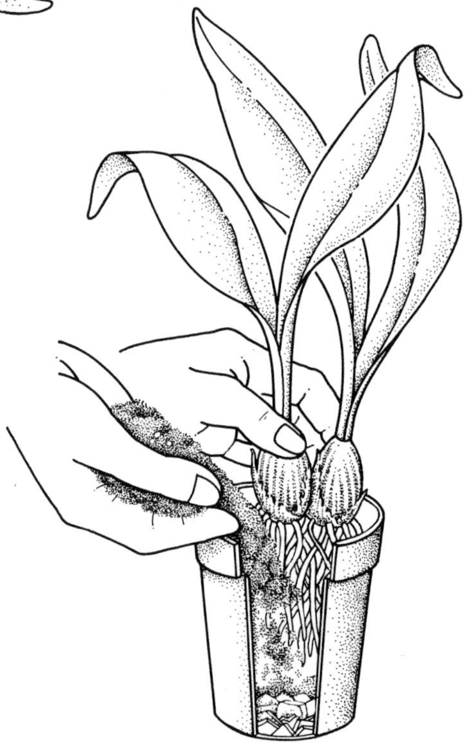

Above: Position the orchid so that the base of the growth is about 2.5cm (1in) below the pot rim. Fill in around the plant with compost.

the compost in which a young plant is growing is still sound, but the orchid's root system has outgrown the pot. The plants should be watered the day before, as this will help to keep the root ball intact when the plant is knocked out of its pot. Select a pot one or possibly two sizes larger, depending upon the size and vigour of the root system, and place crocks and a little compost in the base of the pot sufficient to bring the level of the old compost to just below the rim of the pot. After positioning the plant in its new pot, simply fill in the space around the sides with fresh material. A few gentle taps on the bench, coupled with light pressure around the edges of the compost, will settle the orchid into its larger pot.

Rehabilitating repotted orchids

Preventing dehydration is the biggest problem when repotting. Orchids, with their water-storing pseudobulbs and fleshy roots, are better equipped than most plants to withstand this temporary setback, but a few simple precautions will greatly assist the process of re-establishment. After repotting or potting-on, the plant should be watered thoroughly to settle in the new compost. After this, the pots should be kept slightly drier than usual to allow any damaged or cut root surfaces to form a callus, and to encourage the roots to look for moisture in the fresh compost.

To compensate for this reduction of water to the orchid's roots, the atmospheric humidity should be maintained at a higher level than previously. Indeed, freshly potted orchids—especially those in baskets or mounted on tree fern—benefit from a light overhead spray each morning, and a second misting during the early evening if the day has been warm. If the weather becomes very bright and hot, repotted orchids will need additional shading, although those merely potted-on will not need this extra care.

After approximately three to four weeks, it should be possible to revert to a normal cultural routine as the new roots grow into the fresh compost. The interval between each repotting may vary from a few months to two or three years. Young seedlings benefit by being moved to a slightly larger pot with fresh compost every few months, whereas adult plants are best left undisturbed for several seasons.

However, if the compost has become too decomposed (broken down), or the plant's roots are not happy, a complete repot at the earliest opportunity is often the only solution. Thus it makes good sense to ensure that all the compost used is fresh and in good condition, so that mature orchids may thrive in the same pot for at least two years.

Increasing Your Collection

Apart from achieving new growth there are two main reasons for dividing an orchid plant. First, it may have become unmanageably large so that it no longer fits easily into a container of convenient size. Second, some part of the plant (usually the centre, though occasionally the back section) may have become diseased and/or, by reason of age, defoliated. In monopodial orchids, for example, the lower, older leaves drop, leaving an ugly bare stem.

Every plant is an individual and needs different treatment, but there are two basic techniques, one for monopodial and the other for sympodial growth.

Monopodials — simple division

The main direction of growth in monopodial orchids is from the top of the plant, though some orchids in this group (notably the smaller angraecoids) do produce growth from the base. In general terms, any monopodial orchid that has grown taller than 75cm (30in) becomes an embarrassment to many amateur growers' greenhouses. In places such as Singapore, Hawaii and the West Indies, where they are grown as garden plants or in cut-flower nurseries, these orchids grow to several metres tall. Under greenhouse conditions in temperate areas, however, it is likely that many monopodial orchids approaching 1m (39in) in height will already have lost some of their lower leaves, exposing the woody stem. Aerial roots will have developed on at least the lower two thirds of the plant and to propagate new growth the stem should be cut through immediately below one of these roots, preferably leaving three or four pairs of leaves on the lower section. These leaves will act as a 'sap drawer' (rather like the two or three leaves that should be left beyond the upper truss on a tomato plant), allowing this part of the plant to photosynthesize.

The top part of the plant, removed with its own root system already growing, should be potted into a suitable container, remembering that monopodial orchids in particular like an abundance of fresh air around their roots.

Within six to eight weeks during spring or early summer one or more dormant buds, or 'eyes', situated in the leaf axils of the lower section will have started into growth. These can either be left to develop on the parent, or, when each new growth has initiated its own small root system (which may take several months), they can be removed and potted separately. Exceptionally, the old and by now very woody lower section will produce further new growth, but for all practical purposes it is not worth retaining.

Monopodials — nature's way

On certain monopodial orchids, notably species of *Phalaenopsis* and *Vanda,* plantlets called 'keikis' (a Hawaiian word meaning babies) develop on the flower spikes. (Keikis also develop on some sympodial orchids, such as dendrobiums.) As soon as a keiki possesses an independent root system it is possible to remove it

Vegetative Propagation of Monopodial Orchids

The photographs on these two pages show how a typical monopodial orchid can be divided into three healthy plants. Although all growers like to see their greenhouses full of plants, the temptation to divide plants unnecessarily should be resisted. If divisions of orchids are too small, all their energies will go towards building up plant strength and they will seldom, if ever, produce flowers.

Basic rules

Only propagate vigorous, free-flowering stock; there is little merit in producing additional stock of orchids that were unsatisfactory to begin with.

If it appears that the plant being divided is infected by a virus, heat sterilize the cutting tools by passing the blades through a flame.

When there are signs of fungus or rot in the plant, all cut surfaces should be liberally dusted with captan or a similar fungicide to control the infection.

1 This plant of *Vanda cristata* has become too tall and is an ideal candidate for propagation by division. The top section can be removed by cutting through the stem and the keiki growing in the centre can also be removed and grown into a new plant.

2 When cutting through the stem to remove the top section, ensure that the cut is made cleanly, and immediately below one or more new roots. Any damaged tissue should be trimmed off.

3 The keiki growing on the end of a previous flower spike has developed its own root system and can be used as the starting point for a new plant. To remove it, cut through the flower spike immediately behind the young plantlet.

from the parent plant and pot it up.

A good example of keiki production is shown by the plant of *Vanda cristata* illustrated on this page. A young growth appeared on the end of a short flower spike in early summer, but did not develop a root system until the following spring. While attached to the parent plant the keiki gained all its nourishment through the old flower spike, which remained green. As soon as the keiki produced a healthy root system it was removed from the parent plant and potted up.

Species from the *Phalaenopsis lueddemanniana* group, which originate in the Philippines, will frequently produce young plantlets from the ends or nodes of flower spikes. Unlike dendrobiums, this is not at the expense of flower production; keikis and flowers often appear together.

Right: Phalaenopsis commonly produce keikis, both in the wild and in cultivation, and one parent plant may give rise to many plantlets. This *Phalaenopsis lueddemanniana* keiki has produced an excellent root system and is itself in flower; it is at the ideal stage for removal and potting up.

4 Both the top section of the plant and the keiki should be potted up in coarse bark chips. Most monopodial orchids thrive in baskets because these containers allow ample air circulation for the roots. The polypropylene baskets shown here are pliable and are able to accommodate awkward roots.

5 A vandaceous orchid three months after removal of the top section. Already three new growths can be seen developing in the uppermost leaf axils. The older leaves are turning yellow.

6 The top section six months after division. Removal from the older, lower section has stimulated activity in the younger tissues and healthy new roots produced since the division are able to grow straight into fresh compost. A new stem can be seen growing from near the base of the original one.

7 The top section, now re-established after division, grows vigorously into a sturdy and healthy new plant.

Sympodials—when to divide

During routine cleaning and checking of the orchids you will be able to assess which ones are scheduled for repotting, and it is at this time, prior to the start of the new growth on the leading pseudobulb, that vegetative propagation should be planned.

At the base of all pseudobulbs there are several dormant growing buds, often referred to as 'eyes'. Unless the pseudobulb is very old or the base has become damaged or diseased, these eyes can be stimulated into growth if given the correct conditions. Any sympodial orchid that has more than two or three pseudobulbs behind the leading growth, is sufficiently large to be divided. If you cut through the rhizome between two pseudobulbs some months before repotting time, then it is likely that a new growth will have already started when you remove the orchid from its pot preparatory to repotting. Thus you are well on the way to a second plant.

Deciduous orchids, such as *Thunia, Pleione, Calanthe* and *Cycnoches,* that need to be kept dry during the winter, can be divided before the resting period begins. When the leaves have died back, remove the orchids from their pots, clean off all the compost and dead foliage and/or roots, divide the pseudobulbs singly and then place them in trays. They should be kept in a light airy position, such as a shelf above the staging; until the new growths appear from the base of the pseudobulbs with the onset of spring, when the pseudobulbs can be potted up.

Sympodial orchids without pseudobulbs are equally responsive to this method of propagation, provided the old back growths that have flowered once have retained their foliage. Whereas it is possible to regenerate growth from an old pseudobulb that may have been leafless for two or three years, for all practical purposes any once-flowered growths of, for example, paphiopedilums or masdevallias that have lost their leaves are dead. To compensate for this, the foliage of many pseudobulbless sympodial orchids is more persistent and will remain in good condition for several years after the growth has flowered.

Sympodials—how to divide

The technique for both sympodial types is similar. Orchids that have become too large and are scheduled for division should have the initial cuts through the rhizome made during mid- to late winter, when the plant is least active. Many large plants will have developed naturally into three or four divisions, or leads, merely linked by the common rhizome to the central, frequently leafless, pseudobulbs or old growths. By gently pushing two pseudobulbs apart at a point where the plant will divide, you can cut through the rhizome with a sharp knife or secateurs if there is space. (The rhizome will be growing just below the surface of the compost.) Take care not to cut through any new roots, or to damage the dormant eyes that will subsequently produce the new growth.

If the orchid is particularly rare or valuable, or is a vigorous grower, each

Vegetative Propagation of Sympodial Orchids

Sympodial orchids may or may not have pseudobulbs, but both types can be readily divided provided that the plant is large enough. Before starting assess the situation with regard to both plant size and available growing space. There is no point in pulling a plant into many small pieces as they not only clutter the greenhouse but also—at least for those pieces that manage to survive—will take many years to reach a flowering stage. When splitting a plant try not to destroy its character, and where possible use only healthy and well established plants. The photographs on these two pages illustrate the method used to divide a sympodial orchid with pseudobulbs. The technique for those without pseudobulbs is similar, but only the back stems with leaves should be used: those that have lost their leaves are probably dead or dying. However, most orchids of this type retain foliage on the back stems for many years. Cleanliness is important, always sterilize the blade before each cut is made.

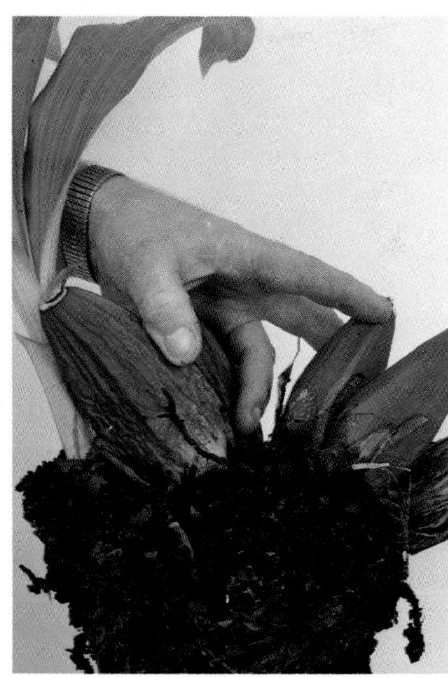

1 During winter assess which plants are ready for splitting and decide where the divisions are to be made. Using a heat-sterilized knife cut through the rhizome at these points. Treat the cut surfaces with fungicide and leave the plant until repotting time. Then, when the plant is removed from its pot, it can be easily split.

2 Carefully remove the growing medium and then trim back all the old dead roots. Whenever possible ensure that each division of the plant has at least two pseudobulbs. Although single pseudobulbs will survive, they will often take many years to grow to a stage where they produce a plant that flowers.

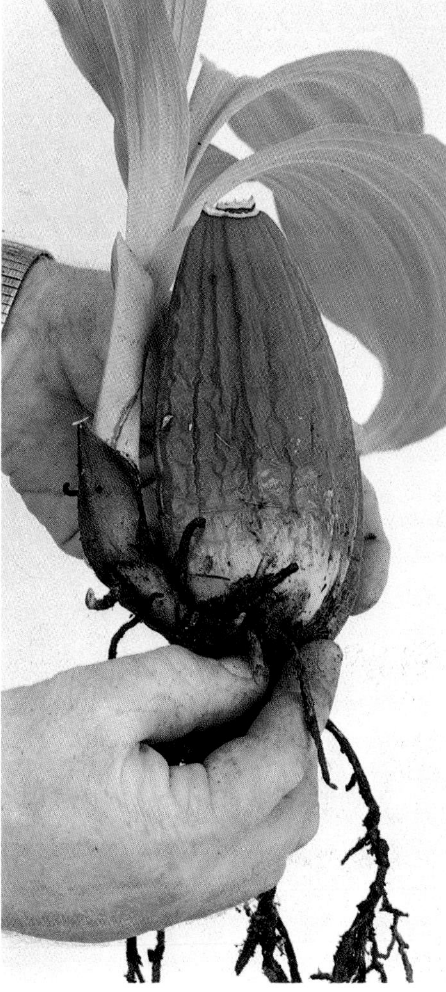

3 Carefully continue trimming the old roots almost back to the base of the pseudobulb. Take your time and be sure not to remove or damage the few new actively growing roots or dormant buds at the base of the pseudobulb. Hopefully, the earlier cutting of the rhizome will have encouraged some of these buds to start growing.

Where to Divide Sympodial Orchids

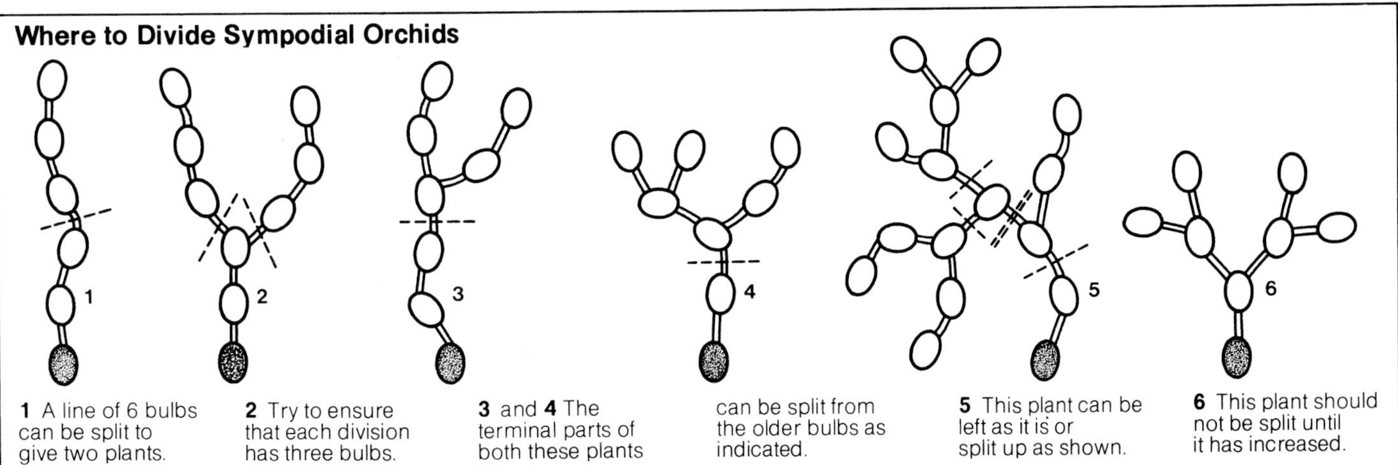

1 A line of 6 bulbs can be split to give two plants. **2** Try to ensure that each division has three bulbs. **3** and **4** The terminal parts of both these plants can be split from the older bulbs as indicated. **5** This plant can be left as it is or split up as shown. **6** This plant should not be split until it has increased.

pseudobulb or growth behind the principal division can be separated by cutting through the rhizome between every back bulb. This method is less likely to succeed with pseudobulbless orchids, and it must be accepted that a new plant starting from a single pseudobulb will probably need to be grown for several years before it produces a flower. Thus, this practice should only be used with plants of particular merit or those that cannot be obtained from any other source.

Apart from being careful not to damage the plant whilst cutting through the rhizome, two other precautions will help to ensure success. The cut surfaces should be dusted with orthocide—a puffer pack is ideal—to prevent any fungal infection entering the plant. Similarly, to prevent the spread of any virus that may be present, heat sterilize the cutting tools—by passing the blades through a flame—after dealing with each plant. After cutting through the rhizome in one or more places, the plant should remain intact in its pot until normal repotting time some months later.

4 The more vigorously growing plants or those from which a large stock is required can be further split into single pseudobulbs, but this should not become a standard practice. Those sympodials without pseudobulbs should never be divided into single stems as their chances of survival are minimal; always split them into twos or threes as a minimum.

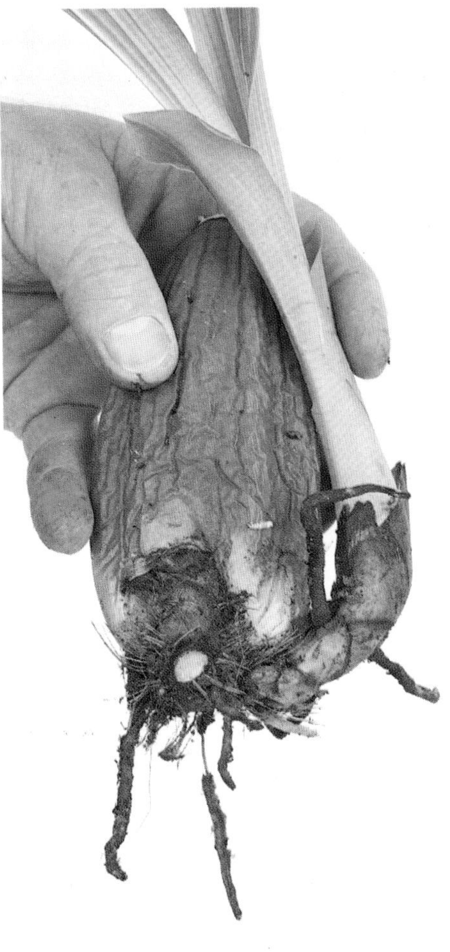

5 The cut face of the rhizome is a site liable to fungal infection and consequent rot. It is important to treat it as soon as it is cut with a liberal dusting of fungicide. This pseudobulb with its actively growing bud is now ready for potting up; it should soon form a healthy and thriving plant.

6 The actively growing part of the parent plant should now be repotted allowing sufficient space for several new pseudobulbs to grow. The removed back bulbs are then potted up. Try to provide a moist atmosphere with little temperature fluctuation. Do not plant the back bulbs too deeply otherwise the shoot may rot before reaching the surface.

Watering and Feeding

When and how to water orchids are questions most frequently asked by first-time buyers, and watering is always the most difficult aspect of culture about which to offer advice. More plants are killed by drowning than any other single cause.

As far as water quality is concerned, orchids can generally be watered safely with ordinary tap water. However, *never* use water that has been through an artificial softener.

Watering from the top

There are many good reasons for not watering orchids from the base of the pot. Most orchid composts, even those based on peat, are of an extremely open nature and thus have a poor capillary action. As a result it is possible for an orchid growing in these composts to stand in at least 2.5cm (1in) of water for more than a month with the top half of the compost remaining dry. If this occurs the roots in the waterlogged lower half of the pot will die through lack of air, whilst those nearer the surface will perish due to lack of moisture—and even orchids cannot thrive for too long without the support of a healthy root system! For similar reasons, orchids have not yet adapted to growing on capillary beds or by hydroculture—methods practised with the majority of houseplants in modern commercial nurseries.

Having accepted that orchids enjoy overhead watering, it is important that water should not be allowed to remain in new growths when they first appear each spring. Different genera tolerate this to varying extents, cattleyas possibly being the toughest. With the exception of several of the bifoliate species, such as *Cattleya bowringiana* and its hybrids, their new growths do not develop an open leaf until the growth is several centimetres high and sufficiently hard to withstand overhead watering. At the other end of the scale, the genus *Lycaste* and its related group start production of their relatively soft, pleated leaves with the emergence of a funnel-shaped growth that is potentially very susceptible to rotting, if water gets inside the growth. Dendrobiums also produce very tender new growths which should be allowed to grow to several centimetres in height, thus hardening the base, before much water is splashed around the pot. Indeed, it is best to avoid all new growths when watering, as there is nothing more frustrating than to see a promising new growth turn to a brown soggy mass as a result of careless watering.

Other areas to keep clear of water are the leaf axils of vandaceous monopodial orchids and, in particular, the crowns of phalaenopsis, which can easily trap water. Paphiopedilums do not seem to suffer problems from water remaining in the new growth, but the flower buds, produced in late summer from within these almost mature growths, will certainly rot if water remains trapped around the bud for long. All watering problems are accentuated by low temperatures, where evaporation is slower, and orchids in a cool house or where night temperature falls below 10°C (50°F) need special care.

How often to water

The interval between each watering depends on several factors—chiefly experience and growing conditions. As a general rule, small pots will dry out faster than large ones, and plastic pots hold more water than clay. Plants will need watering more frequently in hot sunny weather, or if surrounded by dry air, and a large plant will require more water than a small one.

To check whether a plant is in need of watering, if you have a small collection it is not too difficult or time-consuming to lift each plant in turn: those that feel heavy are obviously wet whilst the lighter ones are in need of a drink. You will soon find out which plants dry out more rapidly than others, and after a few weeks you can gradually dispense with the procedure. But even experienced growers will sometimes use this method, particularly with large pots, where the correct moisture content can be difficult to maintain.

Even if the compost at the top of the pot feels dry the bottom may be wet. You can check this by examining the compost through the drainage holes, or by lifting the pot as above.

Very few orchids enjoy their roots being surrounded by constantly moist conditions. In nature these roots are frequently saturated by tropical rain but they often dry out almost completely before the next downpour. To simulate these conditions in the artificial environ-

Below: Be careful to keep water away from paphiopedilum flower buds, as they may rot and spoil your hopes of flowers the next spring.

ment of a greenhouse, it is necessary to allow the compost in the pots to become partially dry between waterings. Orchids with pseudobulbs are capable of withstanding near drought conditions for short periods, and whilst too little water is not being advocated, this would be far preferable to overwatering. Overwatering means giving the plant water too *frequently*— not giving too much water at each watering. Thus, when water is needed, ensure that it washes completely through the pot and does not merely moisten the top level of compost.

In the greenhouse, plants near the edge of the staging will often dry out more quickly than those in the centre, owing to the greater movement of air. This occurs particularly during cold weather when any heating pipes below the staging will be in use. The same will happen when plants are grown in the proximity of a fan, especially if this is a fan heater, and, therefore, all plants should be at least 2m (6.5ft) away from this type of heating device.

Above: Orchids in the direct path of a fan or near a ventilator or louvred panel, where the air flow is greatest, will need more frequent watering. When the heating system is in use, plants at the edges of the staging will become dry more rapidly than those in the middle not directly affected by warm air.

Orchids with an abundance of foliage will obviously lose more moisture through transpiration, and will need watering more frequently than smaller growing varieties. On the other hand, as small pots contain less compost, they will hold a lower reserve of moisture, and therefore need watering relatively frequently. The most frequent watering will be needed by large plants growing in a comparatively small pot, especially when the root system has filled this pot and the plant is growing vigorously.

During the main growing season, from late spring until early autumn, orchids that are in good health and growing vigorously will probably need watering twice or three times a week, depending upon the prevailing weather and greenhouse atmosphere. Plants grown in the house, where the atmosphere is drier, may require watering once a day.

At the other end of the spectrum, the interval between waterings should be increased to a week or even longer in the depths of winter in temperate conditions. Many growers of cool-house plants, such as odontoglossums, most dendrobiums, some laelias and encyclias, do not apply water to the pots during the winter, particularly with the species that are partially or completely resting. Instead, the plants are sprayed overhead during periods of brighter winter weather, to prevent desiccation and to counteract the drying effect of the heating system.

Although it is impossible to give an arbitrary rule on when to water, the following is a helpful guideline: if you are not sure whether or not an orchid needs water during the growing season, apply water, but, if in doubt during the winter months, delay watering until the next watering session.

Reducing water loss

A high humidity around a plant will obviously reduce its rate of water loss through transpiration, thus also reducing the amount of water the plant needs to absorb through its root system in order to thrive. Although orchids enjoy a moist atmosphere more than most other plants, the relative humidity in the greenhouse should be kept in balance with all the other factors, such as temperature and light, and like them should fluctuate during any 24-hour period. Just as it is undesirable to maintain any plants on a 24-hour daylength or at constantly even temperature, it would also be a disadvantage if the humidity were to remain too even.

Left: Automatic watering systems perform a dual function of keeping the greenhouse atmosphere buoyant and the compost moist. They are ideal for young plants, but not for orchids in flower as water may spoil the petals.

Overhead spraying

During spells of warm summer weather, when the plants may have been subjected to temperatures in excess of 32°C (90°F) during the early afternoon, together with a relative humidity of 30 percent or below, it is a positive advantage to spray water over the plants, between the pots, and beneath the staging etc, during the evening. Like having a cool shower after a hot day in the office, the orchids perceptibly recover from the heat of the day. If the air becomes too dry at temperatures much lower than this, the shading/ventilation/moisture retention balance is probably incorrect.

Overhead spraying of plants under glass, whether to increase humidity or to water those orchids growing on rafts, should be restricted either to early morning before the greenhouse temperature becomes too high, or to the evening when the sun's heat is diminishing. There are two reasons for this, both connected with the temperature of the orchid's foliage. When water is applied by overhead spray, it is inevitable that some will remain in the form of droplets for a considerable time. These areas of water will act as a magnifying glass to the sun's rays, thus increasing the chance of burning the foliage. The other problem arises from the effect of cold water on warm foliage. Some orchids, notably phalaenopsis and its allied genera, are particularly sensitive to this and, where the water is more than 11°C (20°F) colder than the foliage, the plant tissue may be damaged. Such tissue then becomes more susceptible to fungal infection. Therefore, it is advisable not to apply cold water to warm foliage.

Misting the greenhouse

One way of overcoming these problems on exceptionally hot, windy days when the air is in danger of becoming extremely dry, is to briefly apply a *very* fine water mist into the greenhouse atmosphere. This is best done early in the morning with a special nozzle attached to the hosepipe. With this method only a very small amount of water is spread onto the foliage, which can dry before the sun's heat causes burning. However, in very bright and hot conditions, avoid even this small amount of overhead water.

Additional devices for the small greenhouse

As with other aspects of culture, the smaller the greenhouse area, the more difficult it will be to maintain reasonable humidity during hot weather. To overcome this problem, additional shading, more efficient ventilation, including low-level apertures, air-circulating fans and more moisture-retentive material on the staging and greenhouse floor, may be necessary. Where normally cooler growing orchids are being cultivated in tropical and subtropical areas, some form of air conditioning may be necessary. Systems are available commercially, or the domestic refrigerator could be adapted to supply cool air for the greenhouse.

Above: To maintain a bouyant atmosphere on very hot days is difficult, but spraying water beneath the staging and between the pots will assist the cooling process.

An alternative method, widely used in the United States, South Africa and Australia, is the adoption of a 'wet-pad' system. This consists of large panels of moisture-retentive material (fibreglass would be suitable), set in vertical wiremesh containers across one end of the greenhouse, with a large extractor fan on the opposite end wall. The fibreglass panel is kept perpetually saturated and the extractor fan pulls in fresh air through open louvres positioned behind the panel. As the air passes through the saturated fibreglass, it is cooled and moistened, thus improving the greenhouse atmosphere. The system may be operated manually, or controlled automatically by the use of thermostats and humidistats. To function correctly, no other ventilators should be open, as no air should be allowed to enter the greenhouse except through the wet-pad.

Feeding orchids

Orchids cannot live entirely on fresh air, and like other plants need moderate amounts of food in order to thrive. In the wild, much of this is provided in the form of gases given off by the decaying matter on the forest floor below—a method that has been adapted successfully by some growers of monopodial orchids in tropical and equatorial regions. The myth that orchids do not require feeding probably arose from the days of sphagnum moss/osmunda fibre compost, as most fertilizers have a harmful effect on the moss and subsequently the whole compost. Modern composts do not provide much food by themselves and even where a base fertilizer is included in the compost recipe this is generally exhausted after about eight to ten weeks.

Orchids do not require a special feed, although liquid fertilizer is preferable as all plants are able to absorb this more rapidly. During the active growing period, from spring to late summer, a high nitrogen feed will encourage rapid growth. To aid the ripening of this growth and to help initiate the flowers, a more balanced fertilizer should be used during the autumn until growth virtually stops during the winter, when little food is needed.

Root feeding

Most compound fertilizers, which include

Below: Applying a fine mist of water into the greenhouse atmosphere first thing in the morning ensures the correct humidity around the plants as day temperatures increase.

ORCHIDS

ANATOMY OF AN ORCHID PLANT

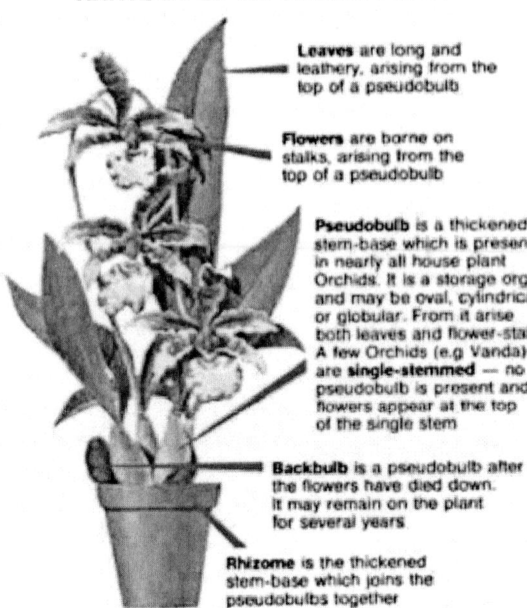

ANATOMY OF AN ORCHID FLOWER

There is a simple basic pattern for all Orchids, but with innumerable variations in the size, shape and colour of the individual parts.

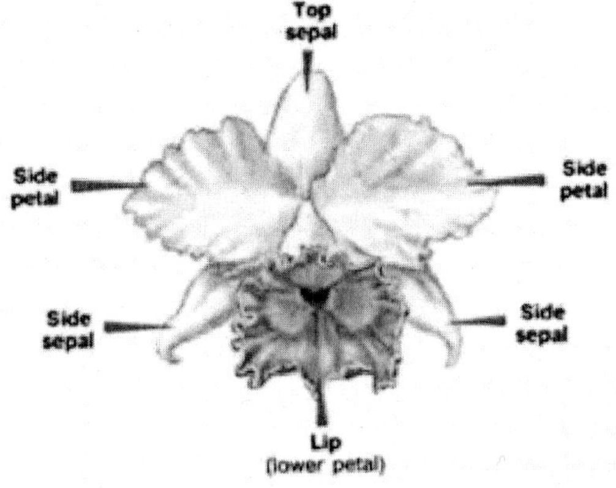

Not too many years ago the idea of growing Orchids in the living room was unthinkable. Since then it has been found that a number will grow quite happily in the home . . . . provided you take a little time to learn about their needs.

Firstly, it is essential to remember that only a tiny fraction of the 100,000 known types are suitable — choose from the 'house plant' group described on the next page and pick an easy one if you are a beginner. You will find specimens in garden centres, department stores etc — look for a well-grown plant which is free from obvious blemishes. It will be pricey as it takes more than 5 years to reach the ready-for-sale stage.

Each type has its own special needs, but there are a number of general rules. You can't just place the plant anywhere. Miniature varieties can be grown in a terrarium (pages 26–28) but the usual home for a potted Orchid is on a pebble tray (page 19). Good light is essential and an east- or west-facing windowsill is ideal if net curtains or other form of sun screen is used — you must protect the plants from unfiltered sunshine. Turn the pot occasionally and move the tray away from the window on frosty nights.

House plant Orchids cannot tolerate hot and stuffy conditions so good ventilation is required even in winter — don't be afraid to stand the pot outdoors on warm and sunny days. Indoors, however, you must avoid cold draughts which can be fatal.

Feed during the summer months. Orchids appreciate being pot-bound but after a few years repotting and division may be necessary. You will require a special Orchid Compost.

SECRETS OF SUCCESS

Temperature: Individual types vary, but the general rule is a day temperature of about 70°F in summer, 60°F in winter and a drop at night of 10°F. Cool nights are important.

Light: Good light, shaded from direct sunlight. Orchids need 10–15 hours of light each day — in winter supplement daylight with artificial light.

Water: Keep compost moist — reduce watering in winter. Use soft, tepid water. With Cattleya and Miltonia let surface dry between waterings.

Air Humidity: Moist air is essential. Mist leaves occasionally.

Repotting: Do not worry if a few roots grow outside the pot. Repot only when growth begins to suffer.

Propagation: Divide plants at repotting time. Leave at least 3 shoots on each division. Stake each newly potted plant.

SPECIAL PROBLEMS

BROWN SPOTS ON LEAVES
Cause: If the spots are hard and dry, the plant has been scorched by the sun. Provide shade; there is no need to remove the spots. If the spots are soft, then a fungus disease is present and the affected parts should be removed immediately.

HORIZONTAL OR DROOPING GROWTH
Cause: Lack of light is the common reason; Orchids need good illumination. If the growth is limp and the light is good then incorrect watering may be the cause of loss of vigour.

MOULD ON LEAVES
Cause: Mildew may develop if the leaves are thoroughly misted under cool conditions and the water does not quickly evaporate.

NO FLOWERS
Cause: When growth is unhealthy any incorrect cultural condition can be the reason. If growth appears healthy then insufficient light is the probable cause.

TERRESTRIAL ORCHIDS ***BLETILLA STRIATA***

COMPOST: Use special orchid compost.

Pot in March, with 2 inches of drainage in each pot. Water freely March to August, moderately August to October, very little or none, afterwards.

TEMPERATURE:
March to September 65 to 75°, September to March 60-65°, Resting period winter. Repot in early spring.

Press the bulbs into the compost but do not cover.

Several flowers will appear at the base of the new pseudo-bulb, on tall slender stems, usually brightly coloured, though not large.

ZYGOPETALUM ORCHIDS

COMPOST: Use special orchid compost.

Repot in spring when the plant reaches 2yrs old, if there is a new flower shoot wait until flowering has finished. Use a pot that is big enough for one years growth. It is usual for the plant to loose one or two leaves at the end of the season. Shake off the old compost from the roots and cut off any dead, soft or black roots. Leave at least 2 bulbs with leaves and 2 older bulbs; these will help to support the plant if it becomes stressed after repotting. It is a good idea to support the plant while the new, damp compost is put around the root ball. As the plants prefer to be free draining, do not pack the compost too tightly. Water sparingly for the first 4 to 6 weeks. Keep the compost evenly moist in the summer and water less in the winter. Use tepid water, rain water if possible. Water more frequently when flowering.

TEMPERATURE:

In winter the temperature should be above 12°C and in the summer 18-24°C is ideal. If the temperature goes above this it may stop the plant from flowering. This plant requires good light but keep out of direct sunlight in the summer.

Information taken from 'The House Plant Expert' by Dr D G Hessayon

nearly all commercially available liquid or solid feeds, have a three-part formula stated on the packet. This gives the ratio of nitrogen (N) to phosphate (P) and potassium (K); thus when growers talk of a 'high nitrogen' feed, the NPK ratio would be 25:15:15 or similar. A 'balanced' feed would be 10:10:10. Minute quantities of other elements are also included, the most important of which is magnesium. A shortage of magnesium in the plant can lead to a chlorotic effect, where parts of the leaves may turn yellow, by breakdown of some cells, which will be attacked by a secondary fungal infection. If you are using a bark-based compost, Dolomite lime watered into the compost every four to six months will also supply the required amount of magnesium.

As a general rule orchids require less feed than most other plants, but it should be given little and often. You will get the best results by applying one of the standard liquid feeds at half to two-thirds strength in three out of every four waterings during the growing season, reducing these applications to one in three during the winter. In warmer climates where the light intensity is good for most of the year orchids may require feeding more often, say at most waterings during the growing season.

Foliar feeding
In recent years, foliar feeding has become more widespread. With this method the fertilizer is diluted in water and then sprayed overhead, either in the early morning or preferably during warm summer evenings. As this form of nutrient is absorbed by the plant through its leaves or aerial roots, spraying in the evening allows a greater time for absorption before the feed is evaporated by the sun's heat.

PESTS AND DISEASES

Orchids are not attacked by many pests, although even the best cultivated plants will be liable to damage from time to time. Prevention is better than cure, and therefore a regular monthly spraying with a systemic insecticide should keep most plants clean. Against this must be weighed the undesirability of spreading potentially harmful chemicals into the atmosphere. Whenever chemicals are used to kill insect pests, remember that most chemicals cannot differentiate between the insects and you—so it is most important to follow the manufacturers' instructions and take all necessary precautions.

Red spider mite

Undoubtedly the most difficult insect pest to eradicate, and consequently the one most commonly seen is the red spider mite (*Tetranychus urticae*). These minute, sap-sucking pests are normally greenish yellow—rather than red—wingless and thrive in warm, dry conditions. They feed on the undersides of leaves, and although they will attack any orchids, the soft-leaved genera such as *Lycaste, Calanthe* and *Catasetum* seem particularly susceptible. Cymbidiums, too, are a favourite diet, especially in smaller greenhouses where at times the temperature may be too high and relative humidity low. With a casual approach to control, this provides an ideal environment for rapid multiplication of the pest.

Plants should be inspected regularly for red spider mite, which is just visible to the naked eye. Any leaf showing a slight whitish mottling on the underside is probably under attack. In severe infestations the leaves will turn yellow and a fine gossamer web can be seen on the underside. Although humid conditions will discourage red spider mite, a regular monthly spraying—using a systemic insecticide alternated with malathion—should be an effective control. Where active colonies have built up, three or four applications at 8 to 10 day intervals should eradicate each generation, as most chemical controls will not kill the eggs.

Alternative methods of control are fumigation, using azobenzene or Naled; or greenhouse aerosols containing malathion. Biological control is also possible using predatory mites, usually available from the local Agricultural Development Advisory Service or the Department of Agriculture, but their introduction would preclude the subsequent use of any chemical control as this would obviously affect both predator and prey.

False spider mite

In recent years, phalaenopsis have frequently been attacked by a false spider mite (*Brevipalpus russulus*), which causes pitting on the upper surface of the leaves. If left unchecked, secondary fungal infection is probable, with the inevitable de-

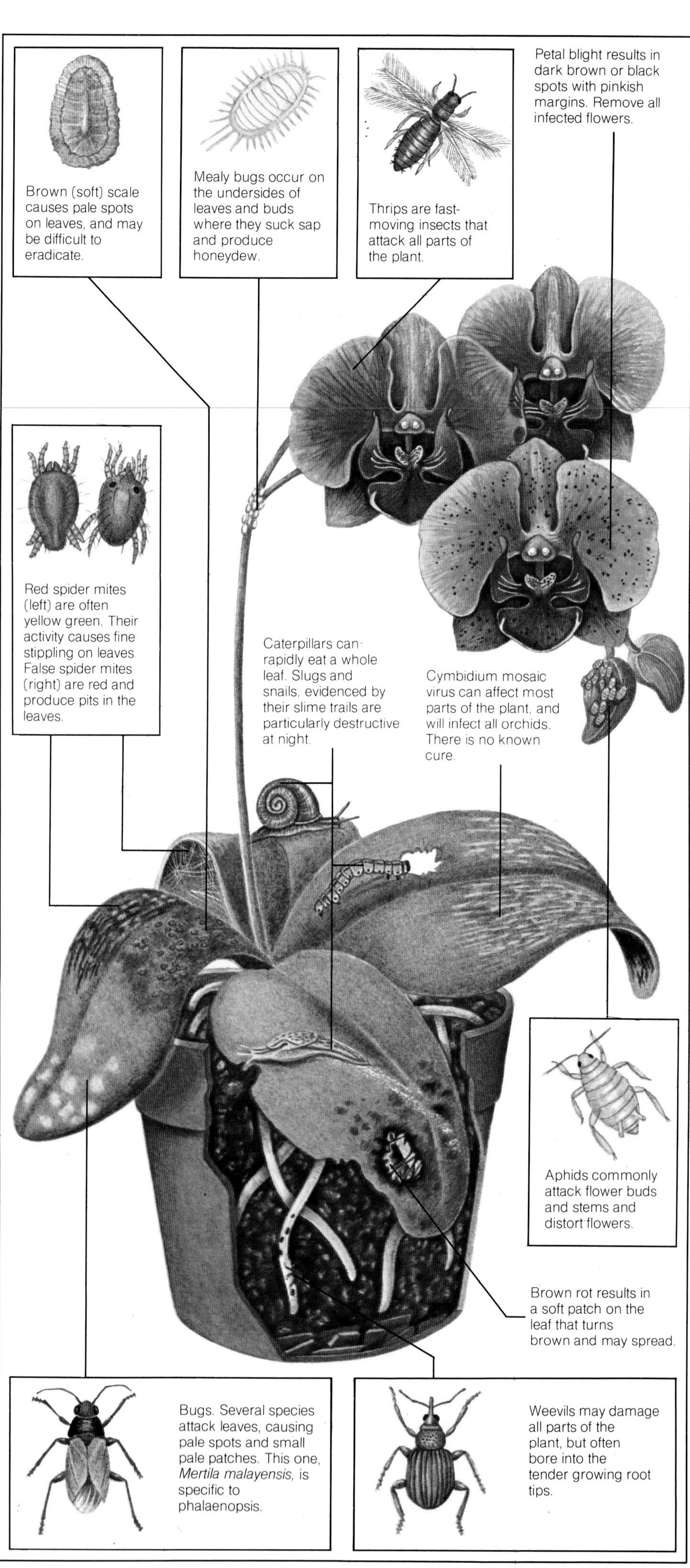

Above: The results of attack by false spider mite show clearly on the upper surfaces of these leaves of *Phalaenopsis*, the only genus to be severely affected by this pest.

Below: Colonies of scale insects may build up in the greenhouse if scrupulous hygiene is not observed. Although they are simple to eradicate, their damage leaves a permanent scar.

foliation of the plant. The treatment recommended above should achieve effective control.

Aphids

Similar treatment should also control the common aphids, although Lindane and liquid derris will be equally effective and will help to avoid a resistance to any one particular chemical building up in these pests. Although many forms of greenfly may appear in the greenhouse, the orchid aphid, *Cerataphis lataniae*, is most commonly found. The pale green aphids are particularly fond of tender young growths and flower spikes, the developing flower bud being especially attractive. Where these buds are attacked, the flower —if it opens at all—will be mottled and distorted.

Mealy bugs and scale insects

These two relatively common pests are more difficult to eradicate because of their protective outer covering. Both the mealy bug (*Pseudococcus longispinus*) and the scale (*Diaspis boisduvalii* or *Coccus hesperidum*; the latter often known as the soft scale), are sap-sucking insects, which feed by puncturing the surface of the leaf. They are clearly visible to the naked eye, being 3.2mm (0.125in) or more in diameter. Mealy bugs are covered with a waxy, whitish substance and frequently hide in the leaf axils of plants. Dendrobiums, especially *nobile* soft cane types, are particularly vulnerable to attack. Scale insects, as the name indicates, are protected by a dome-shaped hard shell, which is resistant to most chemical sprays. Systemic insecticide, which makes the plant toxic to sap-sucking pests, will control both these pests if applied two or three times at intervals of 10 to 14 days. Where only a small number of orchids is involved and infestations are minor, methylated spirit applied with a small paintbrush will clean up the plants.

Slugs and snails

The warm, humid conditions of the greenhouse encourage slugs and snails. Few greenhouses are completely clear of these two invaders, but if cleanliness around the plants and under the staging is normal practice, there will be fewer hiding and breeding places for these mainly nocturnal feeders.

Metaldehyde is the traditional method of control, but liquid and pellet-form slug killers are also currently in use. The liquid has the advantage of treating the compost as well, thus poisoning one of the favourite hiding places. Bait in the form of an upturned potato or grapefruit skin, or even an orchid bloom, is also effective but relies on daily inspection and the disposal of any pests attracted to the bait.

Other pests

Although the pests listed above are the most frequently encountered, thrips, weevils and caterpillars may also cause damage. They can all be brought into an orchid collection inadvertently on new plants, and will inevitably enter through the open ventilators and doors of the greenhouse during summer months. Control is important, as apart from weakening the orchids and spoiling flowers, all these pests are responsible for the spreading of virus diseases. Regular examination of the plants will enable any problems to be handled at an early stage, and a moist yet buoyant atmosphere will discourage them.

Bacterial and fungal diseases

Whereas pests will damage healthy tissue, the main access to the plant for fungal and bacterial diseases is through damaged areas. Therefore, if you experience either of these two problems, dust every cut surface with orthocide powder as a matter of routine. This chemical has proved effective in controlling most forms of 'rots', including 'damping off' problems, in orchids, as in all other plants.

The spores of fungi and bacteria are present in all atmospheres, but will thrive especially where air circulation is poor and the relative humidity high. They will also multiply rapidly where decaying matter is left lying about in the greenhouse—yet another reason for maintaining a high level of cleanliness around the plants.

Many diseases could attack your plants, but where good hygiene is practised and the orchids are carefully observed, all problems will be minimized. Rapid action to eliminate the disease is essential, as all fungi and bacteria spread extremely quickly where conditions are to their liking.

Brown spot

This disease, caused by the bacterium *Pseudomonas cattleyae,* occurs particularly in phalaenopsis and paphiopedilums. An early sign of infection is a soft watery area on the surface of the leaf, which, if left alone, will rapidly turn brown and spread. It is essential to cut out the infected area with a clean, sharp knife, after which the cut surfaces should be dusted with orthocide. Where large numbers of plants are affected, they should be heavily sprayed with a solution of natriphene. Alternatively, all infected plants could be soaked in natriphene or Physan for approximately one hour. Many fungicides and bactericides are available, and those suitable for other greenhouse plants would be ideal for orchids.

Petal blight

This disease is caused by the fungus *Sclerotinia fuckeliana,* and is common on early autumn flowers of phalaenopsis and cattleyas. At first a few small circular spots may appear on any part of the flower. The spots are usually dark brown or black, and on close examination, have a slight pinkish margin. To treat the disease, first remove all infected flowers immediately you notice them, and then ensure that the night-time humidity is not too high. In temperate areas it will probably be necessary to supply a little artificial heat during autumn to prevent the problem spreading.

Virus diseases

Virus has become the 'dirty word' of orchid growers during the past 20 years, and whilst the potential dangers of a virus disease should not be minimized, do not assume that every malformed flower or marked leaf is caused by a virus. In fact many plants that appear healthy may have some form of virus infection, and it is therefore essential that insect pests which spread viruses should be controlled. Many growers sterilize their cutting tools between use on each plant. Although this may seem fastidious, it is certainly advisable to isolate any plant about which you are suspicious.

Symptoms will vary according to the genus attacked and the virus, and plants that are not growing well will show more extreme signs of the disease at an earlier stage. With some genera, notably cattleyas, virus symptoms first become obvious in the flowers, which although they will open normally and appear healthy, will develop colour breaks—irregular stripes or blotches of different colours—in either the petals or sepals after about a week. Isolate suspect plants so that subsequent flowers can be examined for any malformation, which, if present, will almost certainly confirm virus infection. Most orchid nurserymen will advise you if in doubt, but for a more certain diagnosis it will be necessary to have the suspect plant tested. Many commercial tissue laboratories will offer this service.

The only cure for infected plants, be they orchids or others, is to burn them. Hence the importance of thorough pest control and clean conditions within your collection.

Cymbidium mosaic virus

This virus is misnamed, as it will attack almost all orchids. Typical symptoms are chlorotic, or discoloured, areas on the leaf as a result of the breakdown of cells, these marks becoming darker and sunken as the disease advances. The marking often becomes regular, sometimes forming a diamond-shaped pattern on the leaf. On cattleyas and phalaenopsis virus infection often shows up initially as purplish markings, but these too become brown after a few weeks.

Left: Pseudobulb ruptures are invariably caused by small snails and slugs that eat into and eventually hollow out the bulb.

Below: The symptoms of mosaic virus infection show clearly as pale blotches on the petals of this cymbidium.

HELPFUL HINTS

The following advice provides a quick reference to the essential points about orchid cultivation, and is a guide round the pitfalls that occasionally beset the grower.

Plan carefully

Do not be in too great a hurry to start your orchid collection. Evaluate the conditions available before deciding on your first purchases, and preferably visit a few orchid shows and nurseries. Most commercial orchid growers are pleased to welcome newcomers and advise you on the varieties most suitable for your environment, with no obligation to buy plants. The local nursery can also provide you with information about the nearest orchid society, where you will be able to make contact with interested hobbyists. This is extremely valuable, as most of them will have started growing orchids in a similar way, and will therefore be able to offer advice from a comparable level. Remember, however, that there is no *one* correct way to grow orchids.

Time spent planning is recouped many times over, and only when you are certain that a particular orchid will thrive in your situation is it wise to purchase. Buy mature plants initially, from an obviously clean nursery. Lower priced young plants or seedlings may seem a more attractive proposition, but it is important to the success of the venture to have at least some flowers during the first season. Imported species may also be less expensive than those reared at a nursery, but establishing an orchid newly imported from the jungle takes both time and skill, and is best not attempted by the complete novice. Above all, avoid so-called cheap offers in the non-orchid popular press, and those orchids that have been languishing for generations in someone's conservatory. Experience has shown that the former are frequently extremely poor in quality and the latter are probably infested with every possible ailment.

Cultural requirements

Specially constructed orchid houses are not essential; any greenhouse that is satisfactory for the culture of other plants will be adequate for orchids. All electrical installations should be fitted by a competent engineer and kept away from damp areas, preferably well above staging height.

Temperatures

The day temperature should be at least 5.5°C (10°F) higher than the night temperature during winter, and as much as 14-16.5°C (25-30°F) higher in summer. Low nocturnal temperatures—down to 10°C (50°F)—are needed to initiate the flower buds in many genera.

Ventilation

Ventilation, especially from below staging height, should be used at most times except during foggy or extremely cold weather. It is essential to provide adequate ventilation—both high and low level—if a flueless burner is being used to supply heat in the greenhouse. Ventilators should be covered with gauze or fine mesh netting in order to keep out insects and other pests. Field mice are particularly attracted to a warm greenhouse, where they will rapidly demolish the orchid pollens, and anything else that tastes sweet.

Shading

Shading is used to help control the temperature, not necessarily to reduce the light, and therefore all shading material should be applied to the outside of the greenhouse. Internal shading will not reduce the temperature, and in certain circumstances can even increase it by limiting the air circulation.

Insulation

Polyethylene lining installed to insulate the greenhouse in winter is also useful during the summer months. It will assist in retaining humidity, and recent experience has shown that the temperature in uninsulated greenhouses rises more rapidly and remains higher than in insulated greenhouses.

Repotting

Repotting is best completed when the new growth is developing, but try to avoid mid-winter and periods of very hot weather. Plants in bud or flower, or carrying a seed capsule, also prefer not to be repotted. But if a plant looks sick at

Right: To obtain the best display of flowers, try not to turn a plant when the buds are developing, or the flowers may open facing different directions.

any time, examine the roots and compost because a repot may be the answer.

Avoid having a variety of composts in one greenhouse, as this will lead to cultural problems. All orchids, as they join the collection, should be repotted into your chosen standard mixture at the earliest opportunity. Do not keep diseased plants or runts. If the care and attention often lavished on these ailing orchids were redirected towards the thriving plants, the whole collection would benefit.

Water

Rain water is not necessary, though it may be desirable. In city or industrial areas the rain water may be severely polluted. Mains water is not harmful, but *do not* use water that has been softened by means of a conventional salt softener. The sodium in softened water will slowly kill your plants. Some means of water storage, such as a tank fed from the greenhouse roof gutters, is desirable, in case of a temporary drought or water shortage.

Provided the compost is sound, orchids need frequent waterings during the growing season, but far less during the winter. If you are in doubt, orchids are best kept relatively dry. Do not spray or water overhead when the foliage is warm, or when the sun is shining on the plants as the foliage may become burned.

Feeding

Apply liquid fertilizer only in balance with other cultural requirements, such as light and warmth. Do not try to 'push' plants when growing conditions are poor, or when a plant is sick. Feeding is no panacea, and will not compensate for cultural deficiencies.

Plant hygiene

Cleanliness in the culture of plants is essential. Apart from the aesthetic considerations, many weeds make excellent hosts to insect pests and they should not be allowed to grow in the greenhouse. If you wish to cultivate plants under the staging, most fibrous rooted begonias, such as *Begonia rex* and its varieties, also saintpaulias and impatiens, make excellent groundcover plants. Ensure that they too do not become pest-infected, by regularly attending to them.

All new acquisitions, from whatever source, should be thoroughly inspected for insect pests or fungal diseases, which must be dealt with immediately to prevent the problem spreading. Regular spraying with insecticide is advisable, particularly in spring and early summer. Flower buds and new growths are especially susceptible to attack by aphids. It is not a good idea, however, to attempt preventive spraying against fungal attack. There is some evidence to support the belief that more than two applications of systemic fungicide in any one season could restrict the growth of some genera. Therefore use a fungicide only after the disease has appeared, or better still, ensure that the problem is minimized by thoroughly clean culture.

Flower spikes and buds are a delicacy to snails and slugs, and only early preventive action will avoid damage. Apply slug killer just before the spikes are expected, and a 'collar' of cotton wool on the developing spike will prevent these pests from reaching the flowers.

Flower spikes

Some genera or species produce flowers sequentially from the same spike, occasionally over two or even three seasons. Therefore, the flower spike should not be removed—providing the plant is in good health—while it is still green. *Oncidium papilio, Onc. krameranum* and *Paphiopedilum glaucophyllum* produce flowers sequentially, and *Phalaenopsis lueddemanniana, P. violacea, P. cornucervi, Masdevallia tovarensis* and many others will produce flowers in the correct season from spikes several years old, in addition to the current ones.

Be consistent

Above all, do not change your cultural regime after hearing or reading about new techniques. Plants need time to adjust and cannot possibly thrive if the environment is radically changed three or four times each year. It is best to sieve out any cultural advice applicable to your situation, and accept that there are many different routes to success.

Right: During their early development, buds are most susceptible to chemical spray damage. Be careful when applying chemicals, as damaged buds may produce scarred flowers (left).

USING ORCHIDS IN FLOWER

With reasonable care, mature orchid plants will produce flowers regularly in their correct season. Species usually flower once each year at approximately the same period, and although within a single species there will be clones flowering at slightly different periods, each clone will generally come into bloom at a similar time each year. Hybrids are more variable in their flowering habits, many odontoglossums producing flower spikes at 10 to 11 month intervals, whilst phalaenopsis that are in good health will often produce two flower spikes each year. Cymbidiums, paphiopedilums and many other genera are usually more regular in their habits, and it is not unusual to see the same plants in flower on the showbench on identical dates year after year.

Training flower spikes

Orchid flowers do not appear in perfect condition on the showbench by accident or good fortune. Nearly all flower spikes need some form of training in order to present the flowers at their best, and in many cases this preparation should start when the spikes are only a few centimetres high. It is best to place a suitable cane next to each flower spike when it first appears. Marking the spike in this way helps to prevent accidental damage, which can so easily occur during routine watering or handling of the orchid, and the cane provides a suitable support to which the spike may be tied at regular intervals as it develops.

Select a cane of suitable size and strength to support the fully open spike of flowers, and push it into the compost next to the flower spike. Be sure to keep it clear of the base of the plant, where young growths could be damaged, and away from the side of the pot where the majority of the active roots will be found. For cymbidiums, which produce sturdy, heavy flower spikes, a bamboo cane approximately 1.2m (4 ft) long and 1.2cm (0.5in) in diameter should be adequate, while for the more slender spikes on odontoglossums and phalaenopsis, a split cane, 61-91cm (2-3ft) long will be sufficient. If one end of the cane is sharpened to a blunt point it will be easier to push it vertically into the compost.

Make the first tie when the spike is approximately 10-15cm (4-6in) long, using either raffia or a soft green string available from horticultural shops. Young spikes are extremely brittle, and any that are growing horizontally should be gradually trained to the vertical position over a period of several weeks. This would obviously not apply to species such as *Cymbidium devonianum, Coelogyne massangeana* and *flaccida,* and *Odontoglossum citrosmum,* which produce naturally pendulous spikes. In general, species orchids with their daintier flowers and lighter spikes will need far less support than their hybrid cousins. But try to keep all canes and ties to the minimum so that they remain unobtrusive. Approximately three ties should be sufficient for each spike, the top one positioned just above the first flower on the spike, after which the spike should be allowed to arch naturally, and the cane cut back to just above the top tie. In paphiopedilums, the one tie should be positioned just beneath the solitary flower, or, with multi-flowered species, immediately below the top flower.

Orchids in the home

Many orchids that normally grow best in the greenhouse environment can safely be brought into the home when in flower,

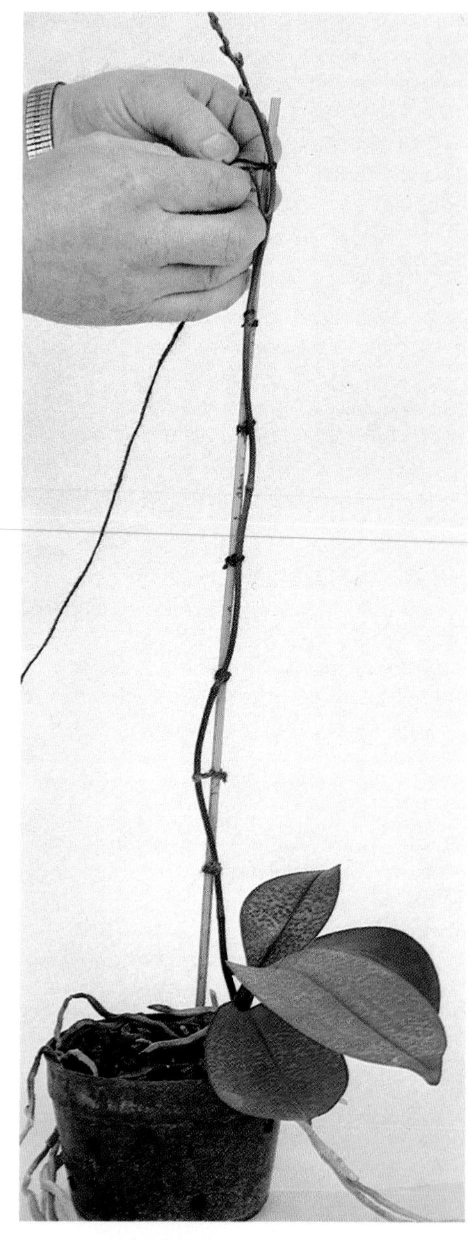

Below and Right: When training flower spikes use soft string; make the first tie near the base and work towards the apex.

Right: Since flowers of the cattleya hybrids are too heavy to be supported by their own stems, they should be tied to the supporting cane.

if a few simple precautions are taken. After all, there is little point in growing orchids merely to decorate the greenhouse!

Try to provide some local humidity around the plant by standing the pot in moist pebbles or similar material. Although these could be put in a saucer, a more aesthetically pleasing effect is obtained if some form of pot-holder or jardinière is used. The space between the plant pot and the outer container can then be filled completely with moisture-retaining material, which will help to keep the root system cool and moist. Even better, is a trough or similar container—the old fashioned, lined wine coolers are ideal—in which several orchids can be grouped with a few ferns or other foliage plants to form a pleasing display. This has the added advantage that several plants growing together will create their own microclimate.

Above: Flowering orchids make fine house plants, and are even more attractive when the flower pots are pleasingly disguised.

Below: A delightful corsage—the green of the fern contrasts beautifully with the delicate pink of the phalaenopsis flowers.

Some areas within the home are unsuitable for orchids. Mantleshelves above hot fires or shelves over radiators may look perfect for the smaller plants, but the rising heat will rapidly cause the plant to dehydrate beyond the point of no return. Areas that are too light, such as a sunny windowsill—and even vandas do not like direct sun through glass—or too dark, excessively draughty or where the temperature fluctuates too frequently, such as a busy hallway, are all harmful to the plants. East or west facing windows are suitable, but if the curtains are drawn across on a cold winter's evening, be sure to bring all the plants into the comfort of the room.

To compensate for the lower humidity indoors, orchids will probably need watering more frequently than in the greenhouse. Plants should be watered thoroughly and it is best to take them to the kitchen or bathroom to avoid spoiling furnishings. Providing that their stay indoors does not exceed three to four weeks, feeding should not be necessary. Similarly, any plants showing symptoms of pests or diseases should be returned immediately to the greenhouse where the trouble can be dealt with.

Orchids in vases

When the last flower on a spike has been open for two or three weeks, the plant will benefit if the spike is cut. This allows the plant to put all its energies into growth, thus ensuring even more flowers for next season. The cut flowers too will last nearly as long off the plant as on, particularly if not placed in the unsuitable areas already described. But do not cut the spike before the terminal flower has been open for at least 8 to 10 days, and as with all cut flowers, orchids will last longer if regularly given fresh water. In the smaller 'specimen' vases, which are ideal for the dainty sprays of many species or a single paphiopedilum flower, the water level drops very quickly and will need daily topping-up. Every few days it is advisable to renew all the water, at the same time cutting a thin slice off the bottom of each spike or flower stem, at a slant, to allow the greatest possible area of stem to absorb the water. Do not crush the stem as often advocated; this merely blocks the capillary passages in the stem and restricts the flow of water, thus shortening the life of the flower.

Corsages and bouquets

Orchid flowers are ideal for buttonholes, corsages or wedding bouquets. What could be more appropriate than white phalaenopsis and dendrobiums mixed with stephanotis and silver foliage to

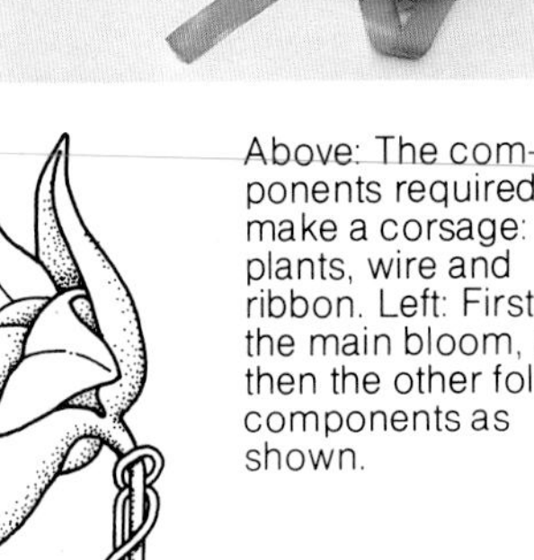

Above: The components required to make a corsage: plants, wire and ribbon. Left: First wire the main bloom, and then the other foliage components as shown.

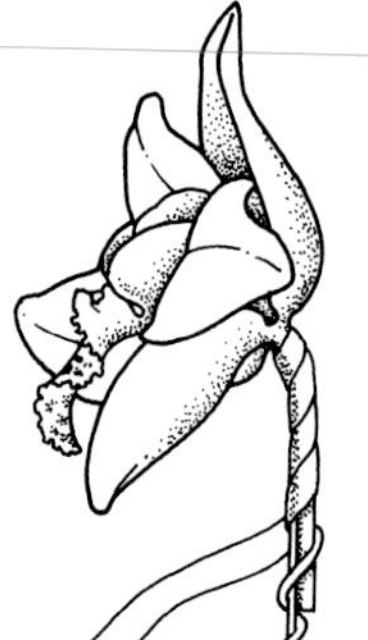

Above and Left: All wires should be covered in green florists' tape as shown (left).

Above and Left: Having brought all the wires of the individual parts together, arrange the foliage to complement the main bloom. Twist the wires together, trim them, and finally tape the 'stem'.

adorn the bridal gown? On a very limited scale, the local florist would probably be happy to purchase good quality, fresh orchid flowers, but although this may provide some funds for the purchase of new plants, orchid growing as a hobby should not be thought of as a paying concern.

To make a single corsage you will need two or three orchid flowers, depending upon size, together with a few small leaves of fern, thin copper wire, florist's tape, and, if desired, a short length of ribbon. To increase durability, all plant material should be stood in deep water overnight before making up the corsage or bouquet. Wire the stem of each flower to increase its length and ensure its correct positioning. Then cover each stem with florist's tape (usually dark green), and arrange the flowers and fern leaves together so that the flowers are just touching and the foliage forms a background. Next, twist the wires from the stems together and round all the stems to hold everything in place. Finally, trim back this central wire 'stem' to within approximately 5cm (2in) of the flowers, and, if you wish, tie the ribbon in a bow around it. If you put the completed corsage into a plastic box and place it in a domestic refrigerator, it will keep perfectly for two or three days.

A similar technique can be used for bouquet making, although instead of single flowers it is preferable to leave the

Right: It is not only the flowers that win an exhibitor a prize, but attention to detail, such as cleaning the foliage.

whole spike intact, allowing the natural presentation of the flowers to predominate.

Exhibiting orchids

For many, the ultimate accolade for their orchids is to gain a prize at an orchid show. But win or lose, there is much to learn and enjoy by exhibiting, and a certain satisfaction in knowing that your orchids have helped in making the show a success. Preparations for exhibiting are not too dissimilar to the normal cultural routine followed by all enthusiastic growers; plants should be maintained in a pest- and disease-free condition, weeds should never be allowed to grow in the pots, and flower spikes always benefit by being trained properly. Extra attention to these details, coupled with a thorough cleaning of the plant and pot, may make the difference between 'just another exhibit' and a 'polished performer'.

Preparing for the show

Dead bracts around the base of pseudobulbs should be split vertically and then each half removed by gently pulling sideways, taking care not to damage any new growths that may be hidden in the base. Any leaves which have died back or have brown tips should be trimmed back in a natural contour, after which the foliage should be sponged with clean water. Before wiping both sides of the leaf with a clean sponge or cloth, hold the base of the leaf to prevent it pulling out. The centre leaves on semi-mature growths of cymbidiums and odontoglossums are particularly vulnerable and, as all foliage is needed for the plant to grow well, care should be taken not to lose any needlessly. Finally, clean the pot and label the plant clearly according to the show schedule.

To transport the plants to the exhibition hall, place the pots in boxes and pack tightly with paper. Where several plants are to travel in the same box, ensure that all the flowers are held apart from each other and any other surface. With large arching spikes it is advisable to insert a second cane into the compost at an angle, so that the end of the spike may be tied to it and held steady.

When staging the plants, ensure that you have complied with the show regulations, and, if in doubt, consult the show secretary, who is there to help make certain that all plants are exhibited to their full potential.

Orchid societies

In all parts of the world there are now orchid societies established to bring together people of similar interests. Many function under the umbrella of a national council, whilst others flourish equally well on an independent basis. There are many advantages to membership, not least the facility to purchase orchid 'accessories' at competitive prices. Regular meetings are held, so the grower is kept informed about current events in the orchid world. Speakers from the commercial sector will frequently attend such meetings, and orchid forums regularly discuss cultural and other questions—basic or more advanced—to the benefit of all. Visits to nurseries and private orchid collections are a normal part of a society programme, as are social events.

But above all, membership of a society offers the opportunity to take a broader view of your hobby, something that is certain to be of benefit to you and your orchids.

Below: A superb display of orchids—the culmination of much painstaking work and effort. Critical attention to culture and detailed preparation have made this a collection to be envied, and as such an inspiration to all other growers.

BREEDING AND TISSUE CULTURE

Since the first manmade orchid hybrids flowered over a century ago, orchidists have been transferring the pollen from one orchid to the stigma of another in the hope of combining the best features of each parent into the resulting seedlings. The process got off to a fine start as *Paphiopedilum* Harrisianum, which first flowered in 1869, is still much used today as a cut flower, and grown by many hobbyists.

Whether it was by chance or inspiration that John Dominy, the chief grower on the famous Veitch nursery at Exeter, crossed *Paphiopedilum barbatum* with *Paphiopedilum villosum,* the results were far reaching. The strong colour of the pod parent, *barbatum* (the plant fertilized) combined with the vigour and tremendous texture of the pollen parent, *villosum* (the plant contributing the pollen) to give richly coloured long-lasting flowers produced on tall stems from a plant that grows and flowers more freely than either of its parents. Appropriately, this first paphiopedilum hybrid was named in honour of Dr John Harris, the Exeter surgeon who had suggested to Dominy the feasibility of pollination—a technique that had previously eluded orchid growers.

The success of hybridization

Once it became certain that orchids would hybridize, many collected plants originally thought to be species were reexamined, and the first natural hybrids were classified.

Even today, some growers ask why, with the vast numbers and diversity found in species and naturally occurring hybrids, do we breed more orchids. There are, of course, many reasons, and possibly the commercial cut flower aspect is of prime importance. To fulfil the requirements of a good cut flower, orchid flowers must be freely produced from compact plants, be well spaced on tall spikes (or, if produced singly as in paphiopedilums, have long stems), be easily packed into boxes (thus arching sprays are less popular than upright spikes) and be sufficiently tough in texture to withstand long journeys, yet still last for weeks in the customer's home. Modern tastes also demand large, rounded flowers.

Unfortunately, not many species or primary hybrids satisfy all these criteria. Thus orchid breeders have sought to combine, for example, the strong colour or lip markings of an otherwise insignificant orchid with the spike habit and flower shape of a more vigorously growing one. Very few of the resulting seedlings will have all the desirable features, but by carefully selecting the best plants for subsequent breeding, hybridizers have succeeded in producing, over many generations, orchids that have most of the good characteristics.

This process of selection is limitless, as new varieties are constantly being demanded by an expanding market. To satisfy the whims of growers in warm climates who wish to cultivate high altitude—thus, cool growing—orchids, there has also been some breeding for temperature tolerance. The cool growing

Hand Pollination of Orchids

From the orchids man has artificially produced many more hybrids than from any other group of commonly cultivated plants. The naturally occurring species and hybrids rely upon insects for transfer of pollen from one flower to the stigma of another. Those insects are attracted by a variety of lures, such as scent, colour and nectar. Some orchids have evolved very highly specialized techniques to ensure that the pollinia are deposited on the correct part of the insect, so that when visiting subsequent flowers the pollen mass is brought into contact with the glutinous receptive surface of the stigma. For synthetic hybrids, however, man has to undertake the pollinating role of these insects.

The plant produced from artificial pollination usually takes many years to reach a flower-

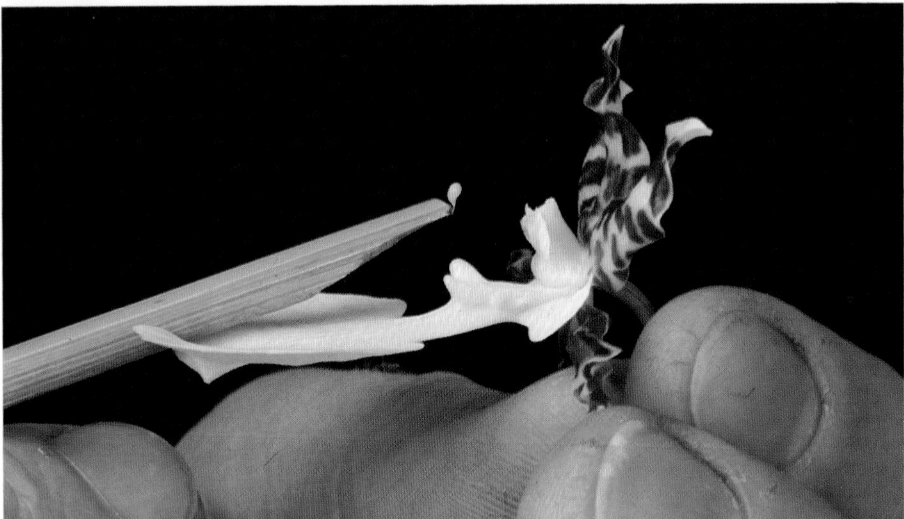

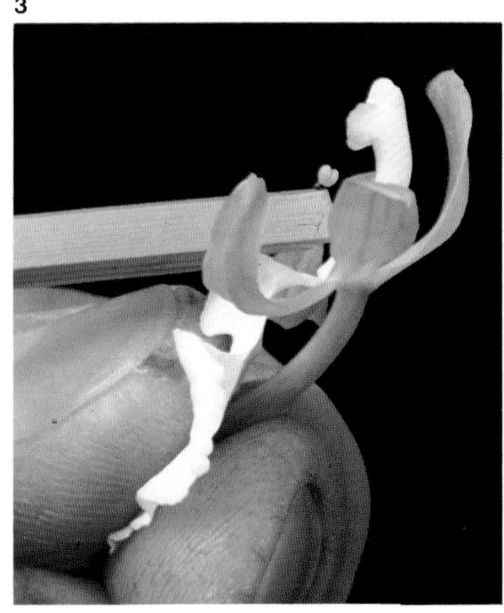

1 First of all decide which plant is to be the pollen parent and which the pod parent. The latter should always be the stronger grower of the two. The pollen masses are found on the column beneath the apex of the cap, except in *Paphiopedilum* and allied genera where there is no cap and they are on either side of the column.

2 Place a small pointed piece of wood, such as a matchstick, under the pollen cap and lift upwards; the cap will fall away leaving the pollinia stuck to the end of the piece of wood. Check that the pollen mass is a clear yellow colour (yellow-brown for *Paphiopedilum* and allied genera) and not infected with mildew.

3 Remove the pollinia of the flower chosen for the pod parent in the same way and either discard or use it for further crosses. Next transfer the pollinia removed from the pollen parent to the pod parent flower.

odontoglossums, for instance, have been bred with the warmer growing Brazilian miltonias to produce flowers that resemble those of odontoglossums, and plants that will tolerate the higher temperatures of tropical areas. *Odontonia* Purple Ace is an example of one of the more successful hybrids.

A more recent reason for breeding is aimed at conservation. By selecting two clones of the same species and crossing one with the other—thus producing a species under cultivation—it is hoped that those species especially endangered in their country of origin will be available to the general public, and even to repopulate depleted colonies in the wild. Luckily, many of these nursery-raised species seem to grow better than their jungle-collected cousins that have to adapt to an unnatural environment.

The commercial orchid industry is reacting swiftly to fill the void created by the Endangered Species Act, which controls the international movement of all orchids—hybrids and species—in an attempt to prevent threatened species from becoming extinct. But while accepting the ideals behind the legislation, far more effort is required from the countries concerned if some species are not to become extinct. Agricultural and mining interests are having a far greater effect on depletion than the relatively small amount of commercial collecting now taking place, and blame for the extinction of species orchids should not be laid solely at the door of orchid growers.

The art of breeding

After successful pollination, in most cases the pollinated flower rapidly wilts and loses much of its colour. Paphiopedilums are a notable exception to this rule, but in all orchids the ovary behind the flower begins to swell and the seed pod, or capsule, develops. This process continues until the capsule is ripe and the seed is ready for harvesting. The time taken to ripen varies even within one genus, from 4 to 14 months, and rather than relying on arbitrary ripening dates, it is best to keep an eye on the individual capsule. The capsules should be removed when the end starts to turn yellow or brown and becomes a little crisp, but before it splits longitudinally.

Seed raising

The seed should be sown immediately, and there are many specialist seed-raising laboratories that offer a good service. Orchid seed is extremely small and needs to be sown in flasks of a chemical agar under sterile conditions. Any bacteria that enter the flask will rapidly spread and ruin the valuable seed. For those hobbyist growers able to supply the necessary sterile conditions, various proprietary brands of sowing medium are available, mostly based on the formula worked out by Professor Lewis Knudson at Cornell University in 1922. For the most detailed information on the subject, see *The Orchids: A Scientific Survey* edited by Carl Withner of the Brooklyn Botanic Garden.

Most orchid seed begins to germinate

ing size, and it is only then that the merit of the new hybrid can be fully assessed. Thus the parent plants should always be chosen from good healthy stock and between them possess all the characters desired in the offspring. Unfortunately, there is no way to ensure that the resulting hybrids will display all the desired characters; it is just a matter of chance.

The photographs on these two pages clearly illustrate the technique for artificially pollinating orchids—having a steady hand is certainly an advantage. After the seed has ripened it is usually sown on nutrient agar gel where it may take several weeks before any signs of germination are visible. With patience and good cultivation techniques (as well as some luck) any orchid grower should be able to produce new and improved hybrids himself.

4

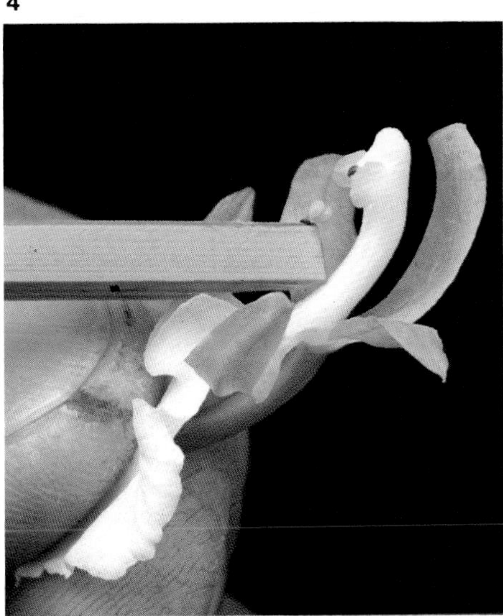

5

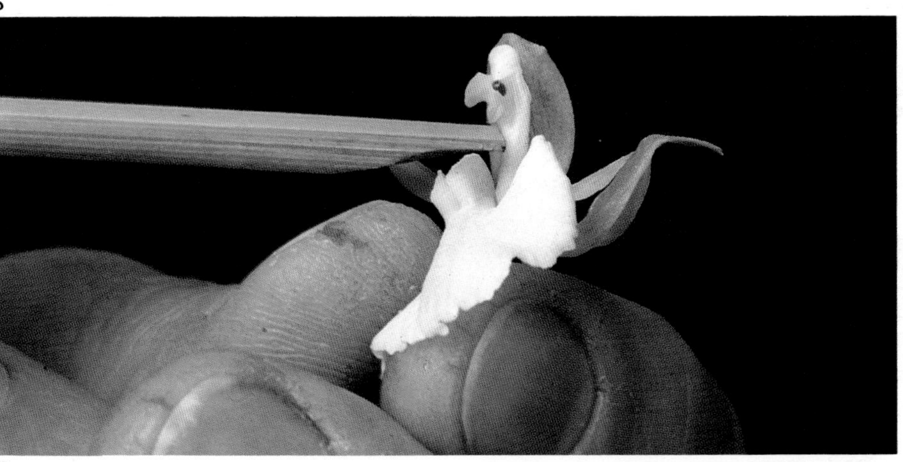

6

4 Introduce the pollinia of the pollen parent into the flower of the female parent, taking care not to damage the flower. Although it is best to have both parents flowering at the same time it is possible to store the pollinia of some orchids for a few months in the dry atmosphere of a sealed and labelled test-tube containing silica-gel.

5 Push the pollinia up on to the stigma—just behind the site from where the pod parent's pollinia was removed. In *Paphiopedilum* and associated genera a 'window' has to be cut in the pouch so that the pollen masses can be placed on the stigma.

6 Once the pollinia has stuck to the glutinous surface of the stigma, the wooden stick can be removed. Finally, label the flower with all the relevant details of the hybridization, such as parents and date of pollination. If pollination has been successful the flower will collapse soon afterwards and the seed pod will swell.

approximately six weeks after sowing, and as the seedlings develop they will need extra space. This is provided by transplanting (replating) the tiny seedlings into fresh flasks of medium, again under sterile conditions, and should be carried out when the first root and growing shoot have appeared on each seedling. On average this will be 15 to 18 weeks after germination. In practice it is similar to 'pricking out' the seedlings of any other plant, and is best completed when the young plants are small. Six to nine months later, the seedlings will have grown sufficiently large to withstand the rigours of greenhouse culture. The seedlings should be carefully removed through the neck of the flask, with the aid of a wire hook, and immediately potted into community pots or seed trays, with seedlings approximately 2.5-5cm (1-2in) apart. As the seedlings grow they should be potted on individually into progressively larger pots.

The science of breeding

As the seedlings come into flower, one or two may prove especially worthy of merit, and consequently become much in demand. In the past, the only method of obtaining a replica of a particular clone was by conventional vegetative propaga-

Left: Orchid seeds should be sown in a flask on sterile nutrient agar gel. These seedlings have germinated and are growing well; the larger ones are ready for potting up.

1

Meristem Culture Techniques

The specialized technique of meristem culture is the most recent practical method of propagating orchids. A meristem is a group of actively dividing cells, from which the various tissues of the plant eventually develop. Meristems are usually found very near the apices of roots and stems.

As sterile conditions are essential at all times and specialized equipment is required, the technique is best carried out by a specialist laboratory service. But for those amateur growers who can provide the necessary conditions, the procedure is illustrated on these two pages. The plant used should be healthy and free from all ailments. First, remove the stem or pseudobulb from the plant using a sterile scalpel, wash off any soil and then sterilize the whole surface by placing it in a 5 percent solution of domestic bleach for up to one hour.

After sterilization, wash the stem or bulb in two changes of sterile deionized water. Next, expose the growing point and cut out the meristem with a sterile scalpel. Place the cut meristem in a flask containing sterile nutrient solution. Stopper the flask with cotton wool to keep out infecting organisms but allow free access of air, and place the flask on a mechanical agitator.

The meristem cells divide, but due to the agitation are unable to organize into shoots and roots and instead form a mass, or callus. When this has grown it can be cut into several small pieces, which, if placed on to sterile nutrient agar gel, will form shoots and roots—young plants—soon ready for potting up.

2

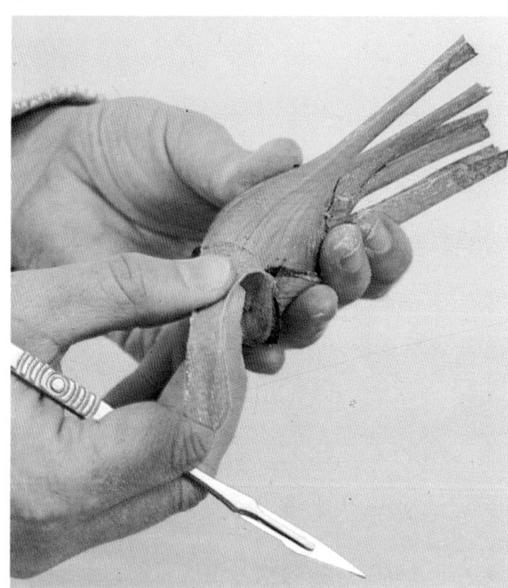

3

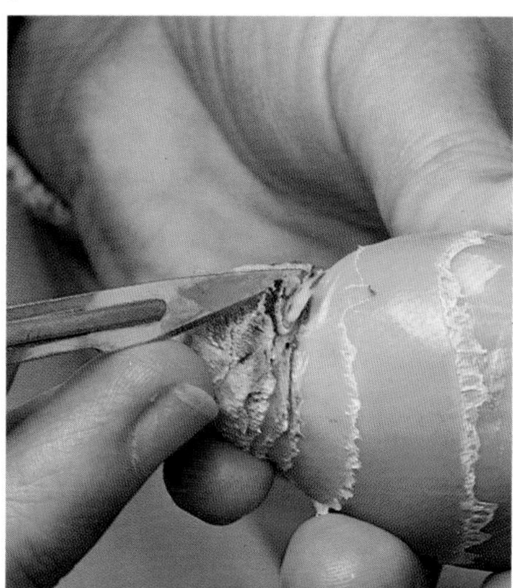

1 At the start of meristem culture of this cymbidium, a pseudobulb is cut from the plant using a sterile scalpel. The operator's hands, as well as the equipment used, must be scrupulously clean at all times. Take care to ensure that, if possible, no compost is removed with the pseudobulb.

2 In the laboratory the leaves are peeled back to expose the young shoots from which the meristems will be taken. Working carefully and patiently these leaves should be completely cut away at their bases and then discarded.

3 With the young shoot exposed, the whole pseudobulb is now sterilized in a weak solution of hypochlorite or domestic bleach. Immersion for 15-30 minutes is usually adequate. The solution is then rinsed off in two changes of sterile deionized water.

tion. This situation changed dramatically in 1961 when Professor Georges Morel of the University of Paris 'meristemmed' the first orchids, using a technique developed with other plants at the University of California 15 years earlier.

Meristem culture

Meristem culture is a highly skilled process, normally performed by orchid specialists. Briefly, the technique is to cut away the apical meristem, which is a minute shoot at the base of a developing young growth. Under sterile conditions this shoot is placed in a liquid medium in a sterile flask, which is then placed on either a revolving wheel or a mechanical agitator. The constant movement inhibits the formation of a growing shoot or root; instead, the apical meristem proliferates into many embryo plants or *protocorms,* which can be divided by cutting. The process may be repeated indefinitely, until the required number of protocorms is produced; these are then replated and grown on as seedlings. By far the most comprehensive review of the considerable literature in this field may be found in *Orchid Biology: Reviews and Perspectives, 1,* edited by Joseph Arditti of the University of California.

If meristem reproduction is properly carried out, the resulting *mericlones* (protocorms derived from the meristem) are free from virus infection at the time of leaving the flask. With very few exceptions, the habit of growth and flower colour will be identical to those of the mother plant and—of importance to the cut flower industry—the mericlones will all flower simultaneously each year. For the hobbyist, meristemming has meant large reductions in the price of top quality orchids, making the very best orchids available to all. For the conservationist, the economic production of species mericlones will help to prevent the extinction of threatened species. The technique of meristem culture is still being perfected, and it is certain that the few genera, such as *Paphiopedilum,* that remain resistant will shortly succumb.

Future trends

Science will not rest on its laurels. One genus of orchids will interbreed only with other genera of the same subfamily and then not always successfully. Thus cymbidiums are unlikely ever to breed with paphiopedilums, for example. However, experimental work is attempting to combine the cells of one orchid with those of an orchid from a different subfamily. Although this is still in its infancy, there are reports that the *protoplasts* (living cells without cell walls) of *Renantanda* have fused with *Dendrobium,* and also with *Phalaenopsis,* under experimental conditions. Whether or not the fused protoplasts can be persuaded to develop into protocorms and eventually strong plants remains to be seen.

But one thing is certain: we are only at the threshold of orchid hybridization and development. Although the past has produced many marvellous plants, the future will be infinitely more colourful, diverse, exciting and rewarding for all who grow orchids.

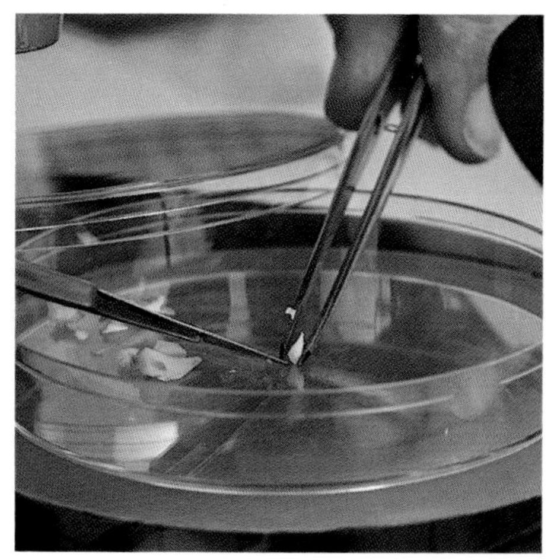

4 Ensuring that all equipment is sterile, the shoot is cut from the pseudobulb and the meristem carefully dissected out. In order to distinguish the microscopic meristem region of the shoot, a stereoscopic dissecting microscope is absolutely essential.

5 The meristem is transferred to a liquid nutrient medium which is continuously agitated to ensure that no shoots or roots develop. Instead a large mass of cells will form. Usually the meristems of virus-infected plants are free from infection, and provided special care is taken it is possible to produce virus-free plants from infected stock.

6 Under the ideal conditions for growth that are available in the laboratory the cell mass can become large. As it has no organized structure it can be cut into several smaller pieces, which can either be grown on to produce another cell mass, or allowed to develop into small plants.

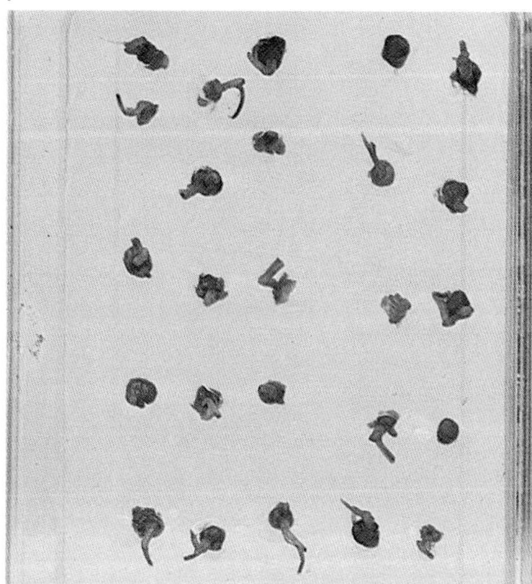

7 If pieces of the cell mass are returned to the shaken nutrient solution, an indefinite supply of material for propagation can be maintained. If, however, pieces are placed on nutrient agar gel (left), they develop into small plants (right), which can eventually be transplanted into a sterile potting medium.

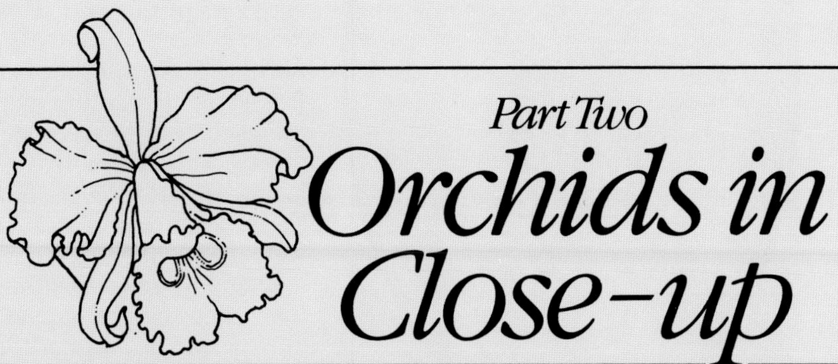

Part Two

Orchids in Close-up

In the early days of orchid growing, when the species were imported from the wild and cultivated, it was thought that the peculiar structure of their flowers would preclude hybridization between the different species. However, in 1854, the first orchid cross was successfully pollinated by John Dominy at the nursery of James Veitch. Once this had been achieved, the pollination of orchid flowers was found to be remarkably easy, and two years later the first hybrid—between two calanthes—flowered. At the time its significance was not fully appreciated, and the hybrid was considered a novelty not to be taken seriously. Further hybrids followed slowly, partly because it was difficult to cultivate the seedlings.

Once these problems had been overcome, growers turned to the more flamboyant species to develop showier hybrids, which began to rival the species for their beauty. Orchid hybridizing has come a long way in the last few decades and today the amateur grower has a wonderful range of superb hybrids from which to choose.

By careful breeding over the years, hybridization has produced a plant that is more vigorous and has a wider tolerance of artificial conditions. The modern hybrid can be perfectly at home on a windowsill, or in a greenhouse. A further advantage of the hybrid over the species is that the flowers are often more exciting, larger and more richly coloured than those of the original species.

Despite the availability of so many beautiful hybrids and their easier cultivation, interest in growing species orchids did not decline at first, partly because they were cheaper to buy. Mature plants could be imported in large numbers and quickly established in the nurseries, so that they were flowering and saleable within a few months of arrival. Compared with the production costs of raising hybrids, some of which took as many as seven years to reach flowering size, orchid species were then relatively inexpensive. For this reason most beginners gained their knowledge from the species rather than the more expensive hybrids.

The days of the inexpensive species are now limited. Many have become extinct or are rare in the wild due to years of over-collecting. In some situations where agriculture has led to the destruction of the virgin forests their habitat has been destroyed. A number of orchids in danger of becoming extinct are now protected by the Endangered Species Act and their export has been prohibited in an effort to save them, although this can be successful only where the plants' natural habitat is preserved. Unfortunately, in many places this continues to disappear at an alarming rate.

The most showy and attractive among the orchid species that have been in cultivation for many years will undoubtedly be raised alongside the hybrids in the nurseries of the world, and in this way they will be saved for the collector. However, as this method is far more costly than importation, their price will be comparable with that of the hybrids, so much of their appeal may be lost. For this reason, only the most flamboyant of the species will be retained, and many of the less exotic flowers will not be seen in collections of the future.

The most popular orchids in cultivation come from those genera that have been hybridized to the greatest extent. Cymbidiums, odontoglossums and cattleyas are examples of these. Among the cymbidiums the hybrids far surpass the species for the size, shape and colour of the flowers, and the colour range has been extended to accommodate every possible shade with the exception of blue. The odontoglossums and cattleyas have not only been hybridized from within their own genus, but have also been interbred with closely allied plants to produce several new manmade genera, with two, three or more genera contained in each hybrid.

Where a variety of plants is grown, it is quite possible to have flowers all the year round. Some orchids, such as cymbidiums, have a decided flowering season, and can be relied upon to bloom during the same month year after year. Others may bloom progressively through the year, for example the *Odontoglossum* hybrids and particularly those of mixed generic breeding, such as the vuylstekearas. Their complicated pedigree contains several different species, all of which may bloom at different times. The resulting hybrid produces its flower spike when the leading bulb has completed the season's growth, regardless of the time of year. It follows that where a bulb can be grown in a period of nine months or so, the plant will bloom as often, the flowers opening at a different time each year. When buying plants, it is always a good idea to enquire whether the plant will bloom consistently each year, or vary its flowering according to the culture it receives. In this way, with careful selection, you can build up a collection of mixed orchids that will give you some plants in flower, whatever the season.

Although the following pages illustrate a wide range of orchid species and hybrids, not all will be available to the grower. Only the best varieties remain consistently in cultivation; others lose favour as better varieties come along. Some grow better in certain parts of the world, and are discontinued wherever they do not thrive. Commercial nurseries will have their own particular varieties available, and those that they consider the most popular. Do not be deterred, however, for your local orchid supplier will be able to advise you on the best varieties, and there are commercial catalogues, which give details of all the current hybrids available.

Left: The modern hybrid orchids are hard to beat for their beauty and ease of culture. *Renanthopsis* Mildred Jameson, with its intriguing speckled flowers, is a stunning example.

CATTLEYAS

Known to devotee growers as 'Queen of the Orchids', the splendour and variety of many cattleya species give this tribe a fair claim to royal status. It is celebrated, too, in literature as providing the symbolic flower in Swann's love affair with Odette in Proust's *Remembrance of Things Past.* Their exotic blooms appear frequently in glossy magazines and on chocolate boxes and greeting cards.

Cattleyas in the wild

There are about 60 wild cattleya species, most of which are epiphytic or lithophytic. They are native to Central and South America, from Mexico to Bolivia, Paraguay and Argentina, and are concentrated in the Andes and the Brazilian forests.

They are found in a range of natural habitats from the dense steamy jungles of the Amazon region, where they anchor themselves to the branches and trunks of trees, to heights of 3,050m (10,000ft) in the Andes, where the night temperature falls to almost freezing. As a result, cattleyas are among the most adaptable of orchid genera.

Cattleyas can be divided into two groups according to growth: unifoliate, with a single large broad leaf and club-shaped pseudobulbs joined by a creeping rhizome; and bifoliate with longer, more cylindrical pseudobulbs, a pair of short leaves and smaller, heavier flowers.

Cattleyas in cultivation

The genus *Cattleya* was founded by Dr Lindley, a well-known botanist, in 1824 and named after William Cattley, an eminent horticulturalist and one of the first amateurs to create a private collection of orchids. The first cattleyas were brought to England from Brazil in 1818, tied round a consignment of other tropical plants. On examination, Cattley realized that these thick-leaved plants were unusual and rescued them. When the first came into flower, it was studied by Dr Lindley, who found it to be an entirely new genus and named if after its owner.

Temperature requirements

To grow cattleyas successfully, it is wise to attempt to emulate the conditions of their natural environment.

Cattleyas are particularly sensitive to changes in temperature. For mature plants, a winter night temperature between 13 and 15.5°C (55-60°F) will be sufficient. Seedlings and some of the more tender species will benefit from slightly warmer conditions, from 15.5-18°C (60-65°F), combined with a higher humidity to encourage growth. Summer temperatures may rise to 26.5-32°C (80-90°F), and will do no harm provided a constant high humidity is maintained.

To ensure good flower production, mature winter and spring flowering cattleyas should be rested for six to eight weeks at the end of the growing season, when the new pseudobulbs are fully developed. At this time watering should be reduced and the humidity lowered by restricting damping down to once daily. Any shading should also be removed, so that the plants can obtain all available light to ripen the pseudobulbs. Summer-flowering cattleyas do not require a rest.

Light and food

In the treetops of their native South American forests, cattleyas grow in filtered light under a canopy of leaves, provided with moisture from mists and wind. Adult plants therefore require sufficient light to encourage strong growths that will mature into hard pseudobulbs, from which the flowers develop (technically about 3,000 foot-candles), but will benefit from shading applied to the outside of the greenhouse in the form of lath blinds or muslin net. This allows full light in bad weather, when the blinds can be raised. Permanent shading in the form of emulsion paint applied to the glass is also widely used, but although this provides good cover, great care must be taken to ensure that when the cattleyas first require protection from the bright sunlight of early spring, the paint is not applied too thickly as to be detrimental to growth. It is advisable to apply it in two sessions, the heavier shading being completed by late spring.

During early spring, after the plants have been repotted and the new root system has developed, and with the growing season well started, cattleyas should be given a supplementary liquid feed (at half the manufacturer's recommended strength as, in common with most orchids, they are weak feeders). Feeding should be done during the morning, when the temperature is rising, as the plant's metabolism is most active during this part of the day. Use a high nitrogen feed every two to three weeks, with a foliar feed every six weeks throughout the summer. This programme can be continued throughout the summer until a pseudobulb has developed, when a phosphate-based fertilizer should be applied to ripen and harden off the bulbs to ensure good flowers, before the plant enters its resting period.

Humidity, water and ventilation

It is very important to maintain a humid atmosphere in the greenhouse by damping down. This prevents the plants from losing water through transpiration, so they do not require heavy watering and its consequent dangers.

Damping down first thing in the morning, when the heating system has dried out the bench and path areas, and the daylight is lifting the greenhouse temperature, will produce a buoyant growing atmosphere. During the summer months this should be done two or three times a day, coupled with light overhead spraying with clean water. Particular care should be taken to make sure that the side glass has been reached with the spray to help bring down the temperature, for it is in this area that pests will appear.

Watering is one of the most important features in the cultivation of cattleyas. No hard and fast rule can be applied, but 'if in doubt leave alone' and water the plant next time, for more plants are killed by overwatering than by any other means.

After repotting, water the pot well, then leave it alone until the plant is almost dry before watering again. If the greenhouse is kept damped down, cattleyas will not require heavy watering. As soon as the new roots have started to probe through the compost, the supply of water should increase. As a general rule cattleyas will require watering about twice a week during the growing season, depending on the size and condition of the plant. During the late autumn and winter months, when the plant is dormant, only sufficient water to stop the pseudobulbs from shrivelling is required; a light watering every two weeks should be adequate.

For the mature or flowering cattleya the movement of air around the plant is important for maintaining its health and flower production. However, small seedlings and plants with not more than three pseudobulbs require more humid conditions and less air should be admitted; the use of an electric fan is beneficial at this early stage.

A good plan is to open up the house when the outside temperature is rising and close it about an hour before the light starts to decrease. Even in winter, the ventilators should be opened during spells of fine weather. Ventilating the house even for a few minutes at this time of year is of great benefit, as it prevents a stagnant atmosphere from developing.

Above: *Cattleya maxima* is native to Ecuador and Peru. Discovered in the early 1800s, it was crossed with *C. intermedia* in 1859 to produce the first manmade cattleya hybrid, *C.* Dominiana.

Composts and potting

Bearing in mind that cattleyas are epiphytes, the rooting compost should be of an open quality to enable the roots to probe freely and to admit air and water. For many years the root masses of the osmunda fern were used, teased out and cut into suitable lengths, and proved to be ideal when used in conjunction with sphagnum moss (one third moss to two thirds fern). Changing circumstances, including the high cost of importing osmunda fibre, have forced cattleya growers to seek a more readily available compost. Many forms of redwood bark are now used; these are easy to obtain and can be used without any additives, but the addition of small lumps of charcoal and perlite will help to keep the compost open and sweet.

Occasionally, during late summer and early autumn, the compost on the surface of a pot will begin to collect moss, which, if allowed to build up, will be harmful to the formation of the cattleya's root system. The moss should be removed and the pot topped up with fresh compost.

Repotting should be carried out after the resting period, when new growth has started to develop from the base of the previous year's pseudobulbs, and new roots are active. As a rule this will be about four weeks after the plant has finished flowering, in winter or early spring.

Cattleyas can be planted in various kinds of pots, pans, baskets and rafts, but most plants purchased are in plastic or clay pots. Provided there is adequate drainage they are ideal. Free percolation will be ensured if the holes at the bottom of the plastic pots are enlarged.

Small cattleya seedlings or divisions are the easiest to repot, as the whole plant can be removed from its outgrown container and merely dropped into its new pot. The repotting procedure is as follows. Clean away any accumulated weed or moss, and trim back dead roots. Select a pot that will allow the plant to fill it to its sides when the new growth is completed; it is important at this stage not to use too large a pot. To obtain anchorage in the compost, cattleya roots adhere to the sides of the container, and new growth will not begin until this process has been completed. When too large a pot is used, this will take some time and, if the plant is watered frequently, the old roots may rot, causing a further check to growth.

Having selected an appropriate pot, put a few broken crocks or polystyrene chippings into the base. Add a layer of compost and place the plant in the pot so that the base of the pseudobulb is about 2.5cm (1in) below the rim. Then fill in around the cattleya with compost, tapping the pot several times to help consolidate the compost around the roots.

Vegetative propagation

When a cattleya has been allowed to grow on for several years, it will be necessary to reduce the number of back pseudobulbs from the growing section. As a rule, four or five pseudobulbs are required for the plant to produce strong flowers.

Using a clean pair of secateurs or a sharp knife, cut cleanly through the rhizome, removing any damaged roots at the same time. Each new section can then be repotted as described, with the cut area to one side of the pot and the roots spread out as much as possible. Tie each pseudobulb to a strong cane placed slightly behind the plant to give stability until the roots have anchored themselves to the sides of the pot.

The back pseudobulbs can also be grown on in small pots, provided they are given adequate drainage. When a small new growth has started, place the pot in the warmest part of the greenhouse and keep the area damped down to create a humid and buoyant atmosphere. A method commonly used to induce this dormant section into life is to place the bulbs in a clear polyethylene bag with a handful of sphagnum moss; seal the neck of the bag and hang it in the apex of the greenhouse roof where it will receive the correct light conditions to initiate growth; this usually takes about six to eight weeks, and while in the polyethylene bag it will be in its own microenvironment. As soon as it produces new growth, set it in a small pot prepared as above and keep it in the warmest section of the house until established.

Pests and diseases

Because of their hard pseudobulbs and tough leathery leaves, few pests attack cattleyas, and those that do can be controlled. Damage is caused mainly by sucking and biting pests.

Thrips attack buds emerging from the sheath when they are very tender, and damage is immediate. Because of their minute size and prompt crawling away at the slightest movement, thrips are difficult to spot, but malathion is effective against them.

Slugs and snails attack the succulent root tips, buds and flowers. Slug pellets help to keep these under control, but a drenching with a liquid slug bait, on the benches and walls underneath the plants, is more effective. A twist of dry cotton wool tucked below the buds will deter these pests.

The common soft scale (*Coccus hesperidum*) and boisduval scale (*Diaspis boisduvalii*) attack cattleyas by injecting their probosces into the pseudobulb or rhizome and withdrawing the sap. Large colonies can build up quickly, and affected plants should be sprayed at once with malathion. Clusters of cottony masses may occur on the undersides of leaves and under the sheathing leaf, and badly infected plants should be cleaned, using a small brush dipped in malathion.

Sickly looking plants that have small white fluffy patches on the undersurfaces of the leaves have been attacked by mealy bugs. If the infestation is on one or two plants, use neat methylated spirit on a small paintbrush, taking care to get behind the sheaths that protect the pseudobulbs and into the apex of the leaf; several treatments will be necessary. The adult bugs can be controlled by spraying with malathion.

Cattleyas occasionally suffer from 'neck rot' which generally attacks the area between the axis of the leaf and the apex of the pseudobulb. The disease may be caused by bacteria or a fungus, and sometimes takes hold very rapidly. If the rot is in its early stages, dip the plant in a solution of natriphine and allow it to dry. After two or three days follow this treatment by using a systemic fungicide spray, such as Benlate. If the plant is badly infected, it might require surgery. Using a sharp knife that has been flamed in a burner, cut away damaged parts of the leaf or bulb and dust the wound liberally with captan. If the trouble is deep-seated, the removal of the pseudobulb down to the rhizome will be necessary. The dormant eye will then produce a new growth and the life cycle will start again.

Growing cattleyas on the windowsill

For those who do not possess a greenhouse, a few cattleya plants, such as *C. skinneri* and *C. forbesii* can be grown on a windowsill or in a glass case made especially for them.

Several species will do well in an east or south facing window that is light all day, provided that the correct environment is created. Light and heat will not be a problem, but it is difficult to provide the right level of humidity indoors. This can be overcome by standing the plant on a tray of damp peat or gravel chippings, kept sufficiently damp for the warmth of the room to create the necessary moisture round the plant.

A glass frame or case can be fitted with artificial light to provide light and warmth during winter, as well as humidity.

Indoor plants should only be watered when the pot is nearly dry, and fertilizers should be applied once every two weeks at half the manufacturer's recommended strength, remembering that the plant will not be subjected to the same light conditions as its counterpart in the greenhouse and will not be able to assimilate this food supply as fast.

Above: Slugs can wreck all your efforts of cultivation in a single night. They are particularly partial to young shoots, buds and flowers.

Species and hybrids

The first hybrid cattleya, C. Dominiana was produced at the renowned Veitch nursery in 1859, by crossing *Cattleya intermedia* with *Cattleya maxima*. Since that time, cattleyas have been successfully crossed with many of their subtribes, including *Laelia, Brassavola, Epidendrum, Broughtonia, Diacrium. Schomburgkia, Sophronitis* and *Leptotes*, to produce a wide variety of forms and colours.

The crossing of a laelia with a cattleya created the laeliocattleya (LC). To produce large flowers with fringed lips, brassavolas were used in the cross, thus creating brassolaeliocattleyas (BLC). Brassavolas are also crossed with cattleyas alone to produce brassocattleyas (BC). Sophronitis has been widely used because of its intense colours, particularly reds, and the roundness of its flower shape. The hybrid with cattleya is known as sophrocattleya (SC). Laelias may also be involved in the cross to produce the multiflowered, more compact sophrolaeliocattleyas (SLC); they may be crossed with sophronitis alone to produce beautiful red-flowering robust sophrolaelias (SL), and sophronitis may be crossed with epidendrums to produce episophronitis. Schomburgkias are more commonly crossed with laelias than cattleyas to produce robust schombolaelias. A quadrigeneric cross between *Brassavola, Sophronitis, Laelia* and *Cattleya* gave rise to the *Potinaria* range, although relatively few outstanding hybrids have been produced from this cross.

Many combinations are possible, and those species and hybrids featured here demonstrate the wide range achieved in flower colour and shape.

Cattleya Species

Cattleya amethystoglossa

◑*Intermediate* ❀*Summer*

Right: A native of Brazil, this species bears clusters of six to eight flowers, 7.5-10cm (3-4in) across, during the summer. The sepals and petals are white suffused with rose-purple and spotted with amethyst. The broad round violet-purple lip has white side lobes. The plant, which is a subject for the intermediate house, has drooping leaves and slender pseudobulbs that can grow to 91cm (3ft) in height.

Photo X ¾

Cattleya aurantiaca

○*Cool* ❀*Summer*

Below: This small bifoliate species comes from Guatemala and neighbouring countries. It has drooping clusters of red-orange flowers, 7.5-10cm (3-4 n) across, produced in summer. The plant is peculiar in that it produces seedpods by self-pollination.

Photo X ⅓

Cattleya bowringiana

◑*Intermediate* ❀*Autumn*

Below: This lithophytic bifoliate, a natural hybrid, was discovered in 1884 growing near streams in Honduras (and named after J. C. Bowring of Windsor, England). It is a highly productive plant and can produce as many as 20 rose-purple, 7.5cm (3in) across, with a deep purple lip, marked with golden yellow in the throat. This plant requires more water than most to support the long pseudobulbs that are slightly bulbous at the base. The flowers open during late autumn, and the plant benefits from a short mid-winter rest after flowering, during which time watering should be withheld.

Photo X ⅓

Cattleya forbesii

◑*Intermediate* ❀*Summer*

Above: This species was discovered in Brazil in 1823. The plant is a bifoliate of dainty growth, with pencil-thin pseudobulbs. It requires a temperature of 13-15.5°C (55-60°F) in the winter, when it should have a resting period. Its yellow or tan-coloured flowers, produced in summer, are 7.5-10cm (3-4in) across, and have a tubular lip with side lobes of pale pink on the outside, and a deep yellow throat marked with wavy red lines.

Photo X ¾

Cattleya loddigesii

◑Intermediate ❀Summer-Winter

Right: The natural home of this lovely species is Brazil, and it should be housed in the intermediate section of the greenhouse. It is typical of the bifoliate group, with slender pseudobulbs and long-lasting rose-lilac flowers, 10-13cm (4-5in) across, whose lobes are dashed with white. Three to five flowers are borne on the flower spike, and the flowering season lasts from late summer to early winter.

A variety of *C. loddigesii* is *harrisoniae* (named after Harrison who introduced it into England). It has much taller pseudobulbs and more richly coloured flowers, produced in spring and summer.

Photo X 1

Cattleya porcia

○Cool ❀Autumn

Above: This free-flowering species bears clusters of pretty pinky lavender flowers, 7.5-10cm (3-4in) across, that open in early autumn. The plants, which should be grown in the cool house, appreciate a distinct rest during the winter months. At this stage, watering should be withheld until the new growth begins and the roots become active in early spring.

Photo X 1/3

Cattleya skinneri

○Cool ❀Winter/Spring

Right: This popular bifoliate species is the national flower of Costa Rica. Flowering from early winter to spring, the plant bears 5 to 10 flowers on a single stem. It requires cool-house conditions, but can be grown successfully on cork, bark or a wooden raft. Each flower is 7.5-10cm (3-4in) across, rose-purple in colour with a splash of white in the throat. A pure white variety, *C. skinneri* var. *alba* (far right) is also grown, but unfortunately has become increasingly rare.

Photo X 1/4

Laelia anceps

○*Cool* ❀*Winter*

Below: This native of Mexico has large showy flowers, 10-13cm (4-5in) across, that open in early winter. They are rose-coloured and grow clustered on tall graceful stems. The flower spikes develop from the apex between the top of a dwarf pseudobulb and the axis of a single leaf. *L. anceps* is a subject for the cool greenhouse and makes an attractive free-flowering plant for the living room. It should be given a dry resting period after flowering.

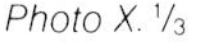

Photo X. ⅓

Laelia purpurata

◐*Intermediate* ❀*Spring/Summer*

Above: This is a free-flowering plant of Brazilian origin that will thrive in the intermediate section of the greenhouse. It flowers in spring and summer and often attains a height of 78cm (30in). It bears several large creamy white flowers, 13cm (5in) across, which have a contrasting velvety, dark crimson-purple lip and yellow throat streaked with magenta.

Photo X ½

Brassavola digbyana

◐*Intermediate* ❀*Summer*

Left: The almost white flower of this remarkable orchid, which has fleshy leaves, is characterized by its enormous deeply frilled lip which makes up most of the flower. Because of this it has long attracted hybridists wishing to reproduce flowers with large lips. It has an added attraction in its lemon fragrance. The apex of the intermediate greenhouse is an ideal position for this sun-worshipping plant, where it will thrive in the air movement at the roof of the house.

Photo X ⅔

Cattleya Hybrids

BRASSOLAELIOCATTLEYA
Crusader
◑*Intermediate* ❀*Winter*
Right: This robust hybrid, which can be grown on into a specimen plant, is the result of a cross between *Brassavola* Queen Elizabeth and *Laeliocattleya* Trivanhoe, and requires intermediate temperature conditions. The large pink flowers, produced in winter, are 20-23cm (8-9in) across. The heavy, round lip is purple with a yellow patch inside the lobes.
Photo X ½

BRASSOLAELIOCATTLEYA
Norman's Bay 'Lows' (FCC/RHS)
◑*Intermediate* ❀*Autumn*
Above: This is probably one of the finest rose-magenta flowered hybrids, produced from a cross of *Brassocattleya* Hartland and *Laeliocattleya* Ishtar. The flowers, which are 20-23cm (8-9in) across, have a splendid frilled lip and lovely fragrance that ensure a place for this superior autumn-flowering plant in the intermediate section of the greenhouse.
Photo X ¼

BRASSOLAELIOCATTLEYA
Norman's Bay ×
CATTLEYA
Triumphans
◑*Intermediate* ❀*Winter*
Right: This spectacular hybrid generally produces two or three beautifully shaped flowers of a heavy texture. They are a rich rose colour, 13cm (5in) across, with large frilled lips of magenta, the side lobes of which are splashed with yellow. Their fragrance is derived from the Norman's Bay influence. This exhibition hybrid, which flowers freely in the early winter, requires a definite resting period after flowering. Watering should be withheld during this period until the new roots and growths have become active.
Photo X ¾

BRASSOLAELIOCATTLEYA
Queen Elizabeth (FCC) ×
BRASSOLAELIOCATTLEYA
King Richard
◑*Intermediate* ❀*Autumn*
Right: The flowers of this hybrid are large, 20-23cm (8-9in) across, pinky lavender in colour with a frilled deep lavender lip, the centre of which is yellow. They are generally borne three to a spike, and open in late autumn. The plant, which has stout pseudobulbs and very broad leaves, is a vigorous grower, requiring intermediate conditions and a period of rest after flowering.
Photo X ¼

CATTLEYA
Bow Bells
◑*Intermediate* ❀*Spring*
Below: This beautiful hybrid is one of the world's most famous cattleyas, bred from the cross of *C.* Edithae and *C.* Suzanne Hye. It produces large heavy flowers, 15cm (6in) across, with pure white overlapping petals and a sulphur-yellow mark in the back of the throat. It is a plant for the intermediate house and requires a rest during the winter after the new growth has matured. The flowers are produced in the spring.
Photo X1⅓

LAELIOCATTLEYA
Amacynth

◑*Intermediate* ❀*Autumn/Winter*

Below: This hybrid, produced by crossing *Laeliocattleya* Cynthia with *Cattleya amabilis,* is a 'semi-alba' (that is, the sepals and petals of the flower are pure white without even a tinge of colour). The purple lip has a frilled edge offset with a faint line of white on the extreme edge. The flowers, which are 15-20cm (6-8in) across, appear in late autumn and early winter, and the plants should be grown in intermediate conditions.

Photo X 1/3

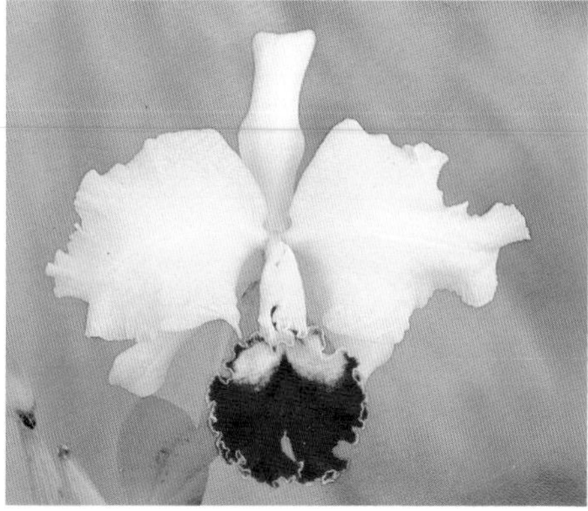

LAELIOCATTLEYA
Chitchat 'Tangerine'

◑*Intermediate* ❀*Summer*

Right: This summer-flowering hybrid is the result of a cross between *C. aurantiaca* and *Laelia* Coronet. The plant, which has clusters of delicate yellow-orange flowers 5cm (2in) across, has slender pseudobulbs and should be grown in the intermediate section of the greenhouse.

Photo X 1 2/3

LAELIOCATTLEYA
Culminant 'La Tuilerie'

◑*Intermediate* ❀*Spring*

Below: Produced from a cross between *Laeliocattleya* De France and *Cattleya* Gaillard, this hybrid has pink flowers, 15-18cm (6-7in) across, with a contrasting petunia-shaped lip delicately trimmed with pink. They open in spring and are heavy in texture and long lasting. This plant should be grown in the intermediate section of the greenhouse.

Photo X 1/3

LAELIOCATTLEYA
Oriental Prince ×
LAELIOCATTLEYA
Olympia
◑*Intermediate* ❀*Autumn*
Right: This lovely hybrid produces 15-20cm (6-8in) flowers with lavender-coloured sepals and petals, and a large frilled, deep purple lip. The plant is a strong grower with stout pseudobulbs and long rhizomes. It requires intermediate temperatures and flowers in the autumn.
Photo X 2/3

LAELIOCATTLEYA
Patricia Purves
◑*Intermediate* ❀*Spring*
Above: This early spring flowering hybrid has deep mauve-purple flowers, 15-18cm (6-7in) across. It requires intermediate conditions, and should be rested in autumn when the pseudobulbs have matured.
Photo X 1/3

POTINARIA
Sunrise
●*Warm* ❀*Autumn*
Right: This hybrid, with its colourful magenta flowers and slightly darker lips, is the result of a quadrigeneric cross (*Brassavola* × *Cattleya* × *Laelia* × *Sophronitis*). The flowers, which open in the autumn, are 13-15cm (5-6in) across and very showy. The plant does best in the warm section of the greenhouse.
Photo X ½

CYMBIDIUMS

The cymbidium is the king of the orchids and without doubt one of the most popular orchids today, both as a plant and a cut flower. The popularity has been earned by the modern cymbidium because it is cool growing, easy and very rewarding to cultivate. It is by far the most popular cut flower orchid in the world because of the long-lasting qualities of the flowers and the immense colour range available.

The genus *Cymbidium* was founded by the Swedish botanist Olof Swartz in 1800. The name *Cymbidium* is derived from the Greek and refers to the boat-like appearance of the lip.

Cymbidiums in the wild

The cymbidium species, of which 50 or 60 are known, are quite diverse and are found growing wild over a wide range from the foothills of the Himalayas to the coast of China, and as far south as Australia. The habitats in which they live vary from tropical rain forests to relatively arid conditions. Most of the cool-growing cymbidium hybrids so widely grown today have been bred from species originating in the foothills of the Himalayas. Species native to other areas have also been used in breeding, particularly to produce the miniature varieties.

Cymbidiums in cultivation

The cultivation of cymbidiums has taken place since the mid-1800s and in those days it was the species which were represented in the various collections.

The first hybrid was registered by James Veitch & Son, in 1889, and was named *Cym.* Eburneo-lowianum (*Cym. eburneum* × *Cym. lowianum*) but during the next 20 years only a further 14 cymbidium hybrids were registered. Most of these early hybrids, with the exception of *Cym.* Eburneo-lowianum, were primarily of botanical interest.

The modern hybrids grow into fairly large plants making hard round pseudobulbs with long strap-like leaves. Flower spikes normally develop in the summer and autumn months and continue developing during a period of up to eight months before coming into full flower. They have been bred to be free flowering and easy to grow in the artificial environment of the greenhouse or home, providing a few simple requirements are met. Mature cymbidiums are easy to grow and bring into flower in both cool and warm climates.

Although cymbidiums will grow well in climates where the autumn and winter night temperatures are above 15.5°C (60°F), they will almost certainly not flower. A substantial drop in night temperature is also important during the summer to initiate flower spike formation.

Temperatures for growth

The species from which the majority of

today's hybrids have been produced were originally discovered in the area around northern India, Burma, Thailand and Vietnam. They grow mainly in the mountainous regions and are subjected to substantial changes in temperature, which can vary during the day from 21-38°C (70-100°F), with cool nights and heavy rains during the wet season.

For mature plants a night temperature of about 10°C (50°F) should be maintained during the autumn, winter and spring months. In the summer months no artificial heat is necessary and the ventilators should be left open day and night unless strong winds make this dangerous. During severe winter weather when the outside temperatures drop below freezing, the indoor temperature may be allowed to fall to 7°C (45°F) without harming the plants. The night temperature should not be allowed to rise above 14 °C (58°F) while the plants have flower spikes, as this can cause bud drop. Certainly nothing is more upsetting than to see the flower buds turn yellow and drop prematurely.

In the winter, a daytime temperature of around 15-18°C (59-65°F) is adequate. Often the problem throughout the rest of the year is to keep the temperature down below 29.5°C (85°F). This can be achieved by a combination of ventilation, shading and humidity control. In cool climates it is only rarely necessary to use artificial heat during the day, even in the winter months.

Ventilation, humidity and shading

In the greenhouse the ventilators should be opened whenever the temperature rises above 15.5°C (60°F) in the winter months and 18.5°C (65°F) during the rest of the year. How much ventilation to give to maintain optimum temperature levels is a matter of judgement, but it is important to avoid draughts. Ventilators should only be opened on the side opposite to the prevailing wind. The use of a fan to circulate the air is also recommended and once installed should be run continuously.

During the sunny spring and summer days it will be beneficial to damp down two or three times during the course of the day. It will also be necessary to damp down when the heating systems are being used continuously to maintain temperature levels, in which case the spraying should take place early in the morning. Do not damp down on dull humid days. Ensure humidity levels are low when the plants are in bloom otherwise the flowers will become spotted. Overhead spraying of the plants is not recommended except on exceptional summer days when you can be sure that the foliage will have dried before nightfall.

Some protection from the sun, given during the late spring, summer and early autumn, will help to lower the temperature and therefore assist with maintaining the humidity. This can be achieved by the use of lath blinds or one of the greenhouse shading materials. The main reason for shading is to prevent the day temperature rising above 29.5°C (85°F) and also to ensure clear coloured flowers that do not fade. Some light shading should be applied from early spring, increased in density through the growing season, lightened again during late summer and finally removed completely in the autumn.

Composts and potting

Various types of composts are used throughout the world. In some countries bark is the predominant constituent of the compost, while in others peat is the main ingredient. A suitable compost would be one based on sphagnum moss peat to which sand, Perlite and bark are added to open up the mix. The pH should normally be slightly acidic, adjusted to around pH 5.5-6.0 by adding limestone and Dolomite lime. Some composts also contain a base fertilizer. For best results, choose a compost containing an even balance of nutrients and trace elements.

Cymbidiums should be repotted in early spring or directly after flowering. Plants should only be repotted when they have filled the pot with roots or where the compost has become sour and the plant has lost its roots.

First clean the plant by removing dead leaf bracts. Check that the root system is sound and that the compost has not deteriorated. If the plant is in good condition select a pot large enough to allow for two years growth. Put chunks of polystyrene or charcoal in the bottom of the pot for drainage, then place the plant in position in the pot and pour compost around the root ball. A few taps of the pot on the bench will ensure that the compost is packed correctly. Apply firm finger pressure down the sides of the pot, then refill to within 2cm (0.75in) of the top.

If the roots are decayed or the compost is sour, remove all the compost and trim back the roots. Any leafless pseudobulbs can be removed by cutting the short rhizome at the base of the bulb with a sterilized knife.

It is often advisable to split plants into divisions of two bulbs with leaves. The repotting procedure is the same as outlined except that more drainage material may be needed in the bottom of the pot. Do not use too large a pot for these divisions—a pot that has room for a year's development is adequate.

Seedlings require more frequent potting than mature plants, but take care not to use too large a pot. Not more than one year's growth should be allowed for, otherwise there is a possibility of the compost becoming sour.

Propagation and division

Plants should be divided during the early spring or directly after flowering. First clean the plant as outlined above, then decide where the plant is to be split. Normally two-leaved bulbs with a new growth make up a division, and cuts should be made with a sterilized knife between the bulbs to sever the short rhizome connecting them. Once all the cuts have been made the plant can be pulled apart. The potting procedure outlined for plants with decayed roots or sour compost should then be followed. You can also increase your stock by removing the leafless pseudobulbs and potting them individually in small pots, which should then be placed in a warm shaded position in the greenhouse. Alternatively, the pot and the bulb could be placed in a polyethylene bag which should then be sealed and hung up in the greenhouse. After a few weeks new growths will develop on most of the bulbs. The polyethylene bag can then be removed and the plants grown on as normal.

The mass propagation technique used by the major cymbidium growers throughout the world is known as meristem tissue culture and is outlined on page 98.

Watering and feeding

Watering is always a difficult subject to offer advice upon, but the golden rule is to allow the compost to become partially dry and then give a thorough watering from the top of the pot, ensuring that the compost is thoroughly saturated. Plants usually require more frequent watering during their active growing season in spring, summer and early autumn, than during the late autumn and winter months.

Newly potted plants in a peat-based compost containing a fertilizer should be given a very thorough watering directly they have been repotted ensuring that the compost is thoroughly wetted. Then they should be allowed to become partially dry and watered as outlined above.

Although the use of fertilizers was frowned upon by the early orchid growers, they are certainly necessary with today's compost. A balanced fertilizer should be given during the late spring and summer months, and a high potassium feed used during the autumn. This feed should be given at about half the manufacturer's recommended strength and carried out at fortnightly intervals.

Pests and diseases

Although cymbidiums are not troubled by many insect pests, the red spider mite causes considerable problems if not controlled. The pest can normally be controlled by one of the recommended proprietary insecticides, such as azobenzine, which will specifically eliminate red spider mite.

Aphids will sometimes attack the flowers and flower buds, but they can be dealt with quickly by spraying with malathion. Scale insects can be more troublesome but a double strength spray of malathion normally kills them.

Slugs and snails occasionally attack the flower spikes and a pellet of metaldehyde and bran placed between the spike and the bulb at an early stage will ensure that no damage is done.

Providing you obtain good clean stock from a reliable source, disease should not present much of a problem. The worst situation would be a plant infected with virus; if you have such a plant it must be destroyed for fear of the problem spreading to other stock.

Fungal and bacterial diseases are not common and will normally only occur where the plants are in a poor condition or if the environment in which the plants are grown is unsuitable.

Looking for flower spikes

Spike hunting is always an exciting time whether you have a large or small collection, as it is then you can speculate on the colourful display for the coming winter and spring months.

It is often difficult for the beginner to distinguish between a flower spike and a new growth. The new growth is invariably broader at the base and flatter than the flower spike. The flower spike tends to be rounder and if *gentle* pressure is applied some 'give' will be detected. Once the flower spike has been located it should be marked with a bamboo cane and tied as it develops.

A word of warning about cymbidiums in flower. The cymbidium is such a generous plant that it will often flower for up to three months. But during this time it is using up most of its resources, so that it is beneficial to remove flower spikes after they have been open for six weeks. This will give the plant an opportunity to produce new growth for the following year's flowering. You can, of course, still enjoy the cut flowers indoors.

Species and hybrids

In the early 1900s several interesting species were discovered in Burma and Indo-China, including *Cym. parishii, insigne* and *erythrostylum.* This group had white to rose-pink flowers and were to be important in the cymbidiums' future development. The earlier discovered species included *Cym. hookeranum (grandiflorum), lowianum, traceyanum, giganteum, i'ansonnii* and *schroderi,* although the last three were not much used in hybridization. The numerous flowers of these species are generally borne on large spikes and tend to be green or brown with some intermediate shades. *Cym. hookeranum* and *lowianum* have been very important in the production of the green-flowered hybrids.

The species *Cym. eburneum* and *insigne* are primarily responsible for the production of the white and pink-flowered hybrids. The autumn to winter flowering types originated from the species *Cym. erythrostylum, hookeranum* and *traceyanum. Cym. traceyanum* is also responsible for imparting some of its yellow colour to the modern yellow hybrids. Although not much used in breeding, *Cym. i'ansonnii* provided the starting point of many of the modern deep pink and red types. Similarly, *Cym. parishii* has had quite an impact on past and present hybrids, often producing varieties with beautiful well marked lips. Such famous cymbidiums as Miretta, Promona and Kittiwake have *parishii* in their backgrounds, and several of their clones have the most outstanding red lips.

When considering cymbidium breeding, mention should be made of H.G. Alexander who began hybridizing cymbidiums in 1907 and was responsible for many fine cymbidium hybrids, the most famous of which is *Cym.* Alexanderi 'Westonbirt' (FCC/RHS) (*Cym.* Eburneo-lowianum × *Cym. insigne.*) This cymbidium has exerted its influence on hybridization from the start and is still important today.

It is interesting to note that most of today's best modern hybrids have the common parents of Alexanderi at some point in their pedigree. This is true of the finest whites, pinks, yellows and greens, and for most of the very finest autumn and winter flowering types.

Cym. Pauwelsii (*Cym. insigne* × *Cym. lowianum*), another hybrid which was to play an important part in hybridization, made its appearance at the same time as Alexanderi. This plant contributed fine qualities of vigorous growth and very large flower spikes to its progeny. The most important hybrid it produced was Babylon (*Cym.* Olympus × *Cym.* Pauwelsii) which, in turn, became the parent of many of the best coloured varieties.

At present, work on cymbidium hybridizing is being carried out in several countries. There are many breeders in Australia, the United States, Holland and England. Some do this on a small scale, while others have vast planned breeding programmes covering the whole colour range and different times of flowering.

Autumn to winter flowering hybrids
The finest autumn to winter flowering cymbidiums will undoubtedly be produced from a combination of the best *Cym. erythrostylum* line crossed with the Lucy Moor lines. This line should produce good quality pastel shades and some fine yellows. For the pink red types *Cym.* Lilliana will be of great importance, and some progeny that have already flowered have shown great promise.

Winter to spring flowering hybrids
The winter to spring flowering types will continue to improve with the use of such parents as *Cym.* Pearl Balkis and Dingwall for whites, and Loch Lomond, York Meradith and the old favourite, Baltic, for greens. For red and orange flowers the most important parent is probably Hamsey 'The Globe'. Some of the Hamsey progeny have already flowered and will be very useful breeding plants for future generations.

A shining star of the future is *Cym.* Howick 'Cooksbridge' (AM/RHS). The clone has very large white flowers of full shape with a very heavy deep crimson banded lip.

The yellow-flowered group remains a problem but Many Waters 'Stonehurst' (AM/RHS) seems to be a possible parent together with Cariga 'Tetra Canary' (AM/RHS). It is important not to forget that some of the autumn to winter flowering cymbidiums are very fine yellows and the best of these crossed with the good winter to spring flowering yellows should produce some very worthwhile results.

Late spring flowering hybrids
There are several fine hybrids available for use in breeding for late spring flowering plants. The most exciting of these is *Cym.* Caithness 'Cooksbridge' (FCC/RHS). This clone has massive light green flowers of perfect shape with a broad attractive lip. The first seedlings have produced some of the finest flowers seen to date. Other interesting parents to look out for are Dingwall 'Lewes' and the old Prince Charles 'Exbury'.

Pure coloured hybrids
An interesting development in recent years has been the appearance of the so-called pure coloured cymbidiums. These plants do not produce red pigment and therefore only three colours are available—white, yellow and green, all without the normal red lip markings. Instead, the markings on the lip are yellow. This line of breeding has been developed from *Cym. lowianum* var. *concolor,* and by crossing and back crossing a fine strain has been built up, although there is still considerable room for improvement.

Most of the work on this type of cymbidium has been carried out in Australia, although recently some very interesting clones have been produced in the United States and England. Recommended hybrids are Sleeping Gold 'Tetragold' (AM/RHS), Pharaoh and several clones of Highland Surprise.

Future trends
In the future novelty type breeding should prove very interesting. This would involve selection for flamboyant colour combinations, such as occur in hybrids like Mavourneen 'Jester' (AM/RHS). Breeding from this clone will hopefully result in plants with beautiful white sepals, red lips and red petals or yellow sepals and a similar combination.

Miniature cymbidiums
The most important miniature *Cymbidium* species used in breeding are *Cym. devonianum, ensifolium, pumilum* and *tigrinum.*

The *devonianum* hybrids are characterized by arching and sometimes pendulous spikes and flowers of green, yellow, bronze or some intermediate shades, many of which have bold lip markings. Some outstanding hybrids from this line of breeding include Touchstone, Miniatures Delight and Bulbarrow (*Cym. devonianum* × *Cym.* Western Rose). The Bulbarrow hybrids have very bold lip markings.

The two most important breeding characteristics of *Cym. ensifolium* are its season of flowering (late summer and autumn) and its fragrance. The progeny from *ensifolium* tend to have inherited the best characteristics of the species. The fragrance of the flowers is striking and can be detected immediately you enter the house. Such fine hybrids as Peter Pan (*Cym. ensifolium* × *Cym.* Miretta) and Ensikhan (*Cym. ensifolium* × *Cym.* Nam Khan) can be recommended.

One of the most important miniature hybrid groups are those bred from *Cym. pumilum.* The most charming plants are found in this group, and the make ideal pot plants, even in the small home. Some outstanding recent hybrids include Lerwick, Stonehaven, Strathavon, Nip × Kurun and Nip × Clarissa: these lovely plants have inherited the best *pumilum* characteristics and have a wide range of flower colours.

Some fine examples of *Cym. tigrinum* breeding are Wood Nymph (*tigrinum* × Sea Foam), Tiger Cub (*tigrinum* × Esmerella) and Tiger Tail (*tigrinum* × Alexanderi). All these hybrids flower in spring (derived from *tigrinum*), and are dwarf, compact plants with short broad leaves and small pseudobulbs. The colour range is rather limited, being mainly green or yellow, but there are some beautiful plants amongst them. Recently improved hybrids have been obtained as a result of breeding from Wood Nymph crossed with a selected standard (non-miniature) cymbidium, Western Rose. These plants

are compact growers, late spring flowering, and range in colour from bronze, yellow and green to pastel pink.

Starting a collection
Assuming that you have the necessary facilities, before starting a collection it would be wise to approach one of the commercial growers who specializes in cymbidiums. If you choose well, it is possible to have plants in flower for more than six months of the year—indeed all year round if you grow hybrids bred from *Cym. ensifolium.* Provided you have room to accommodate them, all cymbidiums make good houseplants.

Do not be afraid to seek the experts' advice on starting a collection and on all aspects of orchid culture. Most of the varieties illustrated here are readily available, but they vary in price according to the size of plant and considered quality of the flower. Do not buy very expensive plants at first. However, you must be sure that the stock is good and robust, for it would be a waste of time and money to start with weaklings.

Below: Because cymbidiums tolerate cool conditions, they make ideal plants for garden rooms and conservatories. Being tall, with flower spikes bearing many blooms, the standard cymbidiums make an impressive display in this large ornamental garden.

Cymbidium Species

Cymbidium devonianum

○Cool ❀Late spring

Above: This miniature species originates from the Himalayas and has been used often in miniature breeding. The flower spikes are pendent, and its progeny tend to have arching spikes. The flowers, which normally open in late spring and early summer, are basically green speckled with red, while the triangular lip is pink spotted with crimson.
Photo x 1

Cymbidium eburneum

○Cool ❀Winter/Spring

Right: Discovered in the 1830s by the botanical explorer William Griffiths, this species is native to the Khasia hills in northern India. It is a compact grower with narrow pseudobulbs, and leaves that can grow to more than 61cm (24in) in length. The erect flower spike arises higher up on the bulb than in most cymbidiums, and several spikes are often carried at the same time. The plant is often erratic in its flowering, producing from one to three, 7.5cm (3in) flowers to each spike. The flowers, which open in winter and early spring, are white to ivory in colour, with a deep yellow band in the middle of the lip, flanked by two yellow keels. Very prominent in hybridization, *eburneum* was one of the parents of the first hybrid cymbidium to be raised in cultivation – Eburneolowianum – which was registered by Veitch in 1889. Whilst it is an important species in breeding, the plant is not a vigorous grower and is a shy bloomer.
Photo x 1

Cymbidium giganteum

○Cool ❀Autumn/Winter

Left: This species was first collected in Nepal in 1821. The name *giganteum* refers to the size of the plant and not the flowers. The leaves, which grow up to 76cm (30in) long, spring from stout pseudobulbs. From 5 to 15 yellow-green flowers, each 7.5-10cm (3-4in) across, are carried on strong spikes. This species is little used in hybridization because of the dull colour and relatively poor quality of its flowers.

Photo x 1

Cymbidium lowianum

○Cool ❀Late Spring

Below: This species was discovered in 1887 in upper Burma, and was also found in Thailand. Its influence is present in almost all of our modern hybrids. The plant, which flowers in late spring, normally carries very large arching sprays of green flowers, up to 10cm (4in) across, with a V-shaped red mark on the lip.

Photo X 1/3

Cymbidium traceyanum

○Cool ❀Autumn/Winter

Below: A very interesting and flamboyant species imported in great quantities from Thailand at the beginning of the century. The number collected in the early years resulted in the virtual disappearance of the plant from its natural habitat. The species is autumn to winter flowering and produces long arching sprays of 10-13cm (4-5in) flowers. The petals are green, heavily striped with dark red, and the white lip is spotted with red. It has been important as a base species for producing spring flowering types and is also in the background of some yellow hybrids.

Photo X 1/4

Cymbidium Hybrids

CYMBIDIUM
Angelica 'Advent' (AM/RHS)
○Cool ❀Autumn/Winter
Below: This superb autumn to winter flowering yellow hybrid (*Cym.* Lucy Moor × *Cym.* Lucense) is fast becoming a very famous breeding plant and is being used by cymbidium hybridists throughout the world. Up to 14 large flowers, 13cm (5in) across, are carried on upright spikes. The petals and sepals are pale yellow and the cream-coloured lip is lightly spotted with dark red, the spotting becoming dense in the throat. This very attractive cymbidium deserves a place in every collection.
Photo x ¼

CYMBIDIUM
Ayres Rock 'Cooksbridge Velvet'
○Cool ❀Winter/Spring
Above: This is one of a new generation of cymbidiums in which the colour range has been extended even further towards the deeper pinks. The interesting breeding of this hybrid (Hamsey × Rodkobb) points the way for the future. The plant illustrated is only a seedling, but should give upright spikes of up to 12 flowers when mature. The flowers, 11cm (4.25in) across, are crimson tinged with white and the lip is a rich dark crimson, boldly edged with white. The plant flowers in winter and spring.
Photo x ½

CYMBIDIUM
Baltic (AM/RHS)
○Cool ❀Winter/Spring
Left: A cross between *Cym.* Riga and *Cym.* Midas, this is one of the most famous breeding plants in the green colour range, and has been responsible for numerous fine hybrids which have gained awards throughout the world. Raised by the famous Dell Park Collection, it will continue to be important for many years to come. The plant is small growing, producing arching spikes of bright green flowers with crimson markings on the cream lip. The flowers are 11cm (4.25in) across and open in the winter and early spring.
Photo x ⅔

CYMBIDIUM
Cariga 'Tetra Canary' (AM/RHS)
○Cool ❀Winter-Spring

Below: This hybrid variety is a mutation of the original *Cym.* Cariga 'Canary' (AM/RHS) (*Cym.* Carlos × *Cym.* Riga), which arose during the tissue culture processes. It is a great improvement on the original, having much rounder greenish-yellow flowers, and a larger lip with heavier crimson and white markings. The plant is free growing and flowers freely from winter to early spring giving up to 12, 11.5cm (4.5in) flowers on semi-arching spikes.

Photo x ½

CYMBIDIUM
Dingwall 'Lewes'
○Cool ❀Late spring

Right: This hybrid is the result of a cross between *Cym.* Pearl Easter and *Cym.* Merlin. Pearl Easter is a superb parent for producing flowers with clear white sepals and petals and the combination with Merlin has produced some very fine late spring flowering whites (the flowering season being derived from Merlin). This plant is free flowering and bears up to 12 large (13cm [5in]) flowers on an upright spike. The petals and sepals are white the lip is marked with red.

Photo x ½

CYMBIDIUM
Fort George 'Lewes' (AM/RHS)
○Cool ❀Winter/Spring

Below: One of the finest, free flowering green-coloured cymbidiums in the world, often giving two spikes per bulb with up to 14 flowers per spike on an upright stem. The flowers, which open in the early spring, are up to 12.5cm (4.75in) in diameter. The bringing together of two of the most famous green-flowered parents (*Cym.* Baltic × *Cym.* York Meradith) has produced an excellent result.

Photo x ½

CYMBIDIUM
Gymer 'Cooksbridge'
○Cool ❀Late spring

Right: This cross between *Cym.* Dorama and *Cym.* Cariga, has produced a late spring flowering hybrid with yellow flowers with deep crimson lips. The flowers can be up to 13cm (5in) in diameter and are carried on upright spikes of up to 24 flowers. The plant is very free flowering, sometimes producing up to three spikes per bulb, and has certainly inherited the very best properties from both its parents.
Photo X 1

CYMBIDIUM
Mavourneen 'Jester' (AM/RHS)
○Cool ❀Winter/Spring

Below: Cymbidiums with lip markings on the petals and sepals (peloric cymbidiums) are very rare. This plant clearly shows the characteristic lip colour and shape taken on by the petals. It is fortunate that the mutation occurred in this particular variety (*Cym.* Sussex Moor × *Cym.* Miretta) because it is in itself a very fine flower. This clone has already been used for breeding but to date none of the seedlings carried the peloric characteristics, although some very fine varieties were produced. The back cross with Sussex Moor has now been made and the results are awaited with anticipation. The plant flowers in winter and early spring, and the flowers are 11cm (4.25in) across.
Photo X 2/3

CYMBIDIUM
Mavourneen 'Tetra Cooksbridge'
○*Cool* ❀*Winter/Spring*
Left: The original plant of Mavourneen 'Cooksbridge' (AM/RHS) was a very fine clone, but this mutation is far superior, having rounder flowers of heavier substance. This plant has erect flower spikes, and blooms during the winter and early spring. The flowers, 11cm (4.25in) across, are moss-green, lightly flushed with pink, and the large lip is rose-pink lightly spotted with dark red.
Photo X ⅔

CYMBIDIUM
Ngaire × Clarissa
○*Cool* ❀*Winter/Spring*
Above: Although there is a quest for flowers of a pure colour, such is the diversity of the cymbidium that some outstanding multicoloured flowers have also been produced by the hybridist. This plant has 11cm (4.25in) flowers carried on erect spikes and blooms during the winter to spring. The petals and sepals are white flushed with rose-pink, and the lip is boldly marked with red.
Photo X ¼

CYMBIDIUM
Pearl Balkis 'Fiona'
○*Cool* ❀*Winter/Spring*
Left: A very beautiful white cymbidium, the result of combining two very famous large-flowered cymbidiums (Pearl Easter × Balkis). Up to 14 flowers, 13cm (5in) across, are carried on upright spikes. The contrasting lip is pale rose-pink spotted with crimson. This is a very fine winter to spring flowering variety.
Photo X ⅔

CYMBIDIUM

Rievaulx 'Cooksbridge' (AM/RHS)

○Cool ❀Late spring

Right: This cross between *Cym.* Rio Rita and one of the world's most famous large-flowered cymbidium parents, *Cym.* Vieux Rose, produced this outstanding deep pink hybrid. The featured plant is free growing and flowering, producing up to 20 large flowers, 11.5cm (4.5in) across, on a semi-arching spike. The plant flowers in late spring.

Photo X 1

CYMBIDIUM

Rincon 'Clarisse' (AM/RHS)

○Cool ❀Autumn

Below: This American plant *Cym.* Pearl × *Cym.* Windsor is famous as a parent for producing high quality early autumn flowering cymbidiums. It imparts its good shape, colour and well marked lips to most of its progeny. The 9cm (3.75in) flowers are white, striped with light pink, and the cream lip is boldly marked with crimson. The shape of the flower is primarily inherited from the species *Cym. erythrostylum* in its background. A worthwhile plant, parent and grandparent of fine progeny.

Photo X 1

CYMBIDIUM
Sparkle 'Ruby Lips'
○Cool ❀Spring
Right: The cross between Vieux Rose and Defiant that produced Sparkle was remarkable for the consistent quality of the progeny. The range of colours obtained includes pink, yellow, orange and green. This particular example has moss green flowers, 11cm (4.25in) across, which are lightly marked with red, and a deep crimson lip. The arching spike can bear up to 20 flowers at a time. The plant is free growing and flowers easily.
Photo X ½

CYMBIDIUM
Stanley Fouraker × Highlander
○Cool ❀Autumn/Winter
Above: An interesting combination of the *Cym. erythrostylum* and *Cym. traceyanum* x *hookeranum* lines of breeding, which has resulted in flowers of good size and shape, in lovely pastel shades with attractive lip markings. This plant, which has white flowers and a pretty pink-spotted lip, flowers in autumn and early winter and carries its blooms on upright spikes. The flowers are 10cm (4in) in diameter.
Photo X ½

CYMBIDIUM
Vieux Rose × Loch Lomond
○Cool ❀Winter/Spring
Right: This hybrid is an interesting combination between a pink flowered and a green flowered cymbidium. Most of the progeny from this cross have green-bronze flowers, though a few pinks are also found. The flowers of this hybrid are pale green, while the large lip is whitish-green, spotted with crimson and yellow in the throat. The spike habit tends to be semi- to fully arching, and the flowers, which are 12.5cm (4.75in) across, open from winter to early spring.
Photo X 1

Miniature Cymbidiums

CYMBIDIUM
Annan 'Cooksbridge' (AM/RHS)
○*Cool* ❀*Spring*

Right: This cymbidium of miniature background (*Cym.* Camelot × *Cym.* Berwick) has some of the deepest, richest coloured flowers seen in the genus. The plant tends to be a little larger than others from this line of breeding but the uniqueness of the 7cm (2.75in) deep crimson flowers more than compensates for the slightly large plant. The upright spikes are normally in full flower in spring.
Photo x ¾

CYMBIDIUM
Bulbarrow 'Our Midge'
○*Cool* ❀*Late spring*

Above: The Bulbarrow hybrids have rightly gained a reputation throughout the world. The crossing of the standard Western Rose with the miniature species, *Cym. devonianum*, resulted in some excellent clones, most of which have flowers with very fine lips of striking colours.

'Our Midge' bears spikes of up to 20 flowers in late spring. The 2.5-4cm (1-1.5in) flowers are soft rose-red with deep crimson lips.
Photo x ⅓

CYMBIDIUM
Lerwick
○*Cool* ❀*Autumn-Spring*

Left: This cross between *Cym.* Putana and *Cym.* Sussex Moor was exceptional for producing fine quality white and pastel shades in the flowers. The plant illustrated, which has pale green flowers and a white lip marked with red, is a typical variety. The plants are very free growing and flower easily from autumn to spring.
Photo x ¼

CYMBIDIUM
Nip × Kurun
○*Cool* ❀*Autumn/Winter*

Right: This very fine autumn to winter flowering second generation *Cym. pumilum* hybrid has inherited the very best qualities from its parents. It is free growing and often produces two flower spikes per pseudobulb. The 6cm (2.5in) flowers are brownish-pink with a crimson-spotted white lip. As many as 16 flowers may be carried at a time on an upright spike.
Photo x ¼

CYMBIDIUM
Peter Pan 'Greensleeves'
○*Cool* ❀*Autumn*

Below: A fine example of *ensifolium* breeding with the clone inheriting the best characteristics from both parents (*Cym. ensifolium* × *Cym.* Miretta). From *ensifolium* the plant has inherited its autumn flowering habit together with a beautiful fragrance, while Miretta has greatly enhanced the quality of the flower. The petals and sepals are soft green, while the lip is heavily marked and edged with deep crimson. The flowers are a little over 7.5cm (3in) across.
Photo x ⅔

CYMBIDIUM
Stonehaven 'Cooksbridge'
○*Cool* ❀*Autumn/Winter*

Below: This second generation *Cym. pumilum* hybrid (*Cym.* Putana × *Cym.* Cariga) is a very good quality, medium sized plant that produces fine strong spikes with up to 25, 7cm (2.75in) flowers. Opening in autumn and early winter, the flowers are cream coloured and the lip is pale yellow, edged with dark red. The plant is very free flowering and easy to grow. Such plants are becoming increasingly popular as high class pot plants for the home.
Photo x ¼

CYMBIDIUM
Strathavon
○*Cool* ❀*Winter/Spring*

Above: For the medium to deep pink shades the cross of Strathavon (*Cym.* Putana × *Cym.* Berwick) produced some excellent progeny and several clones gained awards from the Royal Horticultural Society in Britain. Up to 18 flowers, 7cm (2.75in) across, are carried on upright spikes, and are normally in full bloom during the winter and early spring.
Photo x ⅔

CYMBIDIUM
Touchstone 'Janis'
○*Cool* ❀*Winter/Spring*

Right: This miniature variety is another fine example of *Cym. devonianum* breeding (*devonianum* × Mission Bay). The plants from this crossing tend to be small, free growing and produce beautiful arching sprays of flowers during the winter and early spring. The flowers are bronze with contrasting deep crimson lips and are 2.5-4cm (1-1.5in) across.
Photo x ¼

CYMBIDIUM
Wood Nymph × Western Rose
○*Cool* ❀*Late spring*

Right: Most of the smaller growing cymbidiums tend to flower during the autumn and winter, but this cross between a large-flowered, standard cymbidium and a *Cym. tigrinum* hybrid has produced a late spring flowering miniature. The cross produced a range of colours with attractive lip markings. This particular example is characteristic of the range, having yellow-green petals flushed with light red, and a large cream lip, marked with deep crimson and edged with pink. The flowers are 7.5cm (3in) in diameter.
Photo x ¼

DENDROBIUMS

The beautiful and varied genus *Dendrobium* has always been held in high esteem by orchid growers throughout the world, and is one of the finest groups from the Old World. There are an estimated 1,600 species of dendrobiums, making them the second largest genus in the orchid family, the first place being taken by the strange and intriguing genus *Bulbophyllum.* They are the most important members of the subtribe Dendrobinae, which they share with related species in the smaller and lesser-known genus *Epigenium.*

Dendrobiums in the wild

The genus *Dendrobium* was founded in 1800 by the famous botanist Olof Swartz from a mere half dozen species, which were all that were known at that time. The name is derived from *dendron,* a tree, and *bios,* life—tree life: a good description for these epiphytic plants that exist by clinging to the branches and trunks of host trees. In this situation they thrive on the humidity rising from the jungle floor and on the meagre nourishment obtainable from old leaves and other debris collected in the branches of the trees.

Like other epiphytic orchids, dendrobiums have become beautifully adapted to their aerial existence. They store food and water in swollen stems, or pseudobulbs, that enable the plant to survive through the dry season. In dendrobiums these bulbs have become elongated into canes, often resembling bamboo, leading to the popular name of 'bamboo orchids'. These canes range from a few centimetres to a metre or more in length, the longer canes hanging down from the tree. A mass of aerial roots extends from the base of the plant, often forming a thick mat.

Many of the plants are deciduous, shedding their leaves after one season's growth and remaining dormant throughout the dry season. At the start of the rains they burst forth with new growth and flower buds. The buds appear along the whole length of the bulb on some types and from the upper nodes only on others. It is nearly always the previous year's growth which flowers. At flowering time the completely bare plant, looking like a cluster of dead canes, becomes transformed into a most beautiful display. In some varieties each of the previous season's canes is festooned with delicate and brightly coloured flowers; in others heavy bunches of flowers hang from the nodes of the canes, which become bowed under their weight; other varieties produce large heads of flowers from the upper portions of their canes.

The petals and sepals of dendrobium flowers are of equal size. The colours to be found in the genus are white (often suffused with pink or mauve), golden

yellow and subtle shades of pink, cream and brown; the rounded lip carries a colour which contrasts with the rest of the flower. In many, a delicate fragrance adds to their appeal.

As may be expected from such a vast group of plants, their global range is extensive. They can be found throughout the Himalayas and southern India, through Malaysia and on into China and Japan, and also in parts in northern Australia. They inhabit every type of environment from hot lowland jungles to the snowline of the Himalayas, often in exposed areas provided these enjoy continuous sunshine.

Dendrobiums in cultivation

For ease of culture, dendrobiums can be loosely divided into two main types: the soft-caned, or nobile, type and the hard-caned, or phalaenopsis, type. The former generally require cooler conditions and are therefore more widely grown by amateurs; the phalaenopsis type require more heat to succeed well. Both thrive on plenty of light and humidity.

Dendrobiums enjoy immense popularity wherever orchids are grown. Many of the original native species that delighted our forefathers, and which were grown into huge specimen clumps, are today becoming increasingly rare in cultivation as measures are taken in their countries of origin to protect those which remain. Those species which are still obtainable are distinctive and beautiful and are preferred to the hybrids which have been developed.

Dendrobiums were among the first orchids to be hybridized, a practice which began towards the end of the nineteenth century. In those early days of hybrid orchids, every conceivable cross was made and each new variety was hailed as a botanical wonder. But as the production of hybrids became commonplace, hundreds were obtained from relatively few parents and the results became similar in appearance and of minimal value. Eventually, little progress was made with hybrids from the nobile types, but among phalaenopsis dendrobiums hybridizing has produced some extremely beautiful varieties highly valued for cutting. These are grown in tens of thousands in the warm climates of Malaysia and Thailand.

The seasonal pattern of growth

Dendrobiums start their new growth in the spring, following their resting period. The new growth usually coincides with the formation of the buds along the length or from the top of the previous season's canes. From this time on, the plants, which have remained dry for the duration of the winter months, can be watered regularly. It is advisable to flood the surface of the compost two or three times to ensure that the moisture penetrates throughout the pot.

During the summer months the aim should be to keep the compost continually moist, to ensure a continuous steady rate of growth. Old canes which may have shrivelled slightly during the resting period will quickly become plump again, and the new roots will take up sufficient water for the plant's needs. In addition, they may be lightly sprayed with water several times a day during bright sunny spells. Where the plants are being grown indoors, making spraying difficult, they will benefit from having their leaves sponged over just as often.

During the summer growing season, dendrobiums should be given artificial feed in a liquid form. Any phosphate or nitrate based liquid food is suitable for orchids, but bearing in mind that they are generally weak feeders, and a weak solution is called for. Apply this either to the pot or as a foliar feed sprayed over the plant. This feeding can be given at every third or fourth watering throughout the summer until the slight yellowing of foliage indicates the end of the plant's growth for the season.

Dendrobiums usually complete their annual growth by the autumn months, when the terminal leaf can be seen at the top of the completed cane. When this has been achieved, gradually reduce the watering and feeding to nil over a period of about four weeks. At this time of the year the plants should receive as much light as possible. To ensure flowering in the following spring it is important that the bulbs are sufficiently hardened and ripened by exposing the mature canes to full light. The deciduous varieties will react immediately to the shortening days and cooler temperatures by shedding their leaves, which turn yellow before dropping off. The evergreen types do not show the changing seasons so drastically, and may lose one or two leaves from the oldest canes only. Nevertheless, they too need full light and dry conditions until their reawakening in the spring.

In a greenhouse both deciduous and evergreen varieties should be placed on a shelf for the winter, in a position close to the glass where they can receive full light and be kept partially or completely dry, according to their needs. Indoors it is more difficult to provide the necessary light, but placing the plants in a large, south-facing window of a cool room should suffice. They should not be so close to the glass as to risk damage by frosts on cold winter nights. They can be left in this position until new growth begins in the early spring months.

Temperatures for growth

Dendrobiums have a fast growing season followed by a long resting period. During the summer the cool-growing varieties require a minimum night temperature of 12°C (55°F) with a daytime rise of up to 25°C (80°F), this varying from day to day according to the immediate weather. The warmer-growing types should be kept nearer to 18°C (65°F) at night, again with a considerable rise during the day, which can exceed the cool house temperature for a few hours during the hottest part of the day.

The higher the temperature, the higher should be the humidity, combined with frequent overhead spraying of the foliage. During the late autumn months the plants should be moved to their winter quarters. For the cool-growing types, a winter night temperature of 10°C (50°F) will suit them well, with a daytime rise to at least 16°C (60°F). The warmer growing varieties will require a night time temperature of 16°C (60°F) with a correspondingly higher daytime temperature.

Ventilation

Ventilation is an important aspect of orchid culture, and this is particularly so with dendrobiums, which flourish in a humid but buoyant atmosphere. Regular damping of the surroundings will create a high humidity and this should be maintained throughout the summer months. If the humidity falls significantly when ventilators are opened the remedy is not to allow the ventilators to remain closed, but rather to open them fully on hot sunny days, and to spray extra water round the plants, underneath the staging, and on the paths, until the greenhouse is running with water. In such an environment the ventilators can be brought into full use.

During the summer there will be periods when the ventilators can be left open both day and night, while at other times it will be necessary to close them at night. During the winter the ventilators should be opened on every occasion when this can be done without causing a drastic

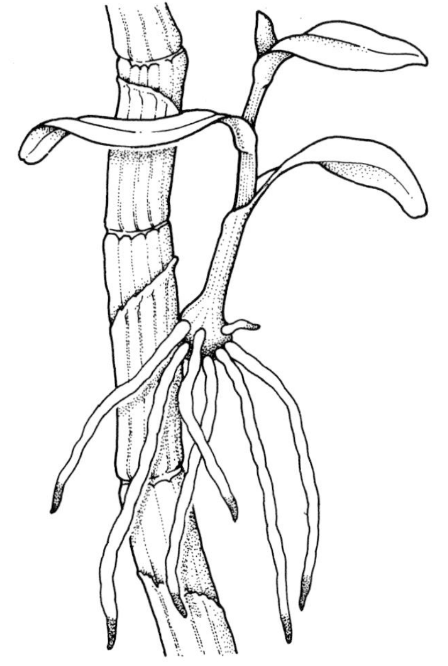

Above: Most dendrobiums propagate themselves by producing young plants from their older canes. When these have sufficient roots they can be removed from the parent plant and potted up on their own.

drop in the inside greenhouse temperature. It will sometimes happen that the ventilators are opened for no more than half an hour before being closed again for the remainder of the day, but this will have been sufficient to freshen the air inside the greenhouse and prevent a stagnant atmosphere, which is detrimental to all orchids.

Potting and composts

Repotting of dendrobiums should always be done during the spring months at the start of the growing season. The ideal time is when the new growth can just be seen at the base of the leading cane, and before the new roots appear. This can sometimes be difficult if the plant is flowering at the same time, and in this case the repotting should be completed immediately after the plant has flowered. Dendrobiums have a fine root system, and they like to be potted in as small a pot as possible. Overpotting can lead to overwatering, resulting in the loss of roots and, in extreme cases, loss of the plant. Plastic pots are quite suitable for dendrobiums, although they can sometimes become extremely top heavy. An alternative method of culture is to grow them on blocks of wood. Dendrobiums are especially suited to this growing method, and they very quickly establish themselves and produce an abundance of aerial roots.

The compost for dendrobiums should be open and well drained. An excellent potting medium is pine bark, and this is usually available from orchid nurseries in various forms. A good, chunky material and not powdered bark should be used. To this can be added a small percentage of sphagnum peat, which will assist in holding moisture in an otherwise very dry compost. A further small percentage of charcoal can also be incorporated to keep the compost sweet. In this basic mixture dendrobiums will grow and thrive.

Vegetative propagation

Most dendrobiums will occasionally produce young plants from a node along the cane. The nobile type are particularly prone to this. These young plants can be removed from the cane when they have roots about 2.5cm (1in) long and one completed bulb. They can be potted up separately and grown on to flowering size. If you require propagations on a more regular basis, remove the older leafless canes (leaving at least four on the main plant) and cut these into pieces about 5cm (2in) long, severing the cane in between the divisions left by the leaves after they were shed. Put the pieces into a community pot with the division on a level with the compost and within a few weeks these will be showing a new growth which in turn can be potted singly when large enough.

Pests and diseases

Provided the greenhouse is kept comparatively free from pests, dendrobiums will remain in a clean and healthy state. Few pests, and even fewer diseases, will attack them. Apart from the general annoyance of slugs and snails, which may enter the greenhouse at any time and must be continually watched for, there may be an unwelcome visit from red spider mite. This pest will attack the undersides of the soft-caned dendrobiums, producing silvery white patches on the undersides of the leaves, particularly the younger ones. The mite is extremely small and difficult to see with the naked eye. It can do considerable harm by sucking the sap of the plant, and if allowed to remain unchecked it will quickly build up into large colonies. Any well-tried insecticide can be used against red spider mite, but the treatment may have to be repeated several times.

Species and hybrids

Of all the many species grown throughout the world, the following short list features a few of the most popular varieties noted for their beauty and ease of culture. All of them are suitable for a beginner provided their particular temperature requirements are catered for. These species are usually obtainable as imported plants from their country of origin, or they may have been raised in the nursery where purchased.

The brief selection of hybrids represents the different *Dendrobium* types that are grown. Although suited to different climates throughout the world, they can be grown together provided different sections of the greenhouse are allotted to suit their particular needs.

Dendrobium Species

Dendrobium aureum

○Cool ❀Winter

Right: This widely distributed species is found throughout India and in the Philippine Islands. The Indian variety is in general cultivation: the Philippino variety may be offered under the name of *D. heterocarpum*. The type produces stoutish bulbs of medium length and is deciduous in winter, when it needs a definite rest. The flowers appear during the earliest months of the year, making it one of the first dendrobiums to flower. The blooms, up to 5cm (2in) across, are creamy yellow with a buff brown lip covered in short hairs. A very pleasant fragrance adds to the great appeal of this free-flowering, cool-growing species.

Photo X 1

Dendrobium fimbriatum var. *oculatum*

○Cool ❀Summer

Below: An extremely beautiful cool-growing, Indian dendrobium, this species produces bunches of bright, buttercup yellow flowers during the early summer months. The flowers, 5cm (2in) across, are striking and the beautifully fimbriated lip carries a rich maroon blotch in the throat. The canes are tall and slender and the flowers appear from nodes on the uppermost portion of the older canes. It is an evergreen plant that sheds part of its foliage in the autumn, after which it should be allowed an almost completely dry rest. Water should be given sparingly if the canes begin to shrivel.

Photo X ¾

Dendrobium chrysotoxum

◑Intermediate ❀Spring

Above: This is one of the showiest of the intermediate range of dendrobiums. The plant is widely distributed throughout southern China, the Himalayas and into Burma and Thailand. It produces stout club-shaped bulbs which carry dark, glossy green foliage from their upper portions. The nodes appear close to the top of the previous season's bulbs, the old bulbs often flowering over several years. The blooms are 5cm (2in) across, and a rich golden yellow, with the well-rounded lip a deeper orange, sometimes with a maroon disc. The highly fragrant flowers last well and are carried in many-flowered, pendent sprays. The plant requires a decided rest during the winter, when it must be given full sun to encourage blooming the following spring.

The species is somewhat variable and is synonymous with *D. suavissimum*, which was at one time considered to be a separate species or a distinct variety of the type.

Photo X ¼

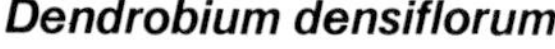

Dendrobium densiflorum

○Cool ❀Summer

Right: Once plentiful, this delightful species is becoming increasingly difficult to obtain. The flowers, up to 5cm (2in) across, are carried in large pendent trusses from nodes at the top half of the club-shaped bulbs. They develop at great speed during the spring months and last for up to ten days in perfection. Their colour is a brilliant golden yellow, the lip similarly coloured and very striking. The plant likes to be grown in the cool greenhouse with a decided rest in the winter. It is an evergreen variety from India which produces stout bulbs that grow to a considerable length.

Photo X ¼

Dendrobium infundibulum

○Cool ❀Spring

Below: This very fine and distinct species produces large, white flowers, 10cm (4in) across, of a soft papery texture. One to three flowers are produced from each node at the apex of the completed bulb. Well-grown plants produce huge heads of long-lasting flowers, the lip stained with bright yellow in the throat. *D. infundibulum* is an evergreen variety and enjoys cool house conditions. In its native India it grows at considerable altitudes. The stems and the sheaths around the young buds are covered in short, protective black hairs.

Photo X 1¼

Dendrobium lituiflorum

◑Intermediate ❀Spring

Left: Originating from India, this elegant species produces long, slender canes which become deciduous during the winter months. The flowers, 5cm (2in) across, appear the following spring along the entire length of the newest canes. Usually occurring in pairs, they vary in colour from almost white to rich amethyst purple, paling towards the centre. The lip is trumpet-shaped with a purple margin. The plant is seen at its best when grown in the intermediate house on bark slabs and allowed to assume a pendent habit. In this way it can also be hung closer to the glass during the winter to gain maximum light. This free-flowering species will produce several new growths in one season and can be grown into a specimen plant within a few years.

Photo X 2

Dendrobium nobile

○Cool ❀Spring

Below: Perhaps the most popular of all the cool-growing dendrobiums, this superb plant from India blooms during the spring. The flowers appear in ones and twos along the complete length of the previous year's bulbs, which are fairly tall and stoutish. The flowers, 5cm (2in) across, are rosy purple at the petal tips, shading to white towards the centre of the bloom. The lip carries a rich maroon blotch in the throat. *D. nobile* is semideciduous and requires a good rest during the winter; water should be withheld until the flower buds have started their development in the spring.

Photo X 1

Dendrobium pierardii

◑*Intermediate* ❀*Spring*

Left: This is a very handsome species from India which produces extremely long, cane-like pseudobulbs that assume a pendent habit unless trained upright in a pot. The plant becomes deciduous during the winter months, when it is important to allow full light to ensure successful flowering the following spring. The 5cm (2in) blooms are produced on the entire length of the previous year's canes and are extremely pretty. They are beautifully coloured a rosy pastel pink, while the rounded lip is creamy yellow, streaked with purple at the base. When in bloom the whole plant becomes transformed for a period of about three weeks.

Photo X ⅔

Dendrobium secundum

◑*Intermediate* ❀*Spring/Summer*

Below: An extremely pretty and distinctive species with a wide distribution down the Malaysian peninsula and into the Philippine Islands. The unusual flowers are individually very small, clustered tightly together into compact sprays 8-10cm (3.5-4in) long. The rosy pink flowers, with an orange blotch on the lip, appear for an extended period through the spring and summer months. A free-flowering evergreen species, *D. secundum* should be grown in intermediate temperature conditions.

Photo X ¼

Dendrobium speciosum

◑●*Intermediate/Warm* ❀*Spring*

Left: A most attractive species from Australia, this plant enjoys warmth and humidity during its growing season, with a decided rest during the winter. It is not unusual for this rest period to last for many months. If ripened sufficiently the plant will bloom profusely in the spring producing a shower of flower spikes, each bearing numerous rather small, densely packed flowers, off white in colour with the lip lightly spotted in purple. The flowers have a delightful fragrance. This species grows exposed to the full sun in the wild, and produces leathery leaves from the top of stout, club-shaped pseudobulbs.

Photo X 1

Dendrobium superbum

●*Warm* ❀*Summer*

Below: One of the finest dendrobiums from the Philippine Islands, this is a deciduous species that produces extremely long canes. The flowers appear during the early summer, along the entire length of the previous year's canes; they are 5-6cm (2-2.5in) across, and a rich magenta purple, the lip a deeper shade. Their powerful fragrance makes this a highly desirable species for the intermediate to warm section of the greenhouse. The very long canes make this species ideal for growing upside-down on a wooden raft.

Photo X 1

Dendrobium transparens

◑*Intermediate* ❀*Spring*

Above: This extremely pretty and free-flowering species from India grows well on bark in a pendent position. Its flowers, produced early in the year along the length of the previous season's canes, are 4cm (1.5in) across and pale rosy mauve, the colour heightening towards the tips of the petals; the lip carries two distinctive purple stains. It is a deciduous species which should be well rested before the next spring flowering season: it grows best in the intermediate section of the greenhouse.

Photo X 3

Dendrobium wardianum

○*Cool* ❀*Winter*

Above left: One of the most handsome of the cool-growing species, this too comes from India. The 5-6cm (2-2.5in) flowers, produced along the length of the previous year's canes, are white, with the petals, sepals and lip tipped with amethyst purple; the lip is also brightly stained with yellow and two maroon blotches at the base. The plant is deciduous and among the first to produce new growth and flowers in the early part of the year. The canes can become tall on a large plant and it grows well on wooden rafts.

Photo X 2

Dendrobium williamsonii

○*Cool* ❀*Spring/Summer*

Left: This is a stout species whose bulbs do not form very tall canes. The numerous flowers appear in early summer from the top of the newly completed bulbs and are ivory white, the lip handsomely marked with brick red. They are 4cm (1.5in) across, fragrant and long-lasting. This evergreen species requires a semi-rest during the winter and does well in the cool house.

Photo X 2

Dendrobium Hybrids

DENDROBIUM
Gatton Sunray (FCC/RHS)
◑*Intermediate* ❀*Summer*

Left: A magnificent hybrid, this is the largest of the cultivated dendrobiums, and requires plenty of growing space. It is a first generation hybrid from the yellow-flowered species, *D. dalhousie-anum,* which is infrequently seen today, but was at one time regularly imported from Burma. The hybrid was registered in 1919 and has enjoyed immense popularity ever since. *D.* Gatton Sunray (FCC/RHS) is extremely robust, the canes growing to a height of 2m (5ft) or more. The extremely large and showy flowers, which appear in trusses during the early summer, are more than 10cm (4in) across and last in perfection for about 10 days. A large plant will produce numerous trusses, each carrying several flowers. This will extend the flowering period, as not all the trusses come into flower at once.

The plant succeeds best in an intermediate greenhouse where it can be given good light and a decided rest during the winter months.

Photo x ¼

DENDROBIUM
Louisae
●*Warm* ❀*Autumn/Winter*

Below: A very popular plant, this evergreen hybrid is widely grown and is readily available on both sides of the Atlantic. The plant was raised in Indonesia and resulted from the crossing of two showy species native to New Guinea, *D. phalaenopsis* var. *schroederanum* and *D. veratrifolium,* both of which bear long sprays of rose-mauve flowers. *D.* Louisae combines the characteristics of both parents and produces long arching sprays of flowers from the top of the bulbs. The 6cm (2.5in) flowers, which are a rich rose-purple, are extremely long lived and appear during the autumn and winter. The plant can be grown in a warm sun room or greenhouse where it enjoys an abundance of light. During the winter resting period it should be allowed to dry out almost completely.

Photo x ⅛

DENDROBIUM
Fiftieth State
●*Warm* ❀*Summer*

Right: This fine hybrid illustrates a completely different type of dendrobium, which has been bred from species of Australasian origin. *D. phalaenopsis*—the famous Cookstown orchid, discovered by Cook and depicted on Australian stamps—was crossed with *D.* New Guinea, a hybrid combining *D. macrophyllum* and *D. atrioviolaceum*—two unusual species not often seen in cultivation. The 6cm (2.5in) flowers of *D.* Fiftieth State are similar in shape to those of *D. phalaenopsis,* although the rich magenta colour of the species appears as overlying veins of soft red in the hybrid. Raised in Hawaii, the plant is warm growing and will succeed in high temperatures and almost full sunlight. It should be watered freely while growing but allowed a complete rest after flowering. The flowers, which open in summer are extremely long lasting and appear on lengthy sprays from the top of the completed bulb.

Photo x ¼

DENDROBIUM
Mousmee
○Cool ❀Summer

Right: Raised from the species *D. thyrsiflorum*, this hybrid resembles the species in appearance and flowering habit. The 5cm (2in) blooms, which are white with a rich yellow lip, are carried on pendent trusses that appear in early summer from the top of the robust canes. An evergreen with stout dark green leaves, the plant will lose an occasional leaf from the oldest canes each year. *D.* Mousmee will grow successfully in the cool section of the greenhouse, but requires abundant light to flower well. It should also be well rested during the winter when the pseudobulbs will shrivel—a process necessary to initiate the production of flowers.

Although not often seen in cultivation today, this is a fine old hybrid well worth looking out for.

Photo x 2/3

DENDROBIUM
Sussex
○Cool ❀Spring

Above: This hybrid results from a combination of three Indian species *D. nobile, D. aureum* and *D. findlayanum,* with *D. nobile* exerting the most influence. *D.* Sussex is cool growing and easy to cultivate, blooming freely in the spring. This hybrid is a good example of what can be achieved by crossing the hybrid *D.* Ainsworthii (*D. aureum* x *D. nobile)* with further nobile hybrids to improve the flower size and shape. Although retaining the appearance and flowering habit of *D. nobile, D.* Sussex has larger flowers (7.5cm; 3in) of fuller shape. The young plant pictured here has only three flowers; when mature the plant will bloom along the length of the previous years' canes, which may remain in leaf for several years.

Photo x 2/3

DENDROBIUM
Tangerine 'Tillgates' (AM/RHS)
◑Intermediate ❀Spring/Summer

Left: Rather different from the 'traditional' cultivated dendrobium, this outstanding hybrid was raised from a little known but beautiful species, *D. strebloceras,* which comes from western New Guinea. Its name means 'crumpled horn' and refers to the long twisting petals. In the hybrid these petals stand erect, closely resembling the horns of an antelope. The plant is more colourful than its parent species, the 7.5cm (3in) flowers having bright orange petals and mustard yellow sepals and lip. Although the plant is little grown outside the tropics, its unusual and delightful flowers make it a desirable addition to any collection. A subject for the intermediate greenhouse, it would not do well as a houseplant, as it requires full light throughout the year.

Photo X 1/6

ODONTOGLOSSUMS

The genus *Odontoglossum* is well represented within the orchid family, containing approximately 300 species and including some of the most beautiful flowers. As a result, it is very popular with orchid growers. Odontoglossums are members of the subtribe Oncidiniae, which also includes such genera as *Brassia, Oncidium* and *Miltonia.*

They are native to the mountainous regions of Central and South America. Although they occur throughout an extensive range between latitudes 15°S and 20°N—which represents an area of the Andes from Peru to Mexico—their occurrence within this range is relatively limited. The main group of species is found at an elevation of between 1,525 and 2,745m (5,000-9,000ft) with some species to be found as high as 3,660m (12,000ft).

The natural environment for *Odontoglossum* species, which should be matched as far as possible in their culture, provides a temperature range from about 5° to 32°C (41-90°F) maximum, the mean annual temperature being about 13°C (55°F). The rainy season is almost continuous, because moisture brought on winds from the Atlantic condenses over the mountain ranges; as the temperature falls at night, mist envelops the region, leaving the plants moist with dew. The fact that these species grow at such heights must always be borne in mind, for continuous movement of air in a fresh, buoyant and moist atmosphere is essential.

Right: Odontoglossums produce some of the most showy flowers of the orchid family. Today's hybrids combine large, richly coloured, long-lasting blooms with vigorous growth and relatively easy cultivation.

A cultural calendar

Winter

In areas with a temperate climate, where the weather in the winter months is liable to be dull and cold and greenhouse conditions can easily deteriorate, careful use of the watering can, damping down and ventilation are essential. Supplementary heat should be in full operation to maintain a minimum night temperature of about 10°C (50°F); if during severe weather the temperature drops below this level, the plants should be kept drier at the root, with a lower atmospheric humidity, as damage is most likely to occur when they are cold and wet. On days when the outside temperature brings that in the greenhouse up to the required 16°C (60°F), you should take the opportunity to ventilate the house and refresh the atmosphere, provided the outside air is not too cold.

Shade should not be required, and any slight reddening of the leaves due to too much light will help to tone up the plants. As the hybrids will still be active during these months, they should not be allowed to become too dry at the roots for long periods; however, this is less dangerous than having the plants wet at the roots for days on end. The majority of species are either fully at rest or in a state of semi-rest in winter, so watering should be restricted to once every three to four weeks, and then applied using a fine rose; experience and observation will determine how much they require. To prevent accidental watering of plants at rest it is a good idea to put a coloured label in the pot; alternatively, resting and semi-resting plants can be moved to a separate corner of the greenhouse.

Repotting and potting can be continued during this period for plants with new growths of about 4-5cm (1.5-2in).

Spring

As weather conditions improve during the spring months, plant growth will pick up in the greenhouse, just as it does outside. This is a period of very active growth for odontoglossums: many new shoots will appear, species will be coming out of their resting period, and correct conditions will be rewarded with strong plants and healthy flowers. The minimum night temperature should be about 10-13°C (50-55°F), and although it is sometimes tempting to turn heating off as warmer weather comes, supplementary heating will still be required. In areas where even late spring nights can be very cold a heater with a thermostat control really proves its worth.

The day temperature should rise to about 16°C (60°F), and up to 21°C (70°F) if the weather is sunny. Keep growth active by being prepared to use some supplementary heat on cold days. Ventilate as much as possible to give the plants plenty of fresh air, but be careful early on in this period not to use too much top ventilation and end up with cold air surrounding the plants; use some bottom ventilation instead. Frequent damping down between pots and under benches will be necessary to ensure that the humidity remains fairly high; growth will be slowed down if the atmosphere becomes too dry.

As the new growths develop, new roots will be produced, and it is important to water correctly to encourage a healthy root system. Too much water at an early stage may rot the delicate new roots; on the other hand, for a plant that is growing well water is essential, so it is a question of achieving the right balance. The compost may be allowed to dry out between waterings, but should not remain dry for more than a day or two. Light feeding every two or three weeks is beneficial during this time, with a heavy watering between feeds to wash out excess salts.

Foliar feed in late spring will also help to tone up the foliage in anticipation of the better weather to come.

The spring can be a difficult time for shading, with days of bright sun when shade is necessary and dull days when every bit of light is needed. As odontoglossums scorch easily, it is prudent to provide permanent light shade at this time of year if you do not have automatic blinds or the time to put on or take off the shade as required. The colour of the foliage at this time should be a dark shiny green with a tinge of red denoting vigorous but not soft growth.

This is the best time of year to repot, ideally when the new growths are about 4-5cm (1.5-2in) long. This coincides with the period of most root activity, when new roots will be able to penetrate and ramify through the fresh compost.

Summer

This is probably the most difficult period of the year for odontoglossums. Normally, supplementary heat should not be required; in fact, high day temperatures can be damaging and proper use of shading, ventilation (including fans) and provision of correct humidity are essential to keep the plant in prime condition.

The minimum night temperature should be about 13°C (55°F), and usually the temperature will remain around this figure naturally. If very cold spells occur the use of thermostatically controlled heating is recommended to ensure that the rhythm of growth is maintained.

The desirable average day temperature lies between 18° and 24 °C (65-75°F) and it is essential to keep the temperature within these limits if optimum growing conditions are to be maintained. The maximum temperature most odontoglossums can tolerate is about 27°C (80°F). Intergeneric hybrids have been bred to withstand higher day temperatures and are therefore more suitable for growing in the warm climates of such places as California and Australia. They are also able to withstand exceedingly hot summers in temperate climates.

Ventilation is necessary during the day throughout the summer to help maintain the fresh buoyant atmosphere and keep temperatures down. The atmosphere must not become too dry and more frequent damping down between pots and under benches will be necessary during hot periods. It is a good idea is to have troughs of moisture-retaining materials, such as Lytag (or perlite), capillary matting or sand, and an automatic damping system (see page 60).

Shading is essential during the summer. The amount of shade required depends on the ability to keep temperatures down. With good control the maximum temperature can be kept down to 24°C (75°F), when 60 percent shade will be adequate; otherwise 70 or 80 percent will be necessary. Extra shading, provided by shade cloth or lath blinds fixed to the outside of the greenhouse, helps to form an insulating barrier and keep the sun's heat out.

During these hottest months of the year, the plants should not be allowed to dry out too rapidly and they should certainly not remain dry for any length of time. Some orchid composts available today drain particularly well, which is beneficial for epiphytic orchids and during the cold damp winter months when it is all too easy to overwater, but extra care must be taken during hot weather to ensure that they do not bake dry. If plants do dry out they can be difficult to moisten again and you can easily be misled into believing that the plant has been well watered when, in fact, the water has merely trickled straight through the compost. Odontoglossums should be watered carefully during this period, little and often. If the compost is in good condition, and you are in any doubt about watering, the rule of thumb is to give them water.

It is not advisable to repot at this time of year, unless it becomes essential, as it is difficult to provide ideal conditions for settling the plants after potting.

Autumn

Autumn, like spring, is a time of good growing conditions and, for the most part, favourable weather. During early autumn there will probably be enough natural warmth to do without supplementary heating, but even so, preparations for heating during the cooler months to come should be made. The minimum night temperature should be about 10-13°C (50-55°F). Daytime temperatures should be allowed to rise to 21°C (70°F), and any excessive rise controlled by ventilation, damping down and shading.

Since it is not a good idea for the plants to enter the cool, dark winter months with soft lush growth, which is liable to be attacked by fungus, this is the time to harden off the foliage. Plenty of ventilation at all times during early autumn (certainly until supplementary heat is needed), reduction of the degree of shading and feeding with a high potassium plant food will help.

Many plants will be producing new shoots and this is therefore a good time for repotting. Select plants that have growths about 4-5cm (1.5-2in) long. Watering should be continued throughout this period for hybrids, but for species that are resting during the winter, reduce the amount of water as the pseudobulbs are completed.

Repotting odontoglossums

Odontoglossums are epiphytic and thrive in a compost that is open and free draining, but which retains moisture at all times, so that plants do not become dry during the growing season. They detest stale, lifeless and waterlogged compost. Bark-based composts, made up of graded pine bark, charcoal, perlite and sphagnum peat or good fresh sphagnum moss, are proving most satisfactory. For young seedlings and adult hybrids a fine moss is probably best as this will not dry out too quickly. Individual species may require different composts. Fertilizers that release their nutrient slowly over a period should not be used, as odontoglossums are not heavy feeders and root burn can easily result.

The best times to repot are spring and autumn, particularly when the new growths are about 4-5cm (1.5-2in) long, coinciding with the period of most active root growth. Potting can be done in summer and winter, but climatic conditions are not so favourable for the aftercare and settling down of the plants.

How often plants should be repotted depends to a large extent on the type of compost used. In bark-based compost the plants should be repotted every two years, and for young seedlings potting every year is advisable.

Potting procedure

Having selected the plant at the right stage of growth, knock it out of its pot and remove the old compost, dead back bulbs and any dead roots (the live roots will be white, green tipped and fleshy when felt gently between finger and thumb; dead roots will be brown, soft and the outer layer of cells will come away easily from the root core.). If the plant has a poor and rotten root system, dipping it in a solution of captan orthocide will prevent the spread of any further rot.

Pot size will be determined by the size of the plant and, in particular, the state of the root system. When potting a large adult plant with numerous bulbs, some of the surface back bulbs can be removed, leaving the plant a minimum of two to three bulbs and new growth.

There should be enough room in the pot for at least one new pseudobulb to form, but the pot should be on the small side rather than too large, as over-potting can lead to poor root action and subsequent deterioration.

First, place a layer of drainage material, such as clean, broken pot, polystyrene chunks or large gravel, in the bottom of the pot. Then, hold the plant so that the base of the bulb is just below the top of the pot with the new growth aimed in the direction of the most room and pour in the compost, working it gently among the roots and tapping the pot occasionally to help it to settle. Firm the compost gently with the fingers without using force: remember the roots are thin and fairly delicate and must be able to grow through the new compost with reasonable ease.

Aftercare of repotted plants

Using a modern compost the actual task of potting orchids is as easy as for any other pot plant, but aftercare is very important to enable them to settle down and continue their growth with a minimum of disturbance.

After potting, water the plant well (particularly if the compost has been stored and is very dry) to moisten the compost. However, it is important at this stage not to overwater and waterlog the compost and so deter new roots. Provide plenty of humidity by maintaining a buoyant atmosphere around the plant, so that it is able to take up all the water it needs through the new roots (which have just been disturbed), keeping water loss through the roots to a minimum. Keep in heavy shade with the maximum temperature below 21°C (70°F) if possible. Subsequent waterings should be light so that the roots are encouraged to search for water and thus build up into a strong system. A diluted foliar feed once a week will be beneficial at this time. Settling down after potting will depend on the state of the root system when repotted and how well you pot, but normally it will take four to five weeks, and after this time normal culture can be resumed.

Vegetative propagation

Odontoglossums are not noted for their ease of vegetative propagation (by division of back bulbs) because many varieties do not readily throw out more than one shoot at a time. Species that produce many new growths (such as *Odontoglossum pulchellum, cordatum, bictoniense, platycheilum* and *stellatum*) can be propagated by division, but do not be tempted to chop up a large specimen plant just to make many small plants, as large specimens should be your ultimate aim.

Each division should be made up of at least two to three bulbs and new growth; smaller divisions could take a year or more to come into flower. Back bulb propagation is another possibility and results can be outstanding. Take two bulbs at a time if possible, as there is then a better chance of getting an 'eye' to start. Pot in a fine bark mix or in sphagnum moss and place in a propagating case, where humidity can be kept high and excessive heat avoided; if a new shoot appears to be careful not to overwater and cause it to rot away. Once roots are visible resume normal cultural practice.

The most effective way of propagating odontoglossums, particularly the hybrids, is to divide the leading pseudobulb and new growth from the rest of the plant. Select a plant that has a growth of 4-5cm (1.5-2in) and, while it is still in the pot, cut through the hard rhizome connecting the newest bulb to the one behind it, then leave it undisturbed in normal conditions. After about eight weeks the bulb behind the severed front bulb and growth will produce a shoot and when this shoot has grown to 4-5cm (1.5-2in) remove both divisions and pot up separately.

Pests and diseases

Aphids are the main insect pests to attack odontoglossums, particularly during the summer months. New shoots and flower buds are especially susceptible. Regular spraying with an insecticide, such as malathion, will help to prevent attack.

Other pests which may attack the soft leaves, include red spider mites and mealy bugs, both of which can be controlled by spraying as above. Slugs and snails may also cause considerable damage to young shoots and flowers, and should be controlled with metaldehyde pellets or powder placed on the surface of the compost.

Provided the greenhouse is kept clean, and your original stock was healthy, odontoglossums should remain disease-free. However, plants may suffer from fungal rot if they remain wet in cold conditions. To prevent this, ensure that there is good air movement around the plants at all times, and reduce damping down during cool weather.

Species and hybrids

Although the species odontoglossums offered growers a superb range, in 1898, C. Vuylsteke in Belgium made the first hybrid, between *O. crispum* and *O. harry-*

Above: *Cochlioda noezliana* has had considerable influence on odontoglossum breeding over the years, contributing towards the brilliant colours of the modern *Odontioda* hybrids.

anum to make *O.* Crispo-harryanum, which opened up a whole new world. Hybridizing advanced quickly and crosses involving other genera were made as early as 1904, setting the scene for a deluge of interest that has lasted through the years to the present time, and their popularity is still increasing rapidly. The hybrids available to the grower today have over 70 years of breeding behind them and are necessarily complicated, but this should in no way deter the enthusiast from exploring the beauties and treasures to be found among them.

Odontiodas result from crossing an *Odontoglossum* with a *Cochlioda. C. noezliana,* the most often used, was introduced because of its brilliant scarlet flowers. Many modern odontiodas are very similar to the odontoglossums because they have been bred back again and again to improve size and form.

There is a wide range of hybrids to choose from; new varieties are being raised all the time, and these quickly supersede the older ones. However, within the various colour groups there are certain breeding lines or parents that have been particularly successful and some of these are given below. The best way to make a selection is probably to visit a nursery, see the plants in flower, and take advice from the experts.

Odontoglossum crispum is the species most responsible for the whites; it produces large, well-shaped flowers—usually white or white with some purple markings. The latter have basically a white background with deep coloured markings. Names to note include: *O.* Stropheon, Connero, Philomel, Ardentissimum, Opheon.

The species originally involved in the production of yellow hybrids were *O. luteo-purpureum, harryanum* and *triumphans.* Today's hybrids are deep golden yellows, often with attractive markings in red or chestnut-brown. Names to note include Moselle, Golden Guinea, Inca Gold, Stonehurst Yellow, Pacific Gold, Cornosa, Ascania.

In the red section the Odontioda hybrids are the most successful. Names to note are: Trixon, Chanticleer, Charlesworthii, Bradshawiae, Memoria Donald Campbell, Trixell, Salway.

Crosses between the large shapely odontoglossums and the brightly coloured odontiodas have resulted in some of the most beautiful colour combinations, ranging from white backgrounds with light markings through to deep rich imperial purples. Names to note include Florence Stirling, Memory, Brocade, Dalmar, Ingera, Memtor, Joe Marshall.

Many other genera have been crossed with odontoglossums and the results have been most interesting; many such crosses involve two or more genera and are therefore quite complicated. The full list of these to date is to be found in *Sander's List of Orchid Hybrids.* The most popular intergeneric hybrids are not only attractive for their flowers, but also are culturally more adaptable. Much breeding is being aimed at producing hybrids that will grow in climates such as Australia, South Africa or California that are normally too warm for odontoglossums and odontiodas. Some of the most popular types are odontocidiums, wilsonaras and vuylstekearas.

Odontocidiums are produced by crossing an *Odontoglossum* with an *Oncidium.* Species such as *Oncidium tigrinum, wentworthianum, leucochilum* and *incurvum* have been very successful, with noted progeny such as *Odontocidium* Tiger Butter, Tigerwood, Tigersun, Crowbrough, Solana, Tiger Hambuhren.

Wilsonaras result from crossing an *Odontioda* with an *Oncidium* or an *Odontioda* with an *Odontocidium.* The same species are generally used. Through the use of odontiodas, many of these crosses produce highly coloured flowers. Examples include: *Wilsonara* Widecombe Fair, Jean du Pont, Tigerman, Celle.

Vuylstekearas result from crossing an *Odontioda* with a *Miltonia* (the pansy orchids). Vuylstekearas are generally very tolerant of excessive heat and normally have the large flamboyant lip associated with the miltonias. Examples are: Vuylstekeara Cambria, Edna Stamperland, Heather Moore.

Odontoglossum Species

Odontoglossum bictoniense

○Cool ✿Summer

Right: This must be one of the easiest and most popular species, and an ideal plant for beginners. Native to Guatemala, it is a very vigorous grower and will quickly grow into a specimen plant. Erect flower spikes appear at the end of the summer, growing quickly in the warm weather to reach heights up to 122cm (48in) and bearing 20 long-lasting flowers on each spike. The flowers open in succession so that there are usually eight or nine out at once over a period of several weeks. The flowers are about 3-4cm (1.25-1.5in) across, yellowy green with brown spots and a striking white or pink lip.

O. bictoniense, which can be grown successfully as a houseplant, requires cool conditions with medium shade and does not need resting in winter, though water should be reduced when flowering has finished, until new growth appears in the spring.

Photo X 1

Odontoglossum cervantesii

○Cool ✿Winter/Spring

Below: This delightful dwarf species comes from Mexico. The total height of pot, bulbs and leaves is only about 15cm (6in) and makes this an ideal subject for growers with limited space.

The flowers are produced on semi-pendent spikes, in winter and early spring, from the new growth as it starts to form a pseudobulb. In comparison to the size of the plant, the flowers are large—about 4 to 5cm (1.6 to 2in) across, beautifully white, almost round and marked with a distinctive band of chestnut rings towards the middle of the sepals and petals.

Being a species with fine roots it does not like to dry out during the growing season and thrives in a fine but free-draining compost. During the winter months water should be reduced and a small amount of shrivelling of the bulb is normal at this time. Give medium shade during the summer.

Photo X 1

Odontoglossum cariniferum

○Cool ✿Winter

Above: Perhaps this Central American species is not as widely grown now as it used to be, but this is probably due to difficulties of supply rather than any other factor. Given cool conditions it grows vigorously and produces long branching spikes which bear brightly coloured flowers, 4-5cm (1.5-2in) across, of dark greenish-brown with yellow tips to the sepals and petals, which open in the winter.

The new shoot appears in spring, developing through the summer growing season until the new bulb starts to form in late summer or early autumn, and it is at this time that the flower spike will first appear. A reduction in watering following the completion of the bulb is necessary and the gradual wrinkling of the bulb during winter is natural. Give medium shade during the growing season and use a medium grade compost.

Photo X ¾

Odontoglossum citrosmum
(syn. ***Odontoglossum pendulum***)
○*Cool* ❀*Spring*

Above: The Mexican species has a distinct growth and flower cycle, which has to be respected if success is to be achieved; perhaps this explains why it has always been sought after but has never quite attained the popularity it deserves.

The plant needs a decided resting period during the winter, following the completion of the previous year's pseudobulb, when water should only be applied to prevent complete dehydration; full light at this time is necessary. Towards the end of the winter the new shoot will appear from the base of the pseudobulb, but the temptation to give water must be resisted as it is from an undeveloping new shoot that the flower spike appears; if water is given too early the new shoot will elongate and grow normally without flowering. It is therefore after flowering that normal watering should be carried out.

The flowers – about 4 to 5cm (1.6 to 2in) – are white flushed with pink and sweetly scented, and borne on pendular spikes, making this an ideal subject to suspend from the greenhouse roof. Give medium to light shade during the growing season and medium grade compost.

Photo X ½

Odontoglossum cordatum
○*Cool* ❀*Spring*

Right: This species is another native of Guatemala which has proved itself as one of the most popular odontoglossums. It is a very vigorous grower and flowers freely in spring. As it readily produces new shoots it can soon be grown into a specimen plant and it is at this stage (with say six or seven flower spikes) that its beauty can be fully appreciated. The spikes are about 18 to 30cm (7-12in) long, bearing flowers of a bright golden yellow with attractive, eye-catching mahogany markings.

This is a thick-root species which can be grown in a medium to coarse compost and is ideal for growing in baskets suspended from the roof. Medium shade is required during the growing season.

Photo X 1

Odontoglossum crispum
○*Cool* ❀*All year*

Above: This is the most familiar species and has contributed more than any other to the development of manmade hybrids; it is a native of Colombia in South America.

Coming from high up in the Andes the plants need medium to heavy shade and cool, moist, humid conditions. The large waxy flowers, up to 10cm (4in) across, vary considerably in presence or absence of marking. Flower spikes develop from the side of the new bulb as it is forming and, as the seasons in its native environment are not clearly defined and growth can start at any time, the flowers may open at virtually any time of year, though spring and autumn are probably the most popular.

Over-collecting in the early days of the orchid craze, which swept England and Europe in the latter half of the nineteenth century, together with destruction of natural habitats during recent years, has made the direct supply almost dry up, but selective breeding of varieties has been continuing for many years and this has ensured that *Odontoglossum crispum* will still be available to enthusiasts without calling on the dwindling wild stocks; moreover, these cultivated plants are of higher quality. As an ancestor, *Odontoglossum crispum* has probably contributed more towards improving the flower size and shape of the *Odontoglossum* and *Odontioda* hybrids than any other species. They should be grown in a fine to medium grade compost, with medium to heavy shade.

Photo X ¾

Odontoglossum grande

○Cool ❀Autumn

Right: Known widely as the 'clown orchid' due to the clown-like figure represented by the column in the centre of the flower, this is certainly one of the most widely grown in this genus, and popular as a houseplant. The flowers are very large up to 15cm (6in) across, yellow with bright chestnut-brown markings. Although it is now classified as a Rossii odontoglossum it is sure to be sold or known as *Odontoglossum grande* for many years to come.

It comes from Guatemala and is distinct from most odontoglossums, with the exception of *O. insleayi, schlieperianum* and *williamsianum,* for it has hard dark leaves and very tough pseudobulbs, and needs a decided rest during the winter months. During the growing season it needs plenty of moisture at the roots but excessive atmospheric moisture can result in unsightly black spotting on the foliage. As the new growth starts to make a pseudobulb towards the end of the summer the flower spike develops and the flowers usually open in autumn. Once flowering is finished and the pseudobulbs have fully matured, watering should be withheld until spring when the new growth appears and starts the whole cycle again. The plants need light shade and should be grown in a medium grade bark compost.

Photo X ¼

Odontoglossum harryanum

○Cool ❀Spring/Summer

Right: A native of Colombia, this is one of the most striking of the odontoglossums. It produces spikes of about 30cm (12in) or more in length with many large 7.5 to 10cm (3-4in) flowers of attractive coppery brown, dappled with yellow throughout, with a large and most distinctive white lip marked in bright lilac. Having been used a great deal during the early days of hybridizing, this species is very similar in its cultural requirements to the modern hybrids, and requires cool conditions, medium to heavy shade and a fine or medium grade bark mix.

Photo X ½

Odontoglossum insleayi

○Cool ❀Autumn/Winter

Above: A native of Mexico this species closely resembles *Odontoglossum grande* and has similar cultural requirements. The flowers are produced in autumn and winter from pseudobulbs that have just formed, they are about 7.5cm (3in) across, yellow with chestnut or reddish-brown markings. They should be grown in a medium grade compost and given light shade, with a rest in winter.

Photo X ⅙

Odontoglossum laeve

○Cool ❀Spring

Below: Opinions differ as to whether this species, a native of Mexico, should be classed as an *Odontoglossum*, an *Oncidium* or a *Miltonia*, but it is usually grown as *Odontoglossum laeve*. It produces long branching spikes and sweetly scented flowers, 5-7.5cm (2-3in) across, yellowish-green with markings of chocolate brown and a distinctive pink or purple lip. This is a vigorous species, producing large plump pseudobulbs at the end of the summer. The plants should be potted in fine or medium grade bark compost and given medium shade; they appear to enjoy a short hard rest after completion of the pseudobulb to initiate flower spikes, after which watering in winter should be kept to about once every three weeks. The spikes develop during the winter and come into bloom during the spring.

Photo X 1/3

Odontoglossum luteo-purpureum

○Cool ❀Spring

Below: This species is a native of Colombia and similar in cultural requirements of *Odontoglossum crispum* and the *Odontoglossum* hybrids, so it requires medium shade and medium or fine bark compost. In spring this attractive species produces long spikes of large flowers, 7.5cm (3in) across, basically yellow with heavy chestnut-brown markings.

Photo X 1/2

Odontoglossum maculatum

○Cool ❀Spring

Above: Very similar to *Odontoglossum cordatum* in both growth and flower habit, the culture should be the same. The flower spikes, about 30-44cm (12-18in) long, are produced in spring, bearing flowers of about 5-7.5cm (2-3in) across, which have a creamy yellow background with brown spots and blotches. Plants should be grown in cool conditions in a medium bark mix and given medium shade.

Photo X 1 1/3

Odontoglossum nebulosum (syn. ***apterum***)

○Cool ❀Spring

Below: This popular Mexican species has flowers about 5-7.5cm (2-3in) across, white with orange-red or brown spots. The spike appears with the new growth and comes into bloom in the spring. The plants have thick fleshy roots so a medium grade bark-based compost is ideal; medium shade is required. The pseudobulbs are soft and fleshy so care should be taken not to overwater as this can result in rot.

Photo X 3/4

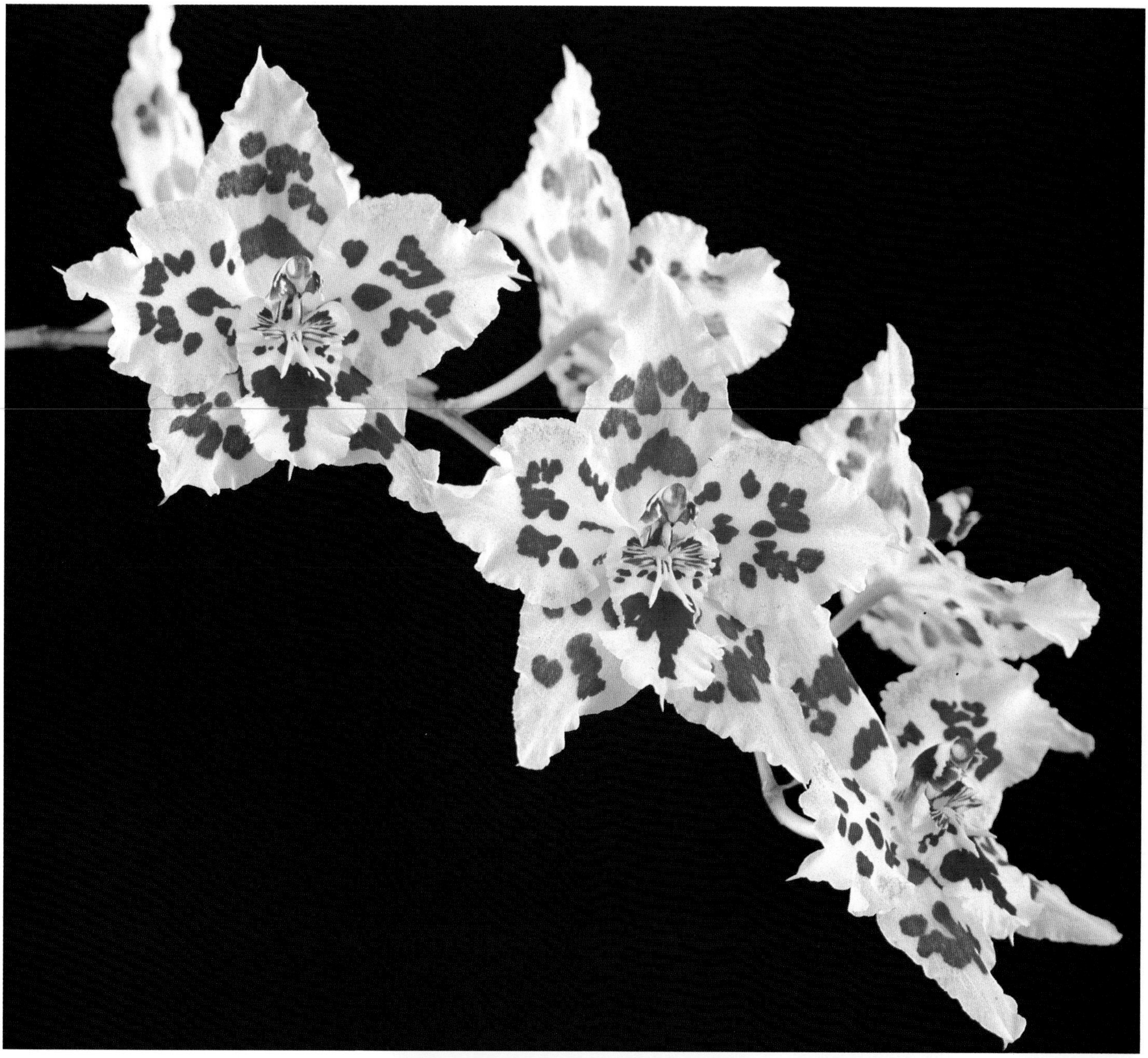

Odontoglossum pescatorei

○Cool ❀Spring and Autumn

Above: This is one of the loveliest of the Colombian odontoglossums with a branching spike and flowers which vary in size but are generally about 7.5cm (3in) across, white with spotting or flushing in lilac rose. Its growth habit and cultural requirements are similar to those of *Odontoglossum crispum;* cool conditions, fine to medium grade bark mix, and medium to heavy shade.

Photo X 1

Odontoglossum pulchellum

○Cool ❀Spring

Right: This is an extremely popular Guatemalan species as it is a vigorous grower. The waxy, white flowers, though small – 1-2cm (0.25-0.5in) across – bloom in masses and have a lovely scent, which explains why it is known as the 'lily of the valley orchid'. It flowers in spring and produces more than one shoot from each pseudobulb, making it ideal for growing into a specimen. The plants are thin-rooted and need cool conditions, a fine grade bark mix, and medium shade in the summer.

Photo X 1

Odontoglossum rossii

○Cool ❀Winter

Left: From Guatemala and Mexico, this is one of the most delightful of the miniature odontoglossums. It is very similar to *Odontoglossum cervantesii* in size of plant and size and colour of flowers, and has similar cultural requirements. The plants are thin-rooted and flourish in cool conditions and a fine bark mix or sphagnum moss which will keep them moist at all times. Medium shade is required during the summer. A typical variety produces flowers in winter, star-shaped, about 3 to 5cm (1.6-2in) across, white with brown markings; rarer varieties are flushed with pink or deep pink. Probably the most popular is the Majus variety which has a much larger flower up to 7.5cm (3in) across. Recent crosses with this species have been very successful and have reawakened interest in this type of breeding.

Photo X 2/3

Odontoglossum stellatum

○Cool ❀Winter

Above: A dwarf species from Guatemala, this has attractive star-shaped flowers, yellow overlaid with brown, with a white or pink lip. These are usually borne either singly or in pairs during the winter months, but on a specimen plant they are produced in abundance, making a fine display. Each flower measures 3-4cm (1.25-1.5in) across. Found nestling among mosses on branches of trees, this species needs a fine bark mix or sphagnum moss, with medium shade during the summer.

Photo X 1

Odontoglossum uro-skinneri

○Cool ❀Winter/Spring

Left: This is a very fine species from Guatemala and Mexico, similar in many ways to *Odontoglossum bictoniense.* This can be a difficult plant to import and is not in abundant supply. The 5cm (2in) flowers, produced in winter and spring, are like those of *Odontoglossum bictoniense* but with a fuller shape and a large deep pink lip. The pseudobulbs and foliage are fleshy, therefore care should be taken with the watering; in particular, watering the new growths should be avoided, otherwise rot will quickly set in. Give medium to heavy shade and grow in a medium grade bark mix.

Photo X 3

Odontoglossum Hybrids

ODONTIODA

Dalmar 'Lyoth Bachus'

○*Cool* ❀*Season varies*

Right: When the highly coloured odontiodas are crossed with large well-formed odontoglossum hybrids the results are a culmination of two lines of breeding, superbly illustrated by this most magnificent of clones, *Odontioda* Dalmar 'Lyoth Bachus' (FCC/RHS). This hybrid has beautiful deep red flowers edged with pale mauve and is 10cm (4in) across. The odontioda parent is Margia, which has been influenced by the *Cochlioda noezliana* in its background, whereas the odontoglossum parent, Mandalum, has *O. crispum* in its immediate ancestry. This hybrid, therefore, requires cool growing conditions.

Photo X 1

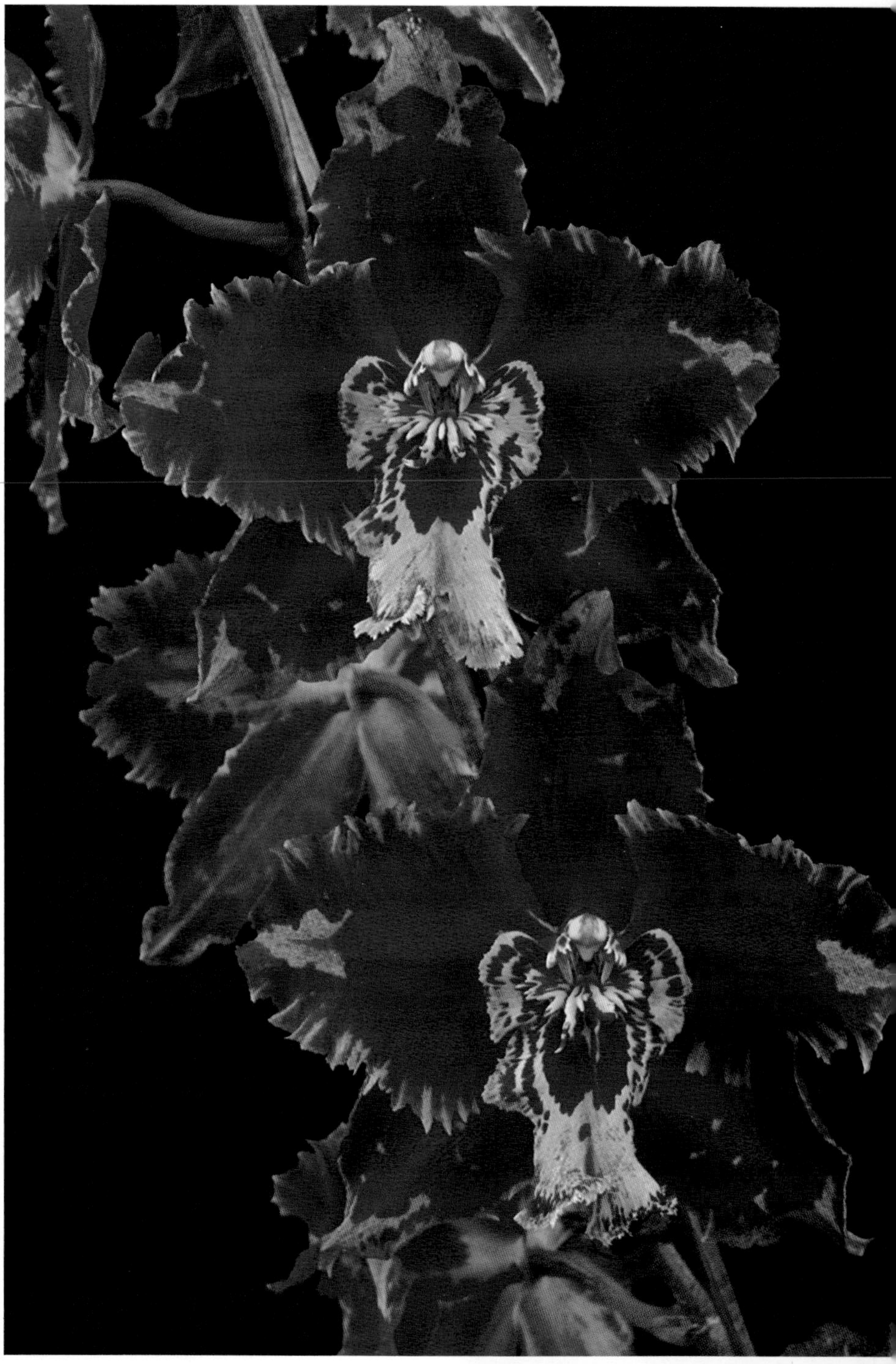

ODONTIODA

Trixon

○*Cool* ❀*Season varies*

Below: Bright red odontiodas have been bred from the diminutive but brilliant scarlet *Cochlioda noezliana*, a cool species that comes from Colombia and Peru. Early crosses produced small flowers, but continual selection and breeding has increased the size and quality of flowers considerably as is amply illustrated by *Odontioda* Trixon, with its 9cm (3.5in) flowers. This is a cross between *Odontioda* Lautrix and *Odontioda* Saxon, and both the parents carry the influence of *Cochlioda noezliana* in their backgrounds. As a result, Trixon can usually tolerate more heat than pure-bred odontoglossums, although it grows best in cool conditions.

Photo X ½

ODONTOCIDIUM

Tigersun 'Nutmeg'

○◑*Cool/Intermediate* ❀*Season varies*

Right: The introduction of *Oncidium* species into the breeding has increased in popularity over the last few years and many hybrids are becoming available. Apart from giving different types of flowers and colours, most of the odontocidiums and wilsonaras will stand more extreme conditions than the pure odontoglossums—which is of great importance to growers in warmer climates or where a mixed collection is cultivated. *Odontocidium* Tigersun is a cross between *Oncidium tigrinum* (a popular scented species from Mexico) and *Odontoglossum* Sunmar, and produces excellent bright yellow flowers, 9cm (3.5in) across, of good substance. This hybrid can be grown in cool or intermediate conditions with a winter minimum night temperature of about 12.7-14.5°C (55-58°F).

Photo X ⅓

VUYLSTEKEARA
Cambria 'Plush'
◑●*Intermediate/Warm* ❀*Season varies*
Above: Every now and again a classic hybrid appears on the scene and *Vuylstekeara* Cambria 'Plush' is surely one of these. Although the cross was made in 1931, it was not until 1967 that the variety 'Plush' received a First Class Certificate from the Royal Horticultural Society, and 1973 when it obtained a First Class Certificate from the American Orchid Society—a unique double for a unique clone. Vuylstekearas are produced by introducing *Miltonia* (the pansy orchids) into *Odontioda* breeding, and they are characterized by large miltonia-type lips and glowing colours. This plant has 9cm (3.5in) dark red flowers, with large red and white lips. Adaptability to various growing conditions has helped to make Cambria popular throughout the world; it is ideal for almost all collections, since it will grow well in cool, intermediate or warm environments.
Photo X ½

ODONTOGLOSSUM
Gold Cup 'Lemon Drop'
○*Cool* ❀*Season varies*
Above: This cross between *Odontoglossum* Chamois Snowcrest and *O.* Croworough Sunrise is a good example of yellow odontoglossum breeding. The flowers are 6cm (2.5in) across, and a bright canary yellow with a few golden brown markings on the lip. The plant, which is proving to be a good parent in its turn, requires cool conditions with plenty of shade during the summer.
Photo X 1⅓

ODONTOGLOSSUM
Stropheon
○*Cool* ❀*Season varies*
Right: A very successful hybrid (*Odontoglossum* Opheon × *Odontoglossum* Robert Strauss), this cross has been highly awarded with two First Class Certificates and two Awards of Merit from the Royal Horticultural Society, and has won numerous awards in the United States. The cross has been characterized by large flowers, 10cm (4in) across, of heavy texture, which usually have white backgrounds strongly marked with deep purplish-red. With its parentage traced back to the cool growing Colombian species of *O. crispum, pescatorei* and *harryanum* this hybrid requires the same conditions as *O. crispum.*
Photo X ½

WILSONARA
Widecombe Fair
○◑*Cool/Intermediate* ❀*Season varies*
Above: This hybrid between the small but many flowered species *Oncidium incurvum* and *Odontioda* Florence Stirling produces long spikes and many 5cm (2in) white flowers, which are heavily marked with pink, and is well suited for the mixed collection. The plant can be grown in cool or intermediate conditions, and will tolerate fluctuations in temperature.
Photo X ½

PAPHIOPEDILUMS

At present, there are in existence some 60 or 70 known species of the genus *Paphiopedilum.* The reason for this approximation in numbers is that taxonomists are not in total agreement as to whether some of these species are in fact true species, or simply sub-varieties.

Paphiopedilum is a subtribe of the family Cypripedilinae, and for many years the genus was referred to as *Cypripedium* by the majority of the world's horticulturalists. In recent years, botanists have classified them as *Paphiopedilum,* so distinguishing them from the true *Cypripedium,* which is found in several countries in the northern hemisphere. The popular name for the paphiopedilum is 'Lady's Slipper' — or variations of this nickname, such as 'Slippers' in Australia, and 'Frauenschuhe' in Germany. The name is derived from the interesting shape of the pouch at the front of the flower, which is made up of two petals joined together, and the resulting cupped formation looks distinctly like a slipper or small shoe.

These fascinating orchids are mostly terrestrial in habit, with some rare examples growing as epiphytes. They are to be found in an intermediate or tropical climate, and in the Far East their habitat ranges from the Himalayas, through Southeast Asia and Indonesia, to Borneo and New Guinea. Some species also grow in the Philippines, and the most southerly point that the genus has been located is the island of Bougainville, from which comes the species *P. bougainvilleanum.* The greatest numbers of paphiopedilums are probably found in Burma and Thailand, and many species of the genus are represented in these two countries.

Our predecessors, who were avid collectors of these species, naturally sent their precious booty home to add to their own orchid collections, or those of their patrons. As many of these first hobbyists were English, the bulk of those first plants was shipped to England. As a result of all this interest, it was also in England that the first hybrid paphiopedilum (or *Cypripedium,* as it was then called) was raised, in 1869. This first hybrid resulted from a deliberate cross between *P. villosum* and *P. barbatum.* Shortly afterwards, in 1870, the first hybrid from *P. fairieanum* × *P. barbatum* also flowered and was named *P.* Vexillarium. By 1871, several more *Paphiopedilum* crosses had entered the scene, and from that time the interest in this genus really took hold, as is more than evident if one takes the time and trouble to look back over some of the old records printed at the end of the last century — books such as *Sander's List of Orchid Hybrids,* or the *Orchid Stud Book* by Rolfe and Hurst.

It was the experience of these early hobbyists that these exotic orchids were quite easy to cultivate, provided one could give them the warm greenhouse situation they needed to simulate their natural habitat. Therefore, they became very popular with wealthy collectors who could afford to keep up these conditions, together with the army of staff needed to run their sometimes vast range of greenhouses. Many of the early hybrids were raised on some of the largest estates in England at the turn of the century, and many of the names of the gardeners and orchid growers concerned with these ventures have been handed down to posterity. They will continue to live on through orchid history in the books that they wrote, the many plants that were named after them (still featuring strongly in the advanced breeding of modern times), or sometimes just in stories of their fame and fortunes that have been handed down to us today.

Owing to the labours of these early growers, the popularity of the paphiopedilum increased rapidly, and no major collection was complete without the largest share of it being made up of species or hybrids of this genus. The *Orchid Stud Book,* printed in 1909, states that . . . 'the hybrids in the Cypripedium group far outnumber those in any other, largely due to the ease and certainty with which seedlings can be raised'. Whilst it should be noted that this particular 'ease and certainty' was comparative for those early days, it is true that work with this genus was found to be much more rewarding than with most others. A great and flourishing business was built up in some of these species and hybrids (also now famous names themselves), and many changed hands for vast sums of money —

Right: The range of paphiopedilums available to the amateur grower is now enormous. The breathtaking colours, shapes and sizes of the long-lasting flowers provide a glorious display throughout the year, in home or greenhouse.

extortionate even by the standards of today's rioting inflation!

Paphiopedilums in cultivation

The culture of the genus *Paphiopedilum* varies, according to the part of the world in which you live. For example, in some countries it is not necessary to build a greenhouse, as the outside conditions are naturally suitable for the plants. Sometimes a shade-cloth roof is all that is really necessary to protect the plants from the full rays of the sun, and happy are the hobbyists who live in places where such a climate is the rule, and no exorbitant bills for heating have to be met.

In temperate climes, of course, a heated greenhouse is an absolute necessity, although in these days of centrally heated houses, some people are having considerable success with growing paphiopedilums in their home environment. For this type of culture, lack of humidity is the main problem, and to aid successful growth, humidifiers or misters are often installed and used regularly to cancel some of the dryness in the air caused by central heating.

Humidity and temperature

For the hobbyist with a greenhouse, it is simple to create the necessary humidity of 60-70 percent, by damping down in the early morning. This involves hosing down the areas below the benches and the paths, thus causing condensation and a sudden rise in the humidity level.

The temperature of the greenhouse for paphiopedilums should be in the intermediate range, varying from a minimum of 18.5-20°C (65-68°F) by day, dropping to a minimum of 12.5-14 .5°C (55-58°F) at night. Although these are the ideal temperatures for paphiopedilums, many amateur growers would find it expensive to keep up such temperatures. It is possible to grow them quite well at lower temperatures, for example, a minimum of 10°C (50°F) at night, rising to whatever daytime temperature may be produced by the heat of the sun. This obviously depends on the season of the year, and temperatures must not be allowed to remain above 29-30°C (84 -86°F) for long periods as this may harm the plants, especially if coupled with a drop in humidity.

Light and ventilation

Paphiopedilums are low light intensity orchids—another reason why they are so popular in countries in the northern hemisphere. In their natural habitat they grow on the floor of the jungle, beneath the shade of low-growing plants. Therefore, to imitate these conditions, diffuse light is necessary. This can be obtained either by shadecloth or green shading painted on the glass, combined with the use of wooden, slatted roller-blinds when

the sun is very strong. When grown in the home paphiopedilums should not be placed on a windowsill that receives direct strong sunlight.

In these warm, humid conditions paphiopedilums will really thrive. However, such an atmosphere may quickly become unhealthy if there is no air circulation. In this case the excess moisture lying around and, in particular, on the plants can cause fungal infection (botrytis) to set in, resulting in the damping off of buds and flowers, often followed by brown rot in the leaves. Good ventilation is therefore absolutely essential. This poses no problems on a warm summer's day, when doors and top ventilators may safely be left wide open. But in winter, when low temperatures outside could harm the plants, electric fans must be used to circulate the air and counteract any unhealthy stagnation.

Composts and potting

The early growers used to grow paphiopedilums in a compost based on osmunda fibre with various additions, such as peat, sphagnum moss, chopped oak leaves and coarse sand. But owing to the world scarcity of osmunda fibre, a suitable substitute had to be found on which to base the potting mix. Having tried various types of peat and bark-based composts, most growers have finally settled for variations on a mixture of fir bark in various grades according to the size of seedling or plant to be potted (fine grades for seedlings, coarse for mature plants), with additions of charcoal, moss and artificial granules of polystyrene.

The actual formula, of course, depends on your particular preference and cultural conditions. The main requisite for the potting medium is that it should be open enough to allow good drainage, whilst still retaining a certain amount of moisture.

Adult (mature) plants should be repotted at least once a year after flowering, and young plants (especially small seedlings) also benefit greatly from being moved on regularly into a larger pot, so that they do not become potbound.

When repotting, always make sure that you remove all the old compost and the dead roots from the plants. If necessary, dust the roots with a fungicide powder, such as orthocide or Benlate, or one of the many brands available from your local stockist.

After repotting, water well to establish the new material, and then do not water again for at least a week to ten days. After this, water infrequently for several weeks, so that the roots have to send out new tips to search for moisture. In hot weather, during this time misting the leaves with a fine spray may help to prevent them becoming dehydrated.

Vegetative propagation

During the repotting process, the plants can be divided if you wish. This practice of propagation should be carried out carefully, otherwise the plant may be severely damaged and eventually die. First, make sure that the root structure extends to both parts of the plant to be divided. If a plant is halved so that the bulk of the roots are retained on the old half, the new front piece will have nothing to rely on and will die.

Carefully place the thumb and forefinger around and between the few growth(s) you wish to remove from the main plant and gently prize the two sections of the plant apart, at the same time endeavouring to make sure that as many roots as possible stay on both pieces. Here again, a light dusting of the wound with a fungal preparation is advantageous. The watering requirements are the same as for newly repotted paphiopedilums.

Watering and feeding

The frequency and amount of watering depends greatly on the general greenhouse humidity and conditions, the type of compost in which the plants are potted and the type of pot used. For example, clay is more thirsty than polypropylene. The plants should be watered twice a week on average, with daily overhead sprays or mistings. You can

Above: These four photographs illustrate a progression through four generations of paphiopedilum breeding, which led to the finest white hybrids in the world – the Miller's Daughters. The line is dominated by three species first used in hybridization at the end of last century: *P. insigne, P. bellatulum* and *P. niveum*. The vigorous growth of the resulting hybrids is derived from *insigne* – a small flowered species – while the full flower shape and predominantly white colour come from *bellatulum* and *niveum*.

P. Astarte (far left) has all three species in its background, and although it has inherited the white colour, the flower is small (4.5cm; 1.75in across). Crossed with *P.* Actaeus, a hybrid with *insigne* in its background, the famous *P.* F.C. Puddle (FCC/RHS) was produced (centre left). This hybrid combines vigour with larger white flowers, and longer flower stems. *P.* F.C. Puddle was crossed with *P.* Chardmoore 'Mrs Cowburn' (FCC/RHS), which also had *insigne* in its background, to produce the Dusty Miller line, of which *P.* Dusty Miller 'Altitude' (centre) is an example. In this line the *bellatulum* and *niveum* influence is obvious in the large, rounded white flowers, which are lightly speckled with pink. Their influence is carried further in the beautiful Miller's Daughters, which were produced from a cross between *P.* Dusty Miller 'Mary' (AM/RHS & GMM) and the yellow-flowered, *P.* Chantal 'Aloha'. P. Miller's Daughter 'Delilah' (above) is a superb example, with its pink pouch and full-shaped, pink-speckled flowers, 12cm (4.75in) across. *Photo X1*

always introduce a foliar feed into the misting process to give plants further benefit during the summer months. It is always beneficial to allow plants to partially dry out between waterings, but do not allow the compost to become parched, as it will then be virtually impossible to re-establish it.

Be careful when watering mature plants, especially in the winter, not to allow the water to lie in the centre of the growths, and thereby damage the buds and flowers with water deposits.

A bark-based compost needs regular feeding with a liquid fertilizer during the summer months, and to a lesser extent in winter. Any liquid brand is suitable if used with caution. The frequency of feeding can be increased, using the recommended pot plant strengths, as the hours of daylight increase, but should be decreased again as winter approaches, because the reduced daylight makes it difficult for the plants to photosynthesize and absorb the nutrients. The compost should be fertilized about once every ten days in summer, reducing to once a month in winter, and washed through with water between feeds to clear the salt deposits.

Pests and diseases

Pests will not often occur in the paphiopedilum house, as the necessarily high humidity is a deterrent to most, such as red spider and white fly. However, paphiopedilums may be attacked by more pests when they are grown as part of a mixed collection in one house. Pests may also be transferred from an infected plant brought into the greenhouse. In such a case, mealy bug and scale insects can be a stubborn problem, but one that is satisfactorily controlled by the use of a systemic insecticide containing dimethoate. Moss fly – whose larvae can cause trouble by chewing up the compost – greenfly and others will also succumb to such an insecticide.

Fortunately, paphiopedilums are tolerant of most insecticides, so careful use of your own preferred brand will probably give good results, but the emphasis must be on 'careful use' – a lackadaisical attitude when measuring quantities of chemicals has had drastic results more than once in the history of orchid growing. It is a good idea to invest in a chemical vaporizer, which has a 'blanket' effect on many insects.

Slugs and snails (including the tiny snails that hatch out in the sphagnum moss when it is brought into the warmth of the greenhouse) will also cause havoc if not controlled. Therefore, a monthly watering with a liquid slug killer is necessary.

You should also be on guard against mice during the late autumn and winter months. They try to get into the warmth of the greenhouse while the weather is cold, and will damage any young buds and flowers around. They also love young pollens and will take seed pods too, so no time should be lost in placing warfarin in the greenhouse, should such a visitor be suspected.

Diseases among these popular plants are not very common, and are best eliminated by precaution rather than cure. If you aim for and achieve a scrupulously clean greenhouse, a sour and dirty atmosphere will not occur, and most troubles will be avoided. Care should, of course, be taken to make sure that there is no contact with infected plants from outside sources.

Bud damp is one of the most common annoyances, but even this may be kept to a minimum by the use of the circulation fans, coupled with careful watering. This last takes the form of not allowing water to lie in the crown of the leaves where the bud emerges. Should the worst happen, and bud rot develop into leaf rot, this can be quickly apprehended by pulling off the leaf (or merely cutting away the affected area if it consists of a small patch), and dusting with orthocide powder. One thorough application is usually quite sufficient to halt most cases of this disease.

Another condition detrimental to good culture is root rot. However, this is something that should never occur when the plants enjoy good drainage and the correct watering technique is applied. In the event of a casualty, the affected plant should be immediately removed from its pot and the old potting medium thoroughly cleaned away, together with the diseased roots. A dusting with orthocide would also be beneficial. The plant should then be repotted in fresh compost in a clean pot, well soaked with water and then left unwatered for a week to ten days. Subsequent watering should be infrequent, as for newly repotted plants.

Species and hybrids

The following list of species and hybrids does not attempt to include all those known in the world, but simply to provide a selection of some of the more familiar and perhaps more common ones. Most of them are subjects for the intermediate house although a few can be grown in cool conditions, and one or two, which grow wild in hotter regions, need more warmth and direct light. The orchid supplier from whom you purchase your plants will be able to provide all the relevant information.

The photographs show the wide variations in flower colour and shape that have been obtained by hybridizers over the years. Many of these have won awards from the Royal Horticultural Society, and some have been awarded the George Moore Medal (GMM) – presented by the RHS for the best paphiopedilum produced each year.

A selection of plants for your own collection can only be made on a personal basis, and no expert can advise on what colour to choose or how much to pay. Therefore, listen to all the good advice you can find, but remember the final choice is always yours!

Paphiopedilum Species

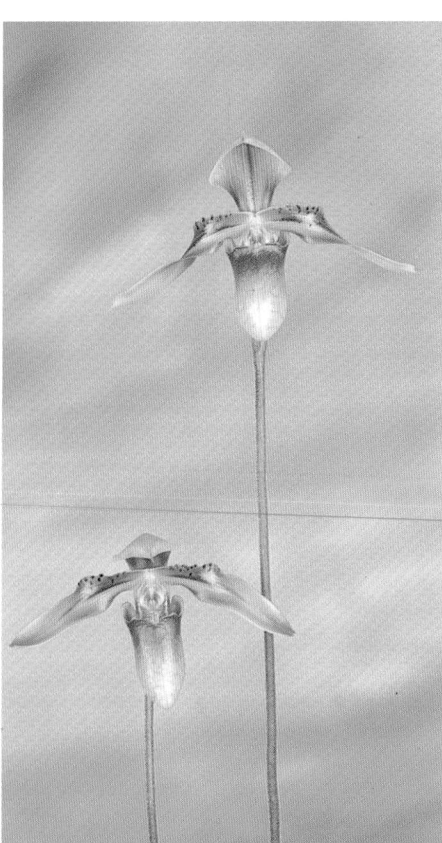

Paphiopedilum appletonianum

◑*Intermediate* ❀*Spring*

Left: This species produces large flowers, 10cm (4in) across, of a greenish-brown colour. It comes from the Himalayas and Thailand and flowers in the spring.

Photo X 1/3

Paphiopedilum barbatum

◑*Intermediate* ❀*Spring-Autumn*

Right: Native to Thailand and Malaysia, this species produces rather stout light green leaves, mottled with dark green. The single flowers, 10cm (4in) across, are borne on a 25cm (10in) stem, and are dark red-brown, with brighter red stripes on the dorsal petal. This species was crossed with *P. villosum* in 1869 to produce the first hybrid paphiopedilum.

Photo X ½

Paphiopedilum bellatulum

◑●*Intermediate/Warm* ❀*Spring*

Below: One of the most beautiful of all the species, this native of Burma and Thailand has broad, fleshy leaves that are distinctly mottled and veined with lighter green. As the flower stem is very short, the lovely 6cm (2.5in) flower often nestles in the foliage. The broad, drooping petals are white or ivory, with maroon spots of varying size and density.

Photo X 2

Paphiopedilum callosum

◑*Intermediate* ❀*Spring/Summer*

Left: This species is a vigorous grower, producing long distinctly mottled leaves. The long-lasting flower is borne on a tall stem, up to 38cm (15in) in length, which makes it very popular with the cut flower trade. The flowers, which open in the spring and summer, are 10cm (4in) across, and coloured in varying shades of purple.

Photo X 1 1/3

Paphiopedilum chamberlainium

◑*Intermediate* ❀*All year*

Below: The long leaves of this Sumatran species are bright green on top and burgundy coloured underneath. The flower stem is very long, 46cm (18in) in length, and produces as many as eight flowers at a time throughout the year. The flowers,5cm (2in) across, vary in colour from yellow to brown, green or red, and have attractive twisted petals.

Photo X 1

Paphiopedilum charlesworthii

◑*Intermediate* ❀*Autumn*

Left: A native of India, this species produces plain green leaves and a single flower on a 15cm (6in) stem. Opening in autumn, the long-lasting flowers are very dainty, 6cm (2.5in) across, reddish-brown in colour with a pretty pink fan-shaped dorsal sepal.

Photo X 1/2

Paphiopedilum ciliolare

◑*Intermediate* ❀*Spring/Summer*

Below: A native of the Philippines, this species has very stout leaves, about 15cm (6in) long and 5cm (2in) wide. The plant bears a single flower, up to 7.5cm (3in) diameter. The petals are greenish pink, with black spots, some of which are hairy. The pouch is greenish brown and the dorsal speal is pale pink, heavily striped with dark green. The flowers open in the spring and early summer.

Photo X 2/3

Paphiopedilum curtisii

◑*Intermediate* ❀*Spring/Summer*

Right: This Sumatran species usually has no more than four leaves, and a single flower, borne on a 20cm (8in) stem. Blooming in spring and summer the 11.5cm (4.5in) flowers are greenish-maroon in colour with small dark purple spots on the dorsal sepals and petals.

Photo X 2½

Paphiopedilum dayanum

◑*Intermediate* ❀*Spring*

Below: The leaves of this species vary in colour from light to dark green and may be mottled. The single, brownish-purple flower, 10-13cm (4-5in) across, is produced in spring on a 30cm (12in) stem. The petals are covered with small purplish warts and long hairs. This species comes from Borneo.

Photo X ⅓

Paphiopedilum delenatii

◑*Intermediate* ❀*Summer*

Below: This species, which comes from Vietnam, has very dark green, heavily mottled leaves. The flowers, produced in summer, and borne on a 20cm (8in) long stem, are 7.5cm (3in) across, and soft rose pink in colour. This is one of the few fragrant paphiopedilums.

Photo X ⅓

Paphiopedilum glaucophyllum

◑*Intermediate* ❀*Spring*

Right: Native to Java, this species has long, bluish-green leaves, and a long flower stem, up to 46cm (18in) in length, which bears a succession of flowers in the spring. The flowers may be 7.5cm (3in) across, and are light green, shading to dark green on the dorsal petals and sepals, with some brownish markings. The pouch is mauve or wine-rose in colour.

Photo X ¾

Paphiopedilum hirsutissimum

◑*Intermediate* ❀*Spring*

Below: The flowers of this Himalayan species are difficult to describe. They are basically purplish in colour, ranging from blackish-purple in the centre of the flower, to bright violet purple at the petal tips. The pouch is brownish-purple. The plant gets its name from areas of black hair on the petals.

Photo X 1

Paphiopedilum insigne

◑*Intermediate* ❀*Autumn-Spring*

Right: This Himalayan species is very easy to grow. It flowers from autumn to spring, producing only one, occasionally two 4.5cm (1.75in) flowers to a stem. The flowers vary in colour from clear greenish-yellow to a brownish-yellow with purple spots on the petals and dorsal sepal. The petals are long, pendulous and twisted.

Photo X ¾

Paphiopedilum lowii

◑*Intermediate* ❀*Spring/Summer*

Right: Similar to *P. haynaldianum*, this species produces from three to five flowers, up to 15cm (6in) across, on one very long stem. The flowers, which open in spring and summer, are basically yellow-green, patched and mottled with dark purple. This native of Sarawak is one of the few epiphytic paphiopedilums.

Photo X ¾

Paphiopedilum parishii

◑*Intermediate* ❀*Spring-Autumn*

Below: This very striking species comes from Burma and Thailand and, like *P. lowii*, often grows epiphytically. The long narrow leaves are very smooth and bright glossy green. The erect flower stem, which can grow to 60cm (24in) in height, bears four to seven flowers, each about 7.5cm (3in) across, from spring to autumn. The twisted petals are long and pendulous, purplish brown in overall colour, and spotted towards the flower centre. The pouch is greenish-brown, and the dorsal sepal greenish-yellow.

Photo X ⅓

Paphiopedilum purpuratum

◑*Intermediate* ❀*Summer/Autumn*

Below: This species, which comes from Hong Kong, has pale and dark green mottled leaves and very distinctive flowers. Opening in summer and autumn, the flowers are 7.5cm (3in) across, and purple-crimson in overall colour. The dorsal sepal is white, striped with purple.

Photo X ½

Paphiopedilum rothschildianum
◑*Intermediate* ❀*Summer*
Above: This species from New Guinea, originally classified as *P. new-guineaense*, is one of the most striking paphiopedilums, and is much sought after by growers. The straight, leathery leaves are bright glossy green and can measure up to 60cm (24in) in length. The long flower stem carries two to five flowers, which can be as much as 29cm (11.5in) across. The flower markings are complicated, the overall colour being cinnamon yellow to greenish-brown, with dark brown stripes on the long petals and pointed dorsal sepal. The plant normally flowers in the summer.
Photo X $\frac{1}{5}$

Paphiopedilum spicerianum
◑*Intermediate* ❀*Autumn/Winter*
Above: A native of Assam, this species has broad-leaves with wavy margins, dark green above and spotted with purple underneath. In autumn and winter one or two 7.5cm (3in) flowers are borne on a 30cm (12in) stem. They are distinctive in markings and shape and play an important role in the breeding of hybrids.
Photo X $1\frac{1}{3}$

Paphiopedilum venustum
◑*Intermediate* ❀*Spring*
Left: The leaves of this species are heavily marbled with grey and green. One or occasionally two flowers, 7.5cm (3in) across, are borne on a 15-23cm (6-9in) stem. The petals and lip are basically yellow-green, tinged with rose-red, and the petals are slightly hairy. The dorsal sepal is white, strongly striped with green. The plant blooms in early spring.
Photo X $\frac{1}{2}$

Paphiopedilum Hybrids

PAPHIOPEDILUM
Cameo 'Wyld Court' (AM/RHS)
◑*Intermediate* ✿*Winter*

Right: A famous 'old' hybrid, this plant is still used in breeding today for its heavily spotted flowers, long flower stems and production of strong seedlings. The flowers are 11.5-13cm (4.5-5in) across, the petals and lip are red-brown, and the dorsal sepal is greenish-white, heavily spotted with red.
Photo X 1

PAPHIOPEDILUM
Chipmunk 'Vermont' (AM/RHS)
◑*Intermediate* ✿*Winter*

Below: The photograph shows clearly how *P.* Chipmunk 'Vermont' (AM/RHS) (centre) has inherited from its parents the strong brown markings and flat, round flower shape of *P.* Dalla (left), and the longer flower stem and larger flower of *P.* Gitana 'Nobilor' (right). The 11cm (4.25in) flowers are borne singly in winter. They are rich green in colour with distinctive chocolate-brown markings.
Photo X ½

PAPHIOPEDILUM
Danella 'Chilton' (AM/RHS)
◑*Intermediate* ❀*Winter*
Below: This plant illustrates one of the most interesting new colours to be produced, and is on the way to achieving the sought-after perfect clear orange. In addition, it is a lovely variety, being vigorous and easy to grow. It flowers in the winter, bearing beautifully shaped flowers on long stems.
Photo X ½

PAPHIOPEDILUM
Honey Gorse 'Sunshine' (AM/RHS)
◑*Intermediate* ❀*Winter*
Left: The first plant to combine the characteristics of both the green and yellow paphiopedilum groups, the 10cm (4in) flowers of this hybrid are dark yellow-green. Deeper emerald green hybrids are now being bred, but this plant will take some beating for its heavy texture – a feature usually lacking in the green colour group.
Photo X 1½

PAPHIOPEDILUM
Miller's Daughter 'Snow Maiden'
◑*Intermediate* ❀*Winter*
Above: This line represents the most advanced breeding for white-flowered hybrids in the world. There is nothing to compare with the perfection of the Miller's Daughter hybrids for flower sizes, shape and vigour. The 13cm (5in) flowers of this particular plant (*P.* Dusty Miller 'Mary' AM/RHS & GMM × *P.* Chantal 'Aloha') are white, lightly speckled all over with pinkish-brown.
Photo X ⅓

PAPHIOPEDILUM
Royale 'Downland' (AM/RHS & GMM)

◑*Intermediate* ❀*Winter*

Right: This hybrid is a seedling from the illustrious *P.* Paeony 'Regency' (AM/RHS) line, and has very large flowers, 15cm (6in) across, borne on long flower spikes. The flowers, which are an interesting colour combination of soft rose-red shaded with green, open in the winter.
Photo X ¾

PAPHIOPEDILUM
Royalet 'Valentine'

◑*Intermediate* ❀*Winter*

Above: An example of how much a modern hybrid (*P.* Paeony 'Regency', AM/RHS) can improve the flower shape and texture of a species parent (*P. barbatum*), in just one generation. The flowers, which are not more than 10cm (4in) across, are rose-red with darker veining, and open in the winter.
Photo X ½

PAPHIOPEDILUM
Small World 'Adventure'

◑*Intermediate* ❀*Winter*

Right: Named in 1959, in honour of the crossing of the Atlantic by four people in a hot-air balloon, this hybrid has proved to be one of the most wonderful parents, giving only its best characteristics to its progeny. (Most of them have 'world' in their names.) The 13cm (5in) flower has warm rich amber-brown petals and lip, with mahogany overtones, and a green-flushed white dorsal sepal spotted with red. Like most paphiopedilum hybrids, the plant flowers in the winter.
Photo X ⅔

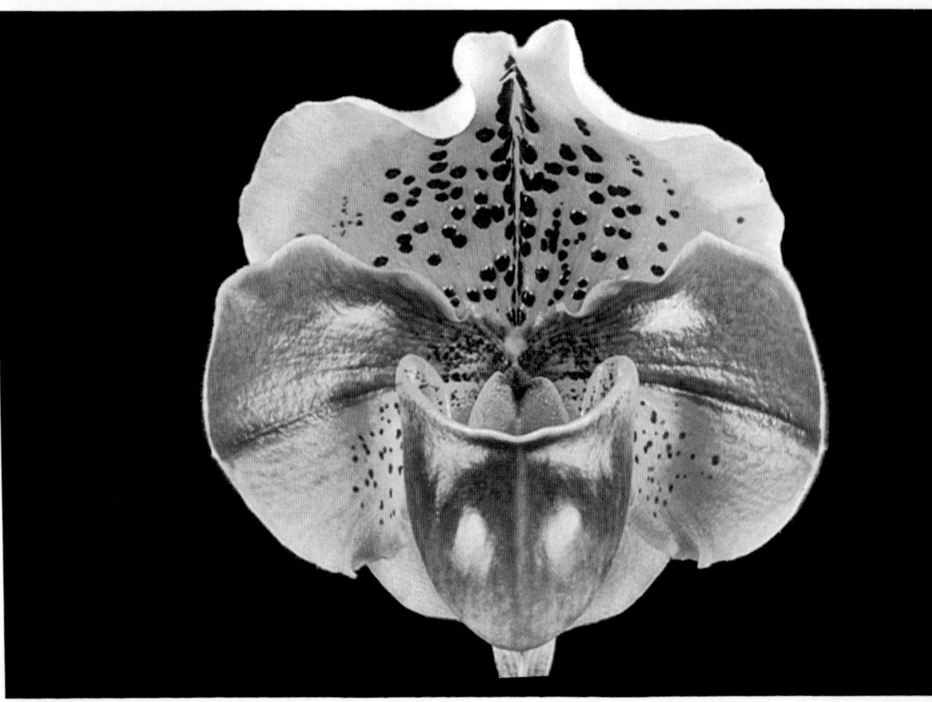

PAPHIOPEDILUM
Silvara 'Halo' (AM/AOS)

◑*Intermediate* ❀*Winter*

Left: An award winner in America, and a member of an extensive and vigorous group of hybrids, this plant has proved to be a useful and productive parent. The flowers, 9cm (3.5in) across, are white marked with yellow in the lip and on the petals, and open in the winter.
Photo X 1

PAPHIOPEDILUM
Vanda M. Pearman 'Downland' (AM/RHS)

◑*Intermediate* ❀*Winter*

Above: A recent cross between *P. delenatii* and *P. bellatulum,* this hybrid combines the rounded flower shape of the latter species with the longer flower stem and delicate colouring of the former. The beautiful 7.5cm (3in) flowers, which open in winter, are basically white, finely spotted with crimson, the spots becoming more dense on the pouch.
Photo X 2/3

PAPHIOPEDILUM
Winston Churchill

◑*Intermediate* ❀*Winter*

Left: One of the most famous of modern paphiopedilums, this plant is generally thought of as an American hybrid because the stock was bought by American breeders in the 1940s. However, it is British-bred and is proving to be a very fine parent. The 13cm (5in) flowers are red, and the white dorsal sepal is spotted with red. The plant blooms in the winter.
Photo X 3/4

PHALAENOPSIS

Phalaenopsis species have a characteristic elegance. Some bear many flowers: for example, on *P. schilleriana*, it is not unusual to find as many as 70 flowers on a single spike. The more flamboyant species have beautifully marked foliage, greys and silver overlying the rich green of a tongue-shaped leaf, and pink or white flowers 7.5cm (3in) or more across. In recent years various hybrids of *Phalaenopsis* have been grown extensively for the cut flower trade, the white flowers being popular for wedding bouquets.

Phalaenopsis in the wild

All species are native to the Far East, but are found specifically in an area stretching from Assam and Burma to the Moluccas and, especially, the Philippines. The name *Phalaenopsis* is derived from *phalaina*, a moth, and *opsis*, the appearance, and was suggested by the Dutch botanist Blume, who, when the first specimen was found in 1852 and named *Phalaenopsis amabilis*, likened them to tropical moths in flight.

Phalaenopsis are epiphytic or lithophytic plants, which grow attached to the branches and trunks of trees, rocks and mossy banks overhanging water, and are almost always found in deep shade. A few species grow so close to the seashore that they receive salt spray at times. (A gardener in charge of an early orchid collection in England, who was particularly successful with this genus, is said to have dressed the gravel of the staging and paths periodically with salt; this could do no harm but it is doubtful whether it had any bearing on his success!)

Three species, *P. lowii*, *P. parishii* and *P. esmeralda*, are deciduous in their native habitat, where they grow on small bushes and limestone rocks. But in cultivation, where they are not subject to such drastic changes in the seasons, they usually keep their leaves. The leathery leaves can be quite large, up to 46cm (18in) long and 7cm (2.8in) wide, and are succulent to the extent that they can store water. The majority of species flourish in the wild where the temperature is naturally uniform, ranging from 24 °C (75°F) at night to 35°C (95°F) during the day, with a rainfull around 2,030mm (80in) a year, so that the atmosphere is nearly always saturated. For this reason *Phalaenopsis* plants do not have pseudobulbs.

The roots are remarkably freely produced and adhere firmly to whatever supports them, be it tree or rock. In cultivation, when the plants are repotted, it is virtually impossible to release the roots from the sides of the pot without leaving half the root covering—and inevitably the growing tip—behind. In *P. schilleriana* and *P. stuartiana* the roots are silver-coloured, wide and flattened, and grow to some length, not so much in search of food as to provide good anchorage. Food is mainly supplied by the humid atmosphere, well laden with contributions from the rotting vegetation below, and absorbed through roots and leaves.

In the natural habitat the flower spikes hang in cascades, as do the long, heavy leaves. The plants are almost continually in flower, and often flower more than once from the original spike. When the first crop of flowers has dropped, branches on the spike will often produce another crop of buds. If you want to use the flowers for decoration, fully cut the spike to just above the uppermost node. The plant will then produce a secondary spike within a short time. Flower spikes are usually staked upright under cultivation.

When conditions are favourable, plants are capable of producing keikis, or 'eyes', which grow into young plants that make their own roots. In the wild it is not uncommon to see large clumps of plants whose flower spikes have produced keikis that have established themselves further along the branch, producing flower spikes of their own.

In some species, including *P. violacea*, *P. amboinensis* and *P. mariea*, after the flowers have been fertilized and the seedpod is being formed, the petals and sepals become thickened and green like the leaves and presumbly function in the same way.

Phalaenopsis in cultivation

The natural environment of *Phalaenopsis* species provides high average temperatures, high humidity and good shade. Therefore, the plants succeed best when an entire greenhouse is devoted to them. The ideal structure is a low-span house, preferably with the first 61cm (2ft) of the building below ground level. Nevertheless, rewarding results are now being achieved in less exacting conditions. When a mixed collection of orchids is being grown it is usually possible to provide a small area which receives more heat, humidity and shade than the rest of the house.

Many hybrids are now being grown successfully in centrally heated homes, but these are generally fully matured plants, comparatively tolerant if humidity is lower than ideal. At least warmth and shade can be provided in home culture, and a tray or saucer of wet gravel will give some immediate humidity. An increasing number of home growers are installing fully automatic growing cases which provide controlled conditions.

Temperatures for growth

Phalaenopsis usually start growing in early spring, when the night temperature should not be allowed to fall below 18°C (64.5°F), with a daytime rise to 24°-27°C (75°-80.5°F). These temperatures should be maintained until late autumn when a reduction in temperature to a minimum of 15°C (59°F) at night, rising to 18°-21°C (64.5°-70°F), will be required. Some variation may occur as the weather outside dictates, and an occasional drop to 10°C (50°F) on winter nights will do no harm provided the plants have not been heavily watered and humidity is low. Some commercial growers use the lowering of the temperature to 10°C to initiate flower spikes if the timing of flower production is important for marketing.

Ventilation

Conventional roof ventilation must be operated with great care: as a rule the ventilators should only be opened on the hottest summer days, when the temperature may rise above 27°C (80.5°F). How much they are opened will depend partly on the direction and force of the wind: draught should be excluded at all costs and the aperture should never be so great that there is a heavy loss in humidity. On the other hand, whatever the season, the overall conditions must be kept buoyant to avoid pockets of stagnant air, and good air movement is especially important during the flowering season. In recent years electrically operated fans have given excellent results.

Shading

During the winter months, when the plants will be in a state of least activity, no shading is required unless there is exceptionally bright weather. But from early spring shading will be necessary. As the important factor is not only to provide shade but to keep the glass cool, the ideal form of shading is one suspended

Right: If shaded from strong sun by blinds during the growing season and given humid conditions, phalaenopsis orchids will provide a colourful display from spring to late autumn.

above the glass, allowing sunlight to filter through. Lath blinds suspended 15-23cm (6-9in) above the glass on a metal or wooden frame have proved satisfactory, as the blinds can be rolled up or down according to weather conditions. A colour wash applied to the glass is less satisfactory as it is liable to wash off and thus require several applications, with the possible risk of scorch occurring between. Where seedlings are grown, heavier shading is required.

Composts and potting

When selecting a compost it is again advisable to remember the native environment and to think in terms of root anchorage rather than of compost as such. As already mentioned, fir or pine bark has the properties required, and can be broken down to a size suitable for the plant to be potted. In general, plants of flowering size are potted in bark crushed to pieces of about 5-12mm (0.2-0.5in); for small seedlings just produced from culture flasks, a much finer grade should be used. In both cases the addition of a little charcoal helps to keep the compost sweet.

Repotting should normally be done during the growing season, but if the condition of the rooting medium has deteriorated badly, the plant should be repotted immediately, whatever the season. Mature plants need fresh material in their second year. Seedlings should be repotted at least twice in the growing season until they have reached full maturity in the third or fourth year.

The potting procedure is simple. After shaking off all the old compost, trim away dead roots and shorten any that are excessively long before settling the plant in its new container and topping up with the selected compost. Polypropylene pots or pans are preferable to the conventional clay. Some growers prefer to use hanging baskets but these dry out more rapidly and will therefore require more frequent watering.

Propagation and division

Generally, vegetative propagation is associated with the *Phalaenopsis* species rather than hybrids and is limited to keikis, or new plantlets produced from the nodes on the flower stalk. In the natural growing conditions of high humidity and heat keikis are formed readily. Under cultivation, they can be cut from the parent plant when a number of roots have appeared and then potted up in the normal way.

Hybrids do not produce keikis as readily as the species, but where more stock is required of a specific clone, this can be achieved by subjecting the nodes to laboratory treatment. This is a highly scientific process and generally practised only by commercial growers (see page 95). New hybrids can be grown from

Above: Phalaenopsis often produce plantlets, or keikis, at the nodes on the flower spikes. When they have formed several roots, these keikis can be cut from the parent plant and potted up.

Below and Right: Be careful not to get water in the crown of phalaenopsis as this will cause rot, which can be devastating. Although the plant appears to be dead, a new shoot (right) may grow if given correct conditions.

seed, but special facilities are required. Details are given on page 94.

Watering and feeding

Because the atmosphere of their native habitat is virtually saturated, it is necessary to maintain very high humidity during the growing season. From early spring to late autumn sprinkling all surfaces with water two or three times a day will help, particularly in the late evening during the height of summer. The overall moisture and general conditions of the greenhouse will determine how often the plants should be watered. As a guide, large plants may require watering once a week, while smaller ones need more frequent attention. The density of the rooting medium is also important, as the denser it is, the more water will be held. The epiphytic nature of phalaenopsis necessitates a compost that retains some moisture, is well aerated, and does not decompose too quickly; for all-round good results, pulverized fir bark is best as it is nearest to natural conditions.

Phalaenopsis are fast-growing plants with no pseudobulbs in which to store food and they therefore require feeding. A fertilizer with a high nitrogen content should be applied at fortnightly intervals, when the plants are watered.

Pests and diseases

The main pests are slugs and snails and you should keep a lookout for these at all times. Occasionally water will lodge in the centre growth of a plant and rot will ensue. If this happens little can be done other than to dry out the area as quickly as possible and treat it with captan. The original plant will be permanently disfigured, but occasionally secondary growths appear from its base.

Species and hybrids

In the following pages, some of the most popular varieties are illustrated. Phalaenopsis are very free-flowering and it is possible with only a small collection to have several plants in flower throughout the year. They are easy to grow provided the few basic requirements are met.

The first species to be discovered, *Phalaenopsis amabilis,* has pure white flowers with a red-spotted lip and yellow throat. This species was used extensively in the early days of breeding, and has provided the backbone of all the present-day high quality white phalaenopsis hybrids.

Although many of the species have pink or white flowers, with hybridization and selective breeding new colours and contrasts are continually being produced, notably the 'peppermint striped' varieties, such as *P.* Hennessy.

Phalaenopsis Species

Phalaenopsis amboinensis

●*Warm* ❀*Spring-Autumn*

Above: There are essentially two forms of *P. amboinensis*. The best known and perhaps more extensively used in breeding has flowers with rich dark brown bars on a pale green base. In the second form the base colour is almost cream with bars of pale mustard yellow. The plants are of compact growth, with pale yellow-green foliage, and tend to produce several flower spikes at the same time, normally 15-30.5cm (6-12in) long. The flowers, 2.5-5cm (1-2in) across, are borne singly over a long period through spring to autumn.

Given appropriate conditions, this species responds well in cultivation. The first hybrid was made with *P. amabilis*, and was registered as *P.* Deventeriana in 1927.

Photo X 1½

Phalaenopsis aphrodite

●*Warm* ❀*Autumn*

Right: This species was first discovered in 1837 in the Philippines, and at that time was thought to be the same as *P. amabilis*. However, as more phalaenopsis were introduced into cultivation and knowledge of the genus increased, *P. aphrodite* eventually came to be recognized as a distinct species. The leaves are deep green with a high gloss. Arching flower spikes, carrying many exceptionally long-lasting blooms of a pure glistening white, 5cm (2in) across, are produced in late autumn. The plants grow well in cultivation.

Photo X 1½

Phalaenopsis lueddemanniana

●*Warm* ❀*Spring/Summer*

Above: This is a free-flowering species, which is easy to grow and one of the most variable of the *Phalaenopsis* genus. The leaves are usually light green, broad and long. The flower spikes, several of which may be produced at the same time, each carry up to 20, 2.5cm (1in) flowers that open in succession throughout spring and summer. The sepals and petals are almost white or yellow, marked with bars or spots ranging from pink to deep purple, and the small lip is usually purple. If the plant is given cooler and more shady conditions when the first buds appear, richer colours will be produced. The flower spikes readily produce keikis at their nodes.

The species has been widely used in breeding with great success, two of the best known hybrids from *P. lueddemanniana* being *P.* Golden Sands and *P.* Cabrillo Star. As the name suggests, *P.* Golden Sands is a fine yellow hybrid, and *P.* Cabrillo Star is a large white bloom heavily spotted with red.

Photo X 2

Phalaenopsis equestris

●*Warm* ❀*Autumn/Winter*

Above: This species (for many years synonymous with *P. rosea*) is said to be the commonest phalaenopsis of the Philippines. It was introduced into England in 1848 by James Veitch. The plant is comparatively compact in growth and has leathery, dull green leaves some 15cm (6in) long and 7.5cm (3in) wide. The very graceful arching flower spikes bear pale rose flowers, 2.5cm (1in) across, with a darker oval lip. The flowers open in autumn and winter.

P. equestris was used as a parent to produce the first manmade hybrid phalaenopsis, *P.* Artemis, in 1892. It still plays a part in modern hybridizing where compact, small-flowered plants are in demand.

Photo X ¾

Phalaenopsis mannii

●*Warm* ❀*Spring/Summer*

Left: This species grows wild at high altitudes in Assam, where *Vanda coerulea* is also found. It is the least flamboyant of the *Phalaenopsis* genus, and not a large grower. The flowers, deep yellow in colour, heavily barred with chestnut-brown and borne on short branched spikes during spring and summer, are about 5cm (2in) across. Although a subject for the warm house, the plant is able to withstand temperatures as low as 7°C (45°F) without being harmed. *P. mannii* has had great influence by contributing yellow flower colour to its hybrids.

Photo X 1¼

Phalaenopsis mariea

○Cool ❀Spring/Summer

Below: Little is known about this species. Closely related to *P. lueddemanniana,* it was found in 1878 growing in the Philippines at high altitudes in deep shade. In cultivation the plant should be grown in the coolest section of the greenhouse.

The flowers, which open in spring and summer, are pale yellow, banded with chestnut and are 2.5-4cm (1-1.5in) across. Although the plant has been little used in hybridization in the past, it is possible that some interesting progeny may result from its use as a parent.

Photo X ½

Phalaenopsis sanderiana

●Warm ❀Spring

Below: It has been suggested that *Phalaenopsis sanderiana* is a natural hybrid between *P. aphrodite* and *P. schilleriana.* But both parents are not found in the same locality, and it is now generally accepted as a species in its own right. The foliage resembles that of *P. aphrodite,* being bright glossy green, and the plant is a strong grower. The flush pink flowers, produced in the spring, are 7.5cm (3in) in diameter, and particularly beautiful.

By 1946 some 17 hybrids of this species had been registered, and it is still being used in breeding today.

Photo X ⅔

Phalaenopsis schilleriana

●Warm ❀Spring

Above: This is the best known of all phalaenopsis, and is held in great esteem. It was discovered in Manilla in 1858 growing on trees, often very high up. The plants fix themselves to the branches and trunks by numerous flattened roots. In cultivation these roots grow to considerable lengths along any firm surface within their reach, and are almost impossible to release without breaking. As they mature they develop a beautiful silver sheen.

As a decorative plant, *P. schilleriana* is hard to beat; the handsome leaves, up to 46cm (18in) or more in length, are deep green, marbled and blotched with grey and silver. The flowers 5-7.5cm (2-3in) across, of a delicate rose purple, are often borne in great numbers during early spring on a branched arching spike, which may grow to 91cm (3ft) in length.

Photo X 1

Phalaenopsis stuartiana

●*Warm* ❀*Spring*

Above: This species is very similar to *P. schilleriana,* and when not in flower it is virtually impossible to tell them apart: the foliage is the same deep green, marbled in grey and silver, and the roots have the same flattened appearance. In the wild it is said to be found always closely associated with water, sometimes close to the shoreline, where the plants are subjected to salt-water spray. The spike habit and quantity of flowers are also like those of *P. schilleriana,* but in *P. stuartiana* the upper sepal and two side petals are white. Of the two lower sepals one half is white and the other heavily spotted with reddish-purple; the orange-yellow lip is also spotted. The overall appearance when in flower is thus distinct and striking. The flowers open in spring.

Many hybrids have been registered from this species, all showing the characteristic spotting, and it is valuable for introducing orange shades to the lip, when crossed with white hybrids.

Photo X ¾

Phalaenopsis violacea

●*Warm* ❀*Summer*

Left: This species, first discovered in 1859, has two distinct types, one from Borneo, the other from Malaya. Although it may not be the easiest species to maintain in good flowering condition, it is nevertheless very attractive, as it combines beauty with fragrance. The 7.5cm (3in) flowers of this plant from Borneo, which have the fragrance of violets, are borne in summer on a short pendulous spike, often in succession. The Malaysian form is smaller and of a fuller shape, about 6.5cm (2.5in) across. The plant requires deep shade and high humidity.

The first hybrid, *P. violacea* × *P. amabilis,* was registered by James Veitch in 1887 as *P.* Harrietiae. In recent years, *P. violacea* has been used extensively in breeding, with great success.

Photo X 2½

Phalaenopsis Hybrids

PHALAENOPSIS
Barbara Moler
●*Warm* ❀*Spring-Autumn*

Right: The parents of this important hybrid are *P.* Donnie Brandt and *P.* Spica (syn. Yardstick). *P.* Spica is the result of a two species cross between *P. fasciata* and *P. lueddemanniana*. *P.* Barbara Moler is a comparatively compact grower, with leaves some 30cm (12in) long and 10cm (4in) wide. The flower spikes, which are long—up to 46cm (18in)—and branched, bear flowers for many months from spring to autumn. Individually, the flowers are 7cm (2.75in) across, and of very heavy texture. There are two colour forms. The best known is white with heavy pink spotting, giving an overall appearance of rich pink. The second form can best be described as yellow; the base colour is greenish-yellow overlaid with yellow-chestnut blotches.

P. Barbara Moler is already proving to be a very important parent in breeding for heavy texture and new colour breaks. *P.* Space Queen is an example of the type of hybrid produced from *P.* Barbara Moler breeding.
Photo X 1

PHALAENOPSIS
Hennessy
●*Warm* ❀*All year*

Below: This hybrid is an example of a peppermint-striped phalaenopsis. The plant is very free-flowering, blooming throughout the year, and the branched spikes may bear up to 30 flowers at a time. The individual flowers are 9-12cm (3.5-4.75in) across, white to light pink in basic colour, with red or pink stripes or, in some forms, spots. The lip varies in colour from deep rosy pink to orange.
Photo X ½

PHALAENOPSIS
Party Dress
●*Warm* ❀*Season varies*

Below: This hybrid produces many small, round pink flowers on branched spikes. Large specimen plants are particularly beautiful.
Photo X ⅔

PHALAENOPSIS
Purbeck Sands
●*Warm* ❀*Season varies*
Above: With this hybrid a new colour was introduced into the genus. The result of crossing *P.* Golden Louis (a small yellow) with *P.* Zada (a rich round pink) has been to produce flowers, 5cm (2in) across, in very pleasing shades from light primrose to mustard pinks. The foliage also carries shades of brick red. Plants are small, compact and free-flowering at any season.
Photo X ½

PHALAENOPSIS
Space Queen
●*Warm* ❀*Season varies*
Left: This hybrid is the result of crossing *P.* Barbara Moler with *P.* Temple Cloud, thus producing beautiful flowers of heavy substance, 9-10cm (3.5-4in) across, soft pink or white, heavily spotted with red.
Photo X 1

PHALAENOPSIS
Temple Cloud
●*Warm* ❀*Season varies*
Below: Resulting from the crossing of two outstanding hybrids, *P.* Opaline and *P.* Keith Shaffer, this hybrid took on the finer points of both parents, producing pure white 11.5cm (4.5in) round blooms of heavy texture, and in turn proved to be a very successful parent. It can be in flower at any season.
Photo X ¾

VANDAS

Few orchids can surpass the beauty and drama of the vandas in foliage or flower. There are about 80 species of evergreen plants, native to China, the Himalayas, New Guinea and northern Australia.

The genus is remarkable for the great differences in the colour and sizes of the flowers. Most vandas have erect leafy stems, evergreen leaves and fleshy roots, and flowers are borne on lateral spikes, produced from the axils of the leaves. Vandas are monopodial orchids, and most are epiphytic. For horticultural purposes the leaves of vandas fall into two categories: terete, or cylindrical, as in *Vanda teres*, and strap-leaved as in *v. coerulea*. (A third group, semiterete, whose leaves are a cross between the two, is sometimes included.)

Vandas have thrived on the Hawaiian islands for many decades because of the islands' climate and ocean breezes, but the plants are not indigenous to Hawaii. Today many hybrids of vandas are available, and the plants are often prized as cut flowers. *Vanda sanderana* and Vanda coerulea are perhaps the two most important species of the genus. The flowers of *V. sanderana* are a beautiful lilac or pink colour; those of *V. coerulea* are noted for their striking blue, and thus this species is frequently cultivated.

The sepals and petals of vanda flowers are similar in size, rounded and rather flat. The lip is affixed to the base of the column; the lateral lobes may be either large or reduced in size, and the middle lobe, a part of which is usually fleshy and ridged, is also variable in form.

Vandas in cultivation

Vandas are highly epiphytic, preferring an arboreal existence on tree trunks and branches. The plants can attain heights of 2.2m (7ft), although the average height indoors is 1.2m (4ft). Their long aerial roots, measuring up to 1.2m, store food and water if necessary during periods of drought. All vandas enjoy the light, and with sufficient sunlight they may bloom two or three times a year, with as many as 50 or more flowers. Most vandas bloom in the winter, although some species come into flower in the late summer or early autumn. A healthy plant can produce as many as three or four flower spikes, each bearing up to 12 flowers that last perhaps three to four weeks on the plant.

Requirements for growth

Because vandas are tall plants, they must have sufficient vertical growing space. Most plants should be grown in the warm or intermediate greenhouse as they thrive on sunlight and heat during the day, doing best at a temperature of 26.5°C (80°F). They can survive lower daytime temperatures if absolutely necessary but not for any length of time. At night, plants should be kept in cooler temperatures: 15.5°C (60°F), if they are to be brought to perfection. Some species, such as *V. coerulea* and *V. kimballiana,* need cool daytime temperatures of about 21°C (70°F).

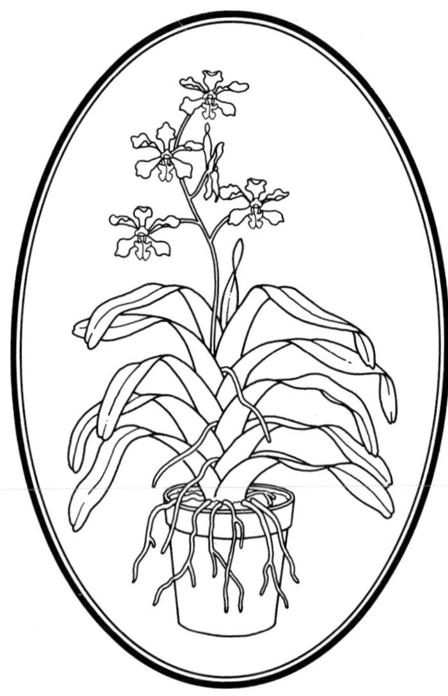

Right: A flamboyant display of vanda orchids at the World Orchid Conference in Bangkok, where they thrive in the warm, sunny climate. Although cultivated commercially, large numbers also adorn many parks and gardens.

Because vandas thrive in sun and bright light it is a good idea to hang plants high up in the greenhouse so that they receive all light possible. And, because the position of the sun in the sky changes with the season, you may need to move vandas around to obtain optimum light at all times.

The higher the temperature, the higher the humidity should be. Vandas require high humidity so daily spraying for most of the year (except in winter) is essential. Minimum humidity for plants should be about 50 percent; in lower humidity plants will not grow well (although they will not die). Higher humidity increases the risk of fungal infection, especially if days are cloudy and conditions wet. Regular damping down of the greenhouse surroundings will create excellent humidity and is especially recommended during summer months. If you are growing vandas at a window in your home, spray-mist plants with water.

A free circulation of air is necessary to keep vandas at the peak of health, as they are naturally arboreal plants and like a buoyant atmosphere. Even in winter, open vents or windows whenever possible (even if for only 30 minutes) without causing a drastic drop in temperature inside the growing area. If you cannot keep vents or windows open, run an electric fan at low speed near, but not directly at, the plants to keep the air moving. Also, try to avoid water becoming lodged in the axils of the leaves as this can cause rot.

Composts and potting

Large-grade fir bark is the accepted growing medium for vandas in containers, but they can also be grown in gravel or charcoal chunks. A good potting mix is fir bark and broken charcoal (half and half). Some growers cultivate plants successfully in cracked bricks, pumice stones or even gritty sand. The selection of the proper growing medium for your plants depends on where you live—in warmer climates you may opt for fir bark, while in cooler climes a mixture of bark and charcoal may be best.

Vandas resent being disturbed, so repot them only when absolutely necessary—about every three years. To remove the plant from a clay pot you will need to break the pot with a hammer because the roots adhere so tightly to the container. Repotting is best done in spring when most vandas are starting new growth (when the root tips are green).

Plants should be potted rather high in the container with only the basal parts of the stem and roots in compost. Plants do best in wooden baskets or clay pots, with additional holes around the base—the more air circulation at the bottom of the pot, the better for the health of the plant. But no matter what potting material is

used or what kind of container, drainage must be perfect.

Although plastic pots may be suitable for other orchids it is best not to use them for vandas. Such pots have a tendency to hold water too long and, furthermore, they are top heavy. They are, therefore, unsuitable for growing such tall plants.

Some growers cultivate vandas on large slabs of wood, and in this situation the plants require daily watering. Osmunda compost is anchored to the slab with wire and the plant roots are tied to the osmunda. It is a tricky method but after several months roots grow into the osmunda and the plants are then securely anchored.

Vegetative propagation

Vandas produce offshoots, or keikis, at various times during the year, usually in the late autumn. When these offshoots are 5-7.5cm (2-3in) high they can be cut from the 'mother' plant, using a sharp, sterile knife, and started in small pots of fir bark. The cut marks should be dusted with charcoal. To ensure maximum humidity, drape polyethylene over four sticks pushed into the container. When the offshoots are 15-18cm (6-7in) tall, move them into larger containers. Now you no longer need the polyethylene cover, but the humidity must be maintained.

If you keep your vandas for several years, and the plants become large (over 1m [39in] in height), new plants can be propagated by cutting off the top of the parent plant. You will need to remove about 30.5-46cm (12-18in) from the top. Make a clean cut on the central stem, and dust both the cut surfaces with charcoal. Place the cuttings in pots of fir bark.

Watering and feeding

During the spring and summer months vandas need plenty of moisture, so flood the pots daily in mid-summer. (Also, hose down any wood slabs if you are using them.) Make sure that containers have sufficient drainage holes because vandas do not like stagnant water.

Their aerial roots should be allowed to hang loose since they are highly specialized moisture-absorbing structures. Vandas require as much water in winter as at other times of the year, but it is best at all times to allow plants to dry out before watering them again.

After flowering, the plants need a resting period of about two weeks. During this time the growing medium should be kept just damp but never bone dry, and spray-misting continued. Increase the amount of watering again in early spring.

Although most orchids do not need much feeding, vandas thrive on plant food, which should be applied at least twice a month in spring and summer. A balanced nitrogen-phosphorus-potassium fertilizer (10-10-5) is best.

Pests and diseases

Vandas are remarkably free of pests and diseases; the leaves are too tough to be chewed by insects. Apart from snails or slugs, which sometimes attack leaves, other common plant pests are rarely found.

Occasionally, vandas develop dark, almost black, streaks, on their leaves. This is generally the result of water remaining on leaves too long or, in some rare cases, it may be due to a virus disease. When due to disease, the black streaks, which are 5cm (2in) in diameter, do not usually affect the plant but they are unsightly.

Species and hybrids

In the last few decades vandas have been used for the production of an incredible number of hybrid orchids and they can be successfully crossed with a large number of orchid groups in their subtribe Sarcanthinae. Crossing *Vanda* with *Ascocentrum,* for example, produces *Ascocenda*; and with *Renanthera, Renantanda.*

The following list is merely a sampling of the many lovely *Vanda* species and hybrids. You can buy your plants from orchid suppliers or, in some cases, at plant shops.

Vanda Species

Vanda sanderana

●*Warm* ❀*Summer*

Above: This magnificent summer-flowering orchid grows to about 61cm (2ft) or more in height, and comes from the Philippines. The leaves are 30-38cm (12-15in) long, and the flower spikes semi-erect with 7 to 20 flowers clustered together. The flowers, 13cm (5in) across, are almost flat, with the upper sepal soft rose to white in colour suffused with whitish-pink, and the lower sepals round, slightly larger, and tawny yellow crossed with red markings. The petals are smaller than the sepals and are white to rose coloured with red blotches near the base; the lip is tawny yellow, streaked with red. Although this species adjusts to varying conditions and will, if necessary tolerate some coolness, it generally grows best in the warmth and sun.

Photo X ½

Vanda coerulea

◑*Intermediate* ❀*Autumn/Winter*

Above: This is perhaps the showiest and most popular vanda for collectors. Blooming in autumn and winter with lovely pale blue flowers, *V. coerulea* is found wild in the Himalayas, Burma and Thailand, growing at about 1,220-1,830m (approx. 4,000-6,000ft). The leaves are leathery and rigid, about 25.5cm (10in) long and 2.5cm (1in) wide, and the flower stems are erect or arching to about 61cm (2ft) with from 5 to 20 flowers per spike. The flowers can be variable in colour, shape and size, but are generally 10cm (4in) across with pale blue sepals and petals and a network of darker markings. The lip is purple-blue marked with white. While most vandas revel in warmth, *V. coerulea* is a subject for the intermediate greenhouse, requiring temperatures between 13° and 18°C (15.5°-64.5°F).

Photo X ½

Vanda cristata

◑*Intermediate* ❀*Spring-Summer*

Right: This small orchid, which grows only to about 25cm (10in), is a good subject for indoor growing. It is native to high altitude areas of Nepal and Bhutan. The leaves are 15cm (6in) long and the flowers waxy and fragrant, about 5cm (2in) across. The sepals and petals are mostly yellow-green, and the entire flower is marked with blood-red longitudinal stripes and spots. Blooming from early spring until mid-summer, this is a fine orchid for those with limited space, and will tolerate evening temperatures of 13°C (55°F).

Photo X 1

Vanda sanderana var. ***alba***

●*Warm* ❀*Summer*

Left: Unusual and pretty, this lighter coloured form of *V. sanderana* is highly prized by collectors and produces rounded flowers, 12.5cm (5in) across, of heavy texture. The upper sepals and petals are white, and the lower sepals are pale mustard yellow. The flowers open in the summer.

Photo X ½

Vanda suavis var. ***tricolor***

●*Warm* ❀*Autumn/Winter*

Below: Coming from Java and Bali, this free-flowering strap-leaved epiphyte bears colourful flowers in autumn and early winter. The stems are densely leafy with curving leaves about 25cm (10in) long and 2.5cm (1in) wide. Flower spikes are horizontal, shorter than the leaves and carry 5 to 10 flowers that vary in shape and colour. Typically they have whitish-yellow sepals and petals barred or spotted with red-brown, usually flushed with pale magenta near the base. The fragrant waxy flowers are about 7.5cm (3in) across. This is an easy vanda to coax into bloom in warm sunny conditions, with temperatures of 25°C (75°C).

Photo X 1

Vanda Hybrids

VANDA
Jennie Hashimoto 'Starles'
●*Warm* ❀*Summer*

Above: This recent cross between *V. sanderana* and *V.* Onomea shows good flower form and is becoming popular with collectors. In the summer, mature specimens may bear as many as 200 flowers, with pink sepals and orange-red petals. This orchid requires growing conditions in the warm house.
Photo X ⅓

VANDA
Nelly Morley
◐●*Intermediate/Warm* ❀*Spring and Autumn*

Right: A semiterete orchid bearing many flowers, this is a cross between *V.* Emma Van Deventer and *V. sanderana.* It has become a very popular hybrid for the collector because it generally blooms twice a year, in spring and early autumn. It requires intermediate to warm conditions.
Photo X ¼

VANDA
Neva Mitchell ×
VANDA
Diane Ogawa
◑●*Intermediate/Warm* ❀*Summer/Autumn*
Right: This recent hybrid shows great promise for collectors because it can be grown in either intermediate or warm conditions. Also, it is a smaller plant, not growing above a height of 61cm (2ft). The mauve flowers are produced in summer or autumn.
Photo X 1/3

VANDA
Onomea 'Walcrest'
●*Warm* ❀*Summer*
Below: This hybrid between *V.* Rothschildiana and *V. sanderana* has proved a robust plant for warm conditions, producing many flowers of pink patterned with reddish-mauve. It grows freely and, although it normally flowers in summer, may bloom twice a year.
Photo X 1/3

VANDA
Patricia Low 'Lydia' (AM/AOS)
●*Warm* ❀*Summer*

Right: Unlike the strap-leaved vandas, the terete-leaved varieties, of which this hybrid is a fine example, have slightly smaller flowers, more widely spaced on the flower stem. The beautiful clear creamy pink flowers, which are 4-5cm (1.5-2in) across, have a striking yellow and red lip, and, characteristically, lack the markings so typical of the strap-leaved varieties. As with all the terete vandas, this plant enjoys warm, sunny conditions which are essential for successful flowering. This hybrid normally blooms in the summer.
Photo X ⅔

VANDA
Rose Davis
◑*Intermediate* ❀*Summer*

Below: This cross between *V.* Rothschildiana and *V. coerulea* has produced a beautiful deep blue flowered hybrid. The 5cm (2in) flowers are similar to those of *V.* Rothschildiana, but are slightly smaller and less rounded. The *V. coerulea* influence has meant that the plant can be grown slightly cooler than most vandas and it will thrive in the intermediate greenhouse. This hybrid may come into flower at any season, but commonly flowers in the summer.
Photo X 1½

VANDA
Rothschildiana
○*Cool* ❀*Winter*
Above: Sometimes called a species but more often known as a hybrid, this cross between *V. coerulea* and *V. sanderana* is a display of nature at her finest. The plant has 25.4cm (10in) leaves, and grows to a height of about 76cm (30in). The flower spikes are arching and crowded with 5 to 10 flowers of intense blue, almost crystalline in texture. The blooms, which are flat faced and appear in mid-winter, are often 12.7-15cm (5-6in) across. This remarkable orchid grows best in the cool house and, once established, can carry as many as three or four spikes of flowers.
Photo X 1/3

VANDA
Thonglor
●*Warm* ❀*Summer*
Left: Raised in Thailand, the 'home' of the vandas, this beautiful hybrid combines the desired qualities of full shape and exciting colour, both inherited largely from the *Vanda sanderana* influence in its background. The rounded, 6-7.5cm (2.5-3in) flowers are rose-mauve, the lower petals and sepals strikingly marked with crimson. This plant, which normally flowers in the summer but may bloom at any season, should be grown in the warm greenhouse.
Photo X ½

A Selection of Species

If you wish to have variety, the cultivation of orchid species will provide you with a glorious range of flower form and colour throughout the year.

While many orchid growers assemble a mixed collection of species and cultivated hybrids, there are some who prefer to grow only species. Should you decide to do the same, your choice of plants will in no way be restricted, for such is the range of species available that the pleasure and challenge of growing them equals if not surpasses that of growing a mixed collection.

Whichever choice you make, it is advisable to start in a modest way. Because there is such a wide range to choose from, amateurs new to orchids are often tempted to start with as many species as they are able to afford, without giving any real thought in advance to individual requirements. This inevitably leads to disappointments and heavy losses.

You should consider three questions before buying any orchid plant:

1. Can you accommodate the plant when fully grown? Some plants grow to a considerable size when mature.

2. Can you provide the correct conditions of temperature, humidity and light known to be required by a particular species?

3. Does the plant provide the type of flowers you favour? A plant should always represent good value for the space it occupies in the greenhouse. Here it is important to remember that, while many orchids produce large and showy flowers, there are a number which have tiny flowers of great beauty. These are often called 'botanicals'.

Plants can be obtained from three main sources. The first, and almost certainly the best for a beginner is the nurseryman who specializes in importing and establishing orchid species. It is always a good idea to start with established plants rather than newly imported divisions that have been taken direct from their natural habitat. Often a great deal of skill is required to acclimatize these plants and encourage them to produce a new root system. Moreover, the time spent in visiting an orchid nursery, seeing the plants growing in a happy environment and drawing on the nurseryman's knowledge and experience, which is readily given, is probably the richest source of information available to a beginner.

A second source is from other amateur growers who have grown plants successfully and taken divisions from them. Rare or less readily available plants can often be obtained in this way. Orchid societies do much to put growers in touch with one another as well as helping to spread useful cultural information.

The third source is direct importation of species from their country of origin, and many growers will want to attempt this when they have gained some experience. The all-important factor here is to be as certain as possible that the source of supply is a reputable one. Here again, contact with other orchid growers, or one of the increasing number of societies, can provide reliable information.

The following section presents a selection of orchid species that are relatively easy to cultivate and which, in conjunction with other species described in this book, represent a good cross-section of orchids found under cultivation today. Both plants and flowers are described using non-botanical language, so that those new to orchids may be able to form an immediate impression of orchid form, size and general habit. The cultural requirements suggested are basic, but should be a sufficient guide to the general needs of each plant.

Left: Cultivating a mixed collection of orchid species is both rewarding and challenging. Many are delicately scented; others mimic the insects that pollinate them.

Aeranthes

Aeranthes is a genus for the discerning grower. The flowers, rarely seen in collections today, are unusual and attract attention wherever they are shown. It is a small group confined almost entirely to Madagasgar and should be grown in the warm house, with shade during the summer months.

Aeranthes are monopodial, producing strong narrow leaves up to 30cm (12in) in length. They are without pseudobulbs and so the plants must never be allowed to become too dry; frequent spraying during the summer months also helps to ensure good condition. The three species mentioned here have a sweet, if not very strong, scent, most noticeable in the early morning or in the cool of the evening. They can be in flower at any season.

Aeranthes arachnites

●*Warm* ❀*All Year*

The flowers of this species are produced in succession on thin, wirelike stems. Only one or two are open at any one time, so that the plant is often in flower for months at a time. Individual flowers are of complex shape, about 4cm (1.6in) across, pale green in overall colour, turning to yellow-green with age.

Aeranthes grandiflora

●*Warm* ❀*All Year*

This species has larger flowers than the former, up to 20cm (8in) across, but on a much shorter stem. *Aeranthes ramosa* is similar but has flowers only about 10cm (4in) across.

Aerides

A popular orchid with the grower, aerides come mainly from tropical Asia. About 50 species have been described. These epiphytic plants grow and flower well in the intermediate or warm section of the greenhouse. Because they make many aerial roots, a high degree of humidity is an advantage, with frequent spraying during the summer months.

The plants resemble the strap-leaf vandas in appearance, with thicky fleshy leaves produced in two rows from a central stem. However, in some cases the leaves and stems are much finer, and almost cylindrical. Many of the species produce their flowers on pendulous, often branching, stems, or racemes, with the flowers surrounding the stem for the greater part of its length. Many aerides are sweet-scented, and the flowers will remain in perfect condition for up to four weeks if the plant can be kept in cooler conditions while in flower.

Aerides fieldingii

●◐*Warm/Intermediate* ❀*Spring/Summer*

This is one of the most free-flowering species of the genus, with drooping, branching spikes often up to 60cm (24in) in length. The flowers, which appear in spring or summer, are about 2.5cm (1in) across and are pinky-white suffused and mottled with rose-mauve. This species is also commonly known as the 'foxtail orchid', are as others (eg *Rynchostylis*), which bear their flowers in a similar way.

Aerides odoratum

●◐*Warm/Intermediate* ❀*Summer*

This is a robust grower, similar in habit to *Aerides fieldingii.* The flowers, which appear in summer, are creamy-white, with the tips of the sepals and petals and the lip blotched with magenta.

Aerides vandarum

●◐*Warm/Intermediate* ❀*Spring*

This species produces very narrow, cylindrical stems and foliage that can grow to a length of 60-90cm (24-26in). The flowers, which are produced in spring, are white in colour and 7.5cm (3in) across; they are carried in groups of one to three on a short stem.

Angraecum

Even though this epiphytic genus is restricted to parts of Africa and the island of Madagascar, some 200 species are known. Although the plants vary greatly in size, the basic colour of the flowers is either creamy-white or white with green. Another common factor is that almost all the flowers produce, from the back or base of the lip, a long spur or nectar-tube.

Angraecums are subjects for the warm house, and being without pseudobulbs require moist conditions and plenty of light. However, some of the smaller-growing plants should be protected from full sun, and for all plants frequent spraying can be a great advantage.

Angraecum sesquipedale

●*Warm* ❀*Winter*

This is the best known of the large angraecums and produces one of the most majestic of all orchid flowers. The plant, which can grow to a height of 90cm (36in), has strap-like, leathery leaves that equal the plant's height in span. The star-shaped flowers, produced two to four on stems that arise from the leaf axils, are 15-18cm (6-7in) across and a beautiful creamy-white in colour. Their most distinctive feature is a greenish spur that may be up to 30cm (12in) in length. The flowers appear in the winter months.

Angraecum eburneum

●*Warm* ❀*Winter*

This winter-flowering species resembles the former in plant habit but the flower spikes are often longer, producing 9 to 12 Flowers of about 10cm (4in) in diameter. The sepals, petals and spur are green and

Above: *Aeranthes arachnites* Photo x 1¼

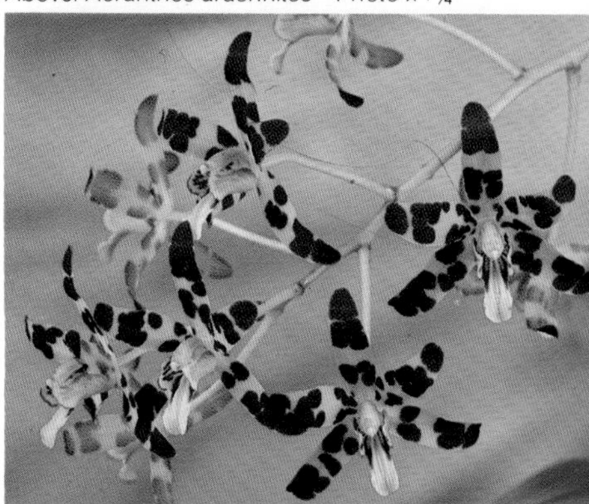

Above: *Ansellia africana* Photo x ¾

Above: *Angraecum eburneum* Photo x 1

Above: *Aerides fieldingii* Photo x ¾

the lip pure white. Curiously, the flowers appear on the stem as if upside-down.

Angraecum distichum
●*Warm* ❀*All year*
This is one of the miniature species in this genus, producing tiny, white, sweet-scented flowers, no more than 6mm (0.25in) in diameter, at almost any time of year.

Angraecum humile is another miniature, whose tiny, star-shaped white flowers are only 3mm (0.12in) across.

Ansellia
●*Warm* ❀*Winter/Spring*
In some cases it is easier to describe an orchid than it is to give it a universally acceptable name. The species within the genus *Ansellia* are very difficult to define, indeed there is common opinion that it is made up of only one highly variable epiphytic or lithophytic species. The genus is indigenous to wide areas of tropical and southern Africa, with considerable differences of habitat, and it is no doubt for this reason that such variation occurs in both plant and flower. Cultural requirements are the same as for vandaceous orchids, although they are sometimes found growing well in intermediate as well as the recommended warm conditions. It is important to give the maximum amount of light at all times.

The plant produces stemlike, cylindrical pseudobulbs up to 60cm (24in) or more in height and 2.5cm (1in) in diameter, narrowing towards the top. The ribbed leaves are produced mainly from the upper part of the stem. An interesting feature of the plant is the way in which the thin roots grow upwards away from the compost to form a thick matted clump covering the rhizome.

The flowers, produced in winter and spring, are basically pale to solid yellow but can be clear, or lightly or heavily spotted and barred with light or dark brown. They are carried on stems, often branching, with up to 40 flowers to each spike; individual flowers are between 2.5 and 5cm (1-2in) across.

The general name in use for this plant is *Ansellia africana*, but it may be listed as *A. confusa*, *A. gigantea*, or *A. nilotica*; because of the colouring of the flowers it is commonly called 'leopard orchid'.

Barkeria
Some taxonomists classify *Barkeria* as a genus in its own right, while others link it with the genus *Epidendrum*. However, the grower will more often than not find the plants described as barkerias, and so for the purpose of identification they are treated here as a separate genus.

Although the conditions in the intermediate house suit these epiphytic plants while they are growing, with plenty of light, warmth and air movement, they like a decided rest in much cooler conditions. By the autumn the pseudobulbs should be fully developed and this is the time to rest the plant in the cool house until the following spring.

Barkerias develop slender pseudobulbs with the leaves and flower spikes growing from the top. They make a number of thick, fleshy aerial roots and so are good subjects to grow on tree-fern or cork bark.

Central America is the habitat for both species mentioned here.

Barkeria skinneri

Intermediate Autumn

This is the best-known species of the genus. The flower spikes, up to 60cm (24in) in height, bear 20 to 30 rose-mauve flowers, the lips of which are often slightly deeper in colour. The flowers are about 4cm (1.6in) in diameter and last for many weeks, generally developing in the autumn.

Barkeria spectabilis

Intermediate Winter/Spring

This species produces shorter pseudobulbs than the former, but the flowers are larger, up to 5.5cm (2.2in) across with six to eight to a stem. The basic colour is rose-lilac, with a broad white lip tipped with magenta.

Bifrenaria

This is a small genus of about a dozen species, coming mainly from Brazil. They are certainly among the easiest of plants to grow, and are often offered in collections for beginners.

While they are usually grown in the intermediate house, with plenty of light, they will also do well in the cool house with a winter minimum of 11°C (52°F). Bifrenarias are epiphytic and will succeed if grown in a pot on the staging, or in wire or wooden baskets suspended from the roof; in either position they should be kept drier at the root when not in active growth. An open compost with good drainage is important.

Most of the species have stout angular pseudobulbs that are yellowish-green in colour, and each of these produces one dark green leathery leaf from the top. The two species mentioned here flower during the spring and summer, and are heavily scented.

Bifrenaria atropurpurea

Intermediate/Cool Spring/Summer

This species produces a stem carrying three to five flowers from the base of the pseudobulb. The flowers, which are 5cm (2in) or a little more in diameter, have purple-red sepals and petals each with a central marking of yellow; the lip is pinky-white or red.

Bifrenaria harrisoniae

Intermediate/Cool Spring/Summer

This is the most familiar species. It produces creamy-white flowers, one or two to a stem, with thick waxy sepals and petals and a lip covered with short, reddish-purple hairs. Each flower can be up to 7.5cm (3in) in diameter.

Brassavola

Brassavolas are very popular with amateur growers, partly because they are easy to cultivate and also for the strange shapes of some of the flowers. The 15 species known are either epiphytic or lithophytic and come from Central and South America.

In many species the pseudobulbs and leaves are very slender and appear as one, both being cylindrical in shape. They are inclined to droop, so the plants are best grown on tree-fern, with just a little compost, and suspended from the greenhouse roof. Brassavolas object to excessive moisture and should be kept quite dry during their lengthy period of rest. They generally do well in the conditions suitable for cattleyas.

The two species described here are very fragrant, especially in the cool of the evening or at night. They can be found in flower at any time of the year.

Brassavola cucculata

Intermediate All year

This plant produces thin, reed-like foliage and drooping pseudobulbs about 38-50cm (15-20in) long. The flower—rarely more than one per pseudobulb—is produced from the base of a leaf on a short stem and has thin, drooping segments about 10cm (4in) long that give it the appearance of a greenish-white spider.

Brassavola nodosa

Intermediate All year

This species has similar growth to the former, but is stouter and shorter and grows upright if planted in a pot. The flowers, often four to five on a stem, are creamy-green and up to 7.5cm (3in) across when fully open. The lip is broad, white with a few purple spots in the throat.

Bulbophyllum

With 2,000 species known, this is the largest genus within the orchid family. Not only are bulbophyllums widely distributed throughout the subtropical and tropical areas of the world, but their vegetative growth habit and flower size and shape are also equally varied. Some flowers for example, are so small that their beauty can only be appreciated with the aid of a magnifier, while others are up to 10cm (4in) in diameter. In most species the sepals are the predominant

Above: *Brassavola nodosa* Photo x 1/3

Above: *Bifrenaria harrisoniae* Photo x 2/3

Above: *Barkeria spectabilis* Photo x 3/4

Above: *Barkeria skinneri* Photo x 2½

Above: *Bulbophyllum umbellatum* Photo x 3

segments of the flower, the petals being so small as to be inconspicuous. Another interesting feature in many species is the hinged lip which gently rocks when the flower stem is moved. The flowers are produced either singly or in a cluster or rosette. They develop on a stem which arises from the base of either a fully or partially developed pseudobulb.

A few species can be grown in the cool house, but the majority require intermediate or warm-house conditions. Being mainly epiphytic or lithophytic plants, they are not deeply rooted, and do best in shallow pots or on tree-fern or cork bark. Good drainage is essential.

Bulbophyllum umbellatum

○Cool ❀Autumn/Winter

This is an Indian species that will grow well in the cool house, flowering in autumn and winter. It produces oblong, ridged pseudobulbs about 5cm (2in) in height, each bearing a solitary leaf. The flowers, each 2cm (0.8in) in diameter, develop as a rosette of five to eight blooms on a single stem. They are creamy-yellow in colour, heavily spotted with red.

Bulbophyllum collettii

◑Intermediate ❀Winter/Spring

Coming from Burma, this is a plant for the intermediate house; it flowers in winter and spring. It has roundish, angular pseudobulbs spaced well apart on a creeping rhizome. The four to six flowers, produced on a flower spike that appears when the new growth is only partly completed, have lower sepals which hang down, as if joined, to a length of 13cm (5in). The top sepal and petals carry tufts of short, fine hairs that flutter in even a slight air movement. The overall flower colour is maroon-red with yellow stripes.

Bulbophyllum longissimum

◑Intermediate ❀Winter/Spring

This is similar to *Bulbophyllum colletti* but has paler flowers. The lower sepals can measure 25cm (10in) in length.

Calanthe

With tall, upright flower spikes and many long-lasting flowers, *Calanthe* is deservedly a special favourite with orchid growers. Given warm-house conditions, it grows easily and is thus a good plant for beginners. Of the 150 species known, most are terrestrials; they come from a wide area, including South Africa, Asia and Central America.

Calanthes divide into two main groups: deciduous and evergreen. The deciduous species produce rather large, angular pseudobulbs with wide, ribbed leaves. During the growing season these plants should be liberally watered and fed until the leaves turn yellow and fall during the early winter months. At this stage watering should be gradually reduced. After flowering, which occurs during the winter months, the pseudobulbs should be repotted in a well-drained compost. Evergreen calanthes grow in similar conditions but do not require a definite period of rest.

Calanthe vestita
●*Warm* ❀*Winter*
This deciduous species produces fine spikes of flowers in winter, ranging in colour from white to deep pink; the lip is often stronger in colour than the rest of the flower.

Calanthe masuca
●*Warm* ❀*Summer/Autumn*
This is a favourite among the evergreen species. It produces violet-mauve flowers with a dark magenta lip, mainly in the summer and autumn.

Ceratostylis

Although 70 species of this genus are known, probably only one is responsible for the name being known to growers.

Ceratostylis rubra
◑*Intermediate* ❀*All year*
This is a very worthy plant to grow since, if left undisturbed, it will develop into a magnificent specimen. It has the great advantage of flowering three or four times a year in flushes. Although only about 2.5cm (1in) across, the solid red flowers contrast well with the dark green foliage. They are produced on very short stalks. A native of the Philippines, this species enjoys good light in the intermediate house; spraying during the summer months is beneficial.

Chysis

The six species of *Chysis* recorded, which come mainly from Mexico, are all epiphytic and semideciduous under cultivation. When in growth the plants require a liberal supply of heat and moisture; when they have shed their leaves they should be transferred to the cool house for a period of rest. During this time they should be kept much drier at the root until growth restarts in the spring, when they can be returned to the warm house.

Growth and form are similar in all the species. A few, often large, leaves grow from the upper half of the spindle-shaped pseudobulbs which may be up to 45cm (18in) long. These either grow horizontally or hang down, so that the plants are best grown in baskets suspended from the greenhouse roof. All three species listed here flower in spring and early summer.

Chysis laevis
●*Warm* ❀*Spring*
This species is perhaps the most colourful of the genus, bearing 8 to 12 flowers, each about 6.5cm (2.5in) across, on a stem produced from the new growth at an early stage of its development. The sepals and petals are yellow, the end third of each segment being marked and sometimes totally covered with orange; the lip is yellow, blotched with dark red.

Chysis bractescens
●*Warm* ❀*Spring/Summer*
The flowers of this species, up to 7.5cm (3in) in diameter, grow rather close together on a single but comparatively short stem produced from new growth. In colour they are white, turning to cream with age; the lip is white on the outer surface and tinged with yellow inside.

Chysis aurea is similar to *C. bractescens* except that the flowers are pale to lemon yellow in colour.

Coelogyne

Although a large genus of well over 100 species, few coelogynes are found in collections today. This is a pity, for they are orchids of great merit. They are, in the main, easy to grow and many species thrive in cool conditions, requiring a warmer environment only during their active growing season.

Many coelogynes are suitable for growing on into specimen plants. However, be warned: a specimen plant of one of the larger-growing species can take up a considerable space in the greenhouse. Fortunately, it is possible to choose from a wide range of smaller growing species, and even a single-growth plant in flower is a valuable addition to any orchid collection.

Coelogyne cristata
○*Cool* ❀*Winter*
Perhaps the most familiar of the genus, this species likes to grow on undisturbed into a specimen plant. The flower spike appears from the centre of the new growth and its snowy-white flowers, broken only by a blotch of golden yellow at the centre of the lip, appear in midwinter and last for four or five weeks.

Coelogyne massangeana
○*Cool* ❀*Spring*
This spring-flowering species bears pendulous spikes of up to 20 flowers, each creamy-yellow in colour with brown markings on the lip.

Coelogyne pandurata
○*Cool* ❀*Spring*
The flowers of this species, produced in spring, can be up to 10cm (4 in) across and are among the largest of all coelogynes. They are green with jet black

Above: *Ceratostylis rubra* Photo x 1½

Above: *Chysis bractescens* Photo x ½

Above: *Calanthe vestita* Photo x ⅓

Above: *Colax jugosus* Photo x 1

Above: *Coelogyne cristata* Photo x 1/3

Above: *Comparettia macroplectron* Photo x 1

hairs partly covering the lip and are borne in beautiful arching sprays.

Colax

The three species of *Colax* have in the past been included in the genera *Lycaste, Maxillaria* and *Zygopetalum,* but are now accepted as a separate genus, only one of which, *Colax jugosus,* is seen in present day collections. This produces such an attractive and unusually marked flower that all must admire it.

Colax jugosus

Intermediate *Spring*

Native to Brazil, this species grows well in intermediate conditions with plenty of fresh air. The plant can easily be accommodated in a small greenhouse for it seldom grows above 30cm (12in) in height. It seems to do best when kept fairly potbound, but the compost must be of an open nature to give good drainage.

The plant develops small oval pseudobulbs, 2.5-5cm (1-2in) in height, narrowing towards the top, and two dark-green leaves 15-23cm (6-9in) long. The flowers, often two but sometimes three to a spike, are about 5cm (2in) in diameter. The sepals and petals are creamy-white, the sepals being clear and the petals heavily blotched with deep purple; the lip is similarly marked. The flowers, which are produced in the spring, last for up to four weeks.

Comparettia

A small but interesting genus, *Comparettia* has less than a dozen species which are found mainly in the Andes region of South America. Although they are rather small plants, the size and number of the brightly coloured flowers they produce make them very rewarding subjects for the amateur to grow.

The plants should be grown in the coolest spot in the intermediate house, and they must be kept well shaded from the full sun. During the growing season they should never be allowed to dry out, and frequent spraying is of great benefit; shallow pots or a fibre-block are suitable, as comparettias are not deeply rooted.

Comparettia macroplectron

Intermediate *Summer*

This is perhaps the best known species. It produces very small pseudobulbs with one or two leaves, 7.5-13cm (3-5in) long, and flowers very freely in the summer. The drooping flower spikes, often 30-38cm (12-15in) long and sometimes longer, are produced from the base of the pseudobulb and carry five to ten flowers, each about 5cm (2in) measured vertically. The sepals and petals are rose-pink in colour, often well spotted with purple, and slightly hooded. The lip is large in comparison with the rest of the flower, pink in colour, and spotted at the base, with fewer spots towards it edge. A spur projects from the base of the lip horizontally towards the back of the flower.

Comparettia coccinea
◐*Intermediate* ❀*Autumn/Winter*
This species resembles *C. macroplectron* in growth habit. The flowers are similar in form but slightly smaller, with three to seven on a stem. Their mixture of bright scarlet and orange attracts the eye at once as they shine out like lights on an autumn day.

Cymbidiella

Only three species of this most attractive orchid are known, all native to Madagascar, and only *Cymbidiella rhodochila* is likely to be found in collections today. At first the genus was linked with that of *Cymbidium*, but it is now widely accepted in its own right.

In the wild this plant is almost always found growing with one particular species of stagshorn fern, and it is often thought that it cannot be grown under cultivation without this 'host' plant. However, this has been disproved many times, although it is not an easy plant to grow: it is most particular about perfect root drainage and is intolerant of any disturbance. Cymbidiellas are subjects for the warm house, provided with an abundance of moisture and good light, though not direct sunshine.

Cymbidiella rhodochila
●*Warm* ❀*Winter/Spring*
This is an epiphytic plant which produces similar growth to that of a cymbidium, but has generally shorter leaves. The flowers—and there can be none more striking—are produced from winter to spring on a stem arising from the base of the pseudobulb. There can be as many as 20, which open in succession, three or four at any one time. Each flower measures about 7.5cm (3in) across and, being of heavy texture, they are long-lasting. The sepals and slightly hooded petals are yellowish-green, the latter thickly spotted with dark green; the lip, in contrast, is crimson, with some yellow and dark green spots in the centre.

Dendrochilum

This genus contains 150 known species, many of which are very attractive. They are frequently given the generic name of *Platyclinis*, but this is now considered to be incorrect. While dendrochilums are native to a wide area of Southeast Asia, those under cultivation come mainly from the Philippines, where they grow in large clumps on rocks and trees.

Although from a warm climate, these plants do well in the cool house with good protection from full sun. Plenty of moisture at the root is required when the plant is in full growth, but drier conditions should be provided throughout the winter, when it is usually at rest.

The plant develops a small oval pseudobulb which produces a solitary leaf. Thin wiry flower spikes arising from the centre of the new growths grow upright at first, then bend over and hang down, producing two rows of tiny flowers, with perhaps as many as 80 on each spike. This gives rise to the name 'chain orchid' often given to these plants. In most species the flowers are fragrant. All can be grown on into specimen plants.

Dendrochilum filiforme
○*Cool* ❀*Spring*
This is a very charming species which produces chains of flowers often reaching a length of 30cm (12in). Individual flowers are not more than 6mm (0.25in) across, and grow very close together on the spike. They are yellowish-green in colour and appear in the late spring.

Dendrochilum cobbianum
○*Cool* ❀*Autumn*
This species produces larger flowers, up to 1.2cm (0.5in) in diameter, creamy-white in colour with a yellow lip, which appear in the autumn.

Dendrochilum glumaceum
○*Cool* ❀*Spring*
The flowers of this species are similar to those of *D. cobbianum*, but they open in the spring, are more star-shaped and grow very close together on the stem. They are straw-coloured and have a strong scent.

Doritis

With only one species recorded, this genus could have been forgotten by growers, but it has been used extensively in hybridization, particularly with the genus *Phalaenopsis*.

Doritis pulcherrima
●*Warm* ❀*All year*
This species, a native of Southeast Asia, is much prized in modern collections and grows well in warm house conditions suitable for phalaenopsis.

In plant habit and appearance it is much like phalaenopsis, but is inclined to grow taller. It has three to four pairs of stiff grey-green leaves, spotted with dark purple on the upper surface.

The flower spikes are held upright and grow to a height of 60cm (24in) or more, producing 10 to 25 flowers which open, a few at a time, on the upper half of the spike. Flowers appear at any season and often more than once in the same year. As

Above: *Cymbidiella rhodochila* Photo X ⅔

Above: *Doritis pulcherrima* Photo x 2¼

Above: *Encyclia mariae* Photo x ⅓

Above: *Dendrochilum cobbianum* Photo x 2

individual flowers last for many weeks, a single spike can bloom for four or five months. The flowers vary widely in size (2-4cm; 0.75-1.5in) and colour; the sepals and petals range from pale rose-purple to deep magenta, with parts of the lip often of a deeper hue.

Encyclia

Opinion is much divided as to whether this is a genus in its own right, but many now accept it to be so and species hitherto included under the generic names of *Epidendrum* and others are today more often listed as *Encyclia*. It is not possible to say with certainty how many species there are, but those known come mainly from Mexico.

The plants should be grown in the cool or intermediate house, with good shading during the summer. A well-drained compost, such as fir bark, is preferable, because the plants should never be too wet at the root; indeed, overwatering kills many of these plants.

Encyclia citrina

○Cool ❀All year

Often known as *Cattleya citrina*, this species prefers the well-shaded cool house; it does best growing downwards from a raft or piece of cork-bark with very little compost. The pseudobulbs and leaves are greyish-green in colour. Single (or occasionally two) pendent, very fragrant and long-lasting flowers are produced at most times of the year. They are lemon yellow with a deeper yellow centre to the lip, and sometimes a white band on the margin.

Encyclia mariae

○Cool ❀Summer

This species is similar in appearance in *E. citrina* but is grown upright in a pot. One to five flowers are carried on a thin stem, each being about 5cm (2in) wide; the sepals and petals are lime green and the very broad lip, which is often the widest part of the flower, is pure white. *E. mariae* is considered to be one of the loveliest of all the summer-flowering orchids.

Epidendrum

The epidendrums are one of the largest genera: over 1,000 species are known, coming mainly from Central and South America. So varied are the plants accepted within the genus, both in vegetation and flower size and appearance, that some groups have been accorded a genus of their own (see *Barkeria* and *Encyclia*). Those that remain within the genus are epiphytic.

Epidendrums seem to divide naturally into two categories: those with oval or rounded pseudobulbs, and those that produce reed-like stems. A common factor in most is that the flower spike develops from the top of the pseudobulb, and the individual flowers open in succession a few at a time, thus keeping the plant in flower for many months. The plants grow best in the cool or intermediate house, depending upon species.

Epidendrum ibaguense
○◑*Cool/Intermediate* ❀*All year*
Often known as *E. radicans,* this is a reed-stem species. The stems, which vary from 60-150cm (2-5ft) in height according to environment, produce rounded leaves and many aerial roots over most of their length. The flowers (2.5cm; 1in) are orange-red or scarlet, the lip flat and very frilled. This is a plant for the cool or intermediate greenhouse, with good light. One successful specimen is known to have flowered continuously for four years.

Epidendrum cochleatum
◑*Intermediate* ❀*All year*
This species, which is a subject for the intermediate house, produces flattened pear-shaped pseudobulbs about 18cm (7in) tall. The flowers resemble the shape of an octopus in water, with their thin green sepals and petals which droop down below the rounded, dark purple, almost black lip. Three or four flowers are usually produced at a time, and the plant may bloom throughout the year.

Epidendrum polybulbon
◑*Intermediate* ❀*Winter*
One of the miniatures within the genus, this species produces small rounded pseudobulbs from a creeping rhizome which, when growing well, develops into a thick mass covering the top of the pot. The plant grows only to about 5-7.5cm (2-3in) in height, and produces one small flower of 2.5cm (1in) in diameter from the top of each leading pseudobulb. The sepals and petals are yellow with brown flushing and the spade-shaped lip is creamy-white. Growing in the intermediate house and flowering in the winter, a specimen plant is a delight to behold.

Eria

Although there are some 500 species of *Eria,* most coming from India or Malaysia, not many are found in collections today. This is surprising as some are very showy and generally they are not difficult to cultivate.

A few species will grow in cool conditions but most do well in the intermediate or warm section of the greenhouse. Some require shade, while others enjoy full light. Most require a period of rest at the completion of their growing season and will flower more freely if this can be given in cooler conditions than those in which the plant has been grown. The three species mentioned here come into flower in winter and spring.

Eria javanica
◑●*Intermediate/Warm* ❀*Winter/Spring*
This is a particularly showy species. The pseudobulbs are about 7.5cm (3in) in height, and produce two upright leaves, 30-60cm (1-2ft) in length. An erect flower spike develops to a height of 60cm from the top of the pseudobulb, and many well-spaced flowers are produced. These are about 4cm (1.5in) across and creamy green in colour.

Eria coronaria
◑●*Intermediate/Warm* ❀*Winter/Spring*
In this species slender stem-like pseudobulbs up to 20cm (8in) in length produce two broad leaves from the apex. Short spikes carry three to five beautifully fragrant flowers 2.5-4 cm (1-1.5in) across, which are creamy white in colour with the upper surface of the lip deep purple, marked with yellow.

Eria rhynchostyloides
◑●*Intermediate/Warm* ❀*Winter/Spring*
This species is similar in growth to *E. javanica,* but can produce four or five flowering spikes from one pseudobulb; these arch to about 20cm (8in) and carry many tiny, pink-white flowers, set densely in a cylindrical arrangement.

Eulophia

Most of the 200 known species of *Eulophia* come from tropical and subtropical Africa, and almost all are terrestrial. The genus can be divided roughly into two groups according to vegetation and flower form.

In the first, the plants have a broad, pear-shaped pseudobulb which produces fairly long deciduous leaves that fall when the growing period is completed. The sepals and petals of the flowers are small in comparison with the lip, which is the main attraction.

Plants in the second group develop thinner, cigar-shaped pseudobulbs and, in common with most orchids, retain their narrow leaves for a number of years; their flowers are smaller and more uniform than those in the first group. Both the species listed below flower during the summer, *E. paivaeana* being found also in autumn and winter.

Eulophia guinensis
●*Warm* ❀*Summer*
This species belongs to the first group and is probably the most familiar. After a cool, dry rest throughout the winter the plant should be brought into the warm house and encouraged into growth by light and watering. When growth is still in progress, the flower spike appears and

Above: *Gomesa crispa* Photo x 2

Above: *Eria javanica* Photo x 1

Above: *Eulophia guinensis* Photo x 1

Above: *Epidendrum ibaguense* Photo x 4

Above: *Huntleya burtii* Photo x 1¼

grows to a height of 60-90cm (2-3ft), producing 6 to 15 flowers. The lip is 2.5-4cm (1-1.6in) in diameter, spade-shaped and rose-pink with darker veins. The sepals and petals are recurving, short and narrow, dullish-purple in colour with green veins.

Eulophia paivaeana

●*Warm* ✿*Summer-Winter*

This species belongs to the second group, and keeps its leaves, which are similar in appearance to those of cymbidiums, for two to three years. The pseudobulb is conical, about 7.5cm (3in) in height, and produces a flower spike from the base. This spike seems to grow continuously, producing well-spaced flowers up to 2.5cm (1in) across, which have greenish sepals shaded with brown and bright yellow petals and lip. This is a plant for the warm house.

Gomesa

○◐*Cool/Intermediate* ✿*Spring/Summer*

Although there are about ten species of this epiphytic orchid available to growers, only one, *Gomesa crispa,* is seen in any numbers today. It is a Brazilian plant and is very attractive when well grown, but its growing conditions require particular attention.

It is a plant for both the cool and intermediate house, requiring some protection from full light during the summer months. Free drainage for the root system is of great importance and for this reason it is a good subject to grow on a raft or piece of cork-bark. If grown in a pot, a coarse material, such as fir bark, should be used. As the plant grows upwards, away from the pot, the roots should be allowed to grow outside, where they should gain sufficient nourishment from the atmosphere. Spraying during the summer is helpful.

The plant produces pseudobulbs and leaves similar to those of odontoglossums, only paler in colour. The flowers are carried on arching sprays, up to 23cm (9in) long, and there are often two sprays to a pseudobulb. The sweetly scented, lime-green flowers, about 1.25cm (0.5in) across, are densely clustered on the spike and appear during the spring and summer.

Huntleya

There are probably three or four species in the genus, but only *Huntleya burtii,* also known as *H. meleagris,* is seen in collections.

These plants come from Costa Rica and Brazil, and grow best in the intermediate house. The named species has a reputation for being rather difficult to maintain in good condition, but failure is often due to one of two reasons. The first is that many growers have a tendency to keep the plant in too warm and humid an environment, causing it to rot; the second is that the new growths which develop part way up the stem are often mistakenly removed and repotted as a complete plant, which they are not. It is far better to allow the plant to grow into a clump, and to let the roots from the new growths develop as aerial roots.

Huntleya burtii
◑Intermediate ❀Summer

The plant grows without pseudobulbs. The leaves, about 30cm (12in) in length, develop from a central stem in the form of a fan. Single flowers 6.5-7.5cm (2.5-3in) across, are produced on a 15cm (6in) stem. The sepals and petals are approximately equal in size and uniform in marking; at the base they are greenish-white, changing through yellow to a reddish-brown marked with yellow. The lower half of the lip is reddish-brown, graduating to white in the upper part. These flowers, which are seen mainly during the summer, are thick and waxy in texture and last well.

Laelia

Some 75 species of *Laelia* have been recorded, almost all from Mexico and the northern parts of South Africa. While in appearance both plant and flower are similar to the cattleyas, with which many intergeneric hybrids have been made, it is a delightful genus in its own right, and is favoured by many growers. As with cattleyas, its flower spikes are produced from the apex of the pseudobulb.

Because of the varied conditions found in the natural habitat of these plants, some do best in the intermediate house, while others prefer cooler conditions. Moderate light is required and a well-drained compost is important as no laelia does well if there is an excess of water at the root; the majority require a definite period of rest when little or no water should be given.

Laelia anceps
○Cool ❀Winter

This is a cool house plant, which generally flowers in winter. It has angular pseudobulbs, each bearing a single leaf. A flower spike, growing erect to 60cm (2ft) or more, produces two to five flowers, each about 10cm (4in) across. They are pale or deep rose-pink in colour, the lip being a darker hue than the other segments.

Laelia purpurata
◑Intermediate ❀Winter/Spring

The orchid is the national flower of Brazil and deserves the honour. Growing to a height of 4.5-60cm (1.5-2ft) including the leaf, the plant produces a short spike of two to six flowers, each 13-18cm (5-7in) in diameter. Very variable in colour, the narrow sepals and petals range from white to pale purple, with a frilled deep purple lip.

Laelia cinnabarina
◑Intermediate ❀Winter/Spring

This species has thinner pseudobulbs, which are darker in colour than most, as is the leaf. Five to twelve orange-red flowers, each about 5cm (2in) across, are produced on a 23cm (9in) spike.

The last two species flower during the winter and spring.

Lycaste

Between 30 and 40 *Lycaste* species are known, including both terrestrial and epiphytic plants, most of which come from Central America. Many are also deciduous, losing their leaves during the winter, when they produce their flowers. Although these vary in size, in all species the sepals open wide and are longer than the petals, which are inclined to remain partly closed.

The plant needs moisture and warmth when in full growth, but take care not to get water on the large, broad leaves as they tend to develop brown spots if this occurs. Cooler and drier conditions are essential when the plant is at rest and in flower, the flowering season being winter or early spring.

Lycaste aromatica
●Warm ❀Winter/Spring

As the name suggests, this species is heavily scented. The bright, orange-red flowers, 5cm (2in) across, often appear at the same time as the new growth, and are carried singly on a stem about 15cm (6in) long. There may be as many as ten flowers to each pseudobulb.

Lycaste deppei
●Warm ❀Winter/Spring

This species produces fewer but larger flowers than *L. aromatica,* up to 11.5cm (4.5in) in diameter. The sepals are mid-green spotted with reddish-brown, and the smaller petals are pure white. The lip is yellow in colour and also spotted with reddish-brown.

Lycaste virginalis
●Warm ❀Winter/Spring

The flowers of *L. virginalis*, also known as *L. skinneri*, are even larger—up to 15cm (6in) across. The colour varies from all-white (which is rare) through pale to deep pink, and the lip is often spotted with crimson.

Masdevallia

This is one of the most fascinating orchid genera, as remarkable for the uniformity of its vegetation as for the diversity of form and colour of its flowers. Three hundred species are recorded, growing mainly in the higher altitude areas of Mexico, Brazil and Colombia. The structure of the flowers is in contrast to that of many orchids, as the sepals are very large in comparison with the other segments of the flower, which can only be seen under close examination.

Because of the high-altitude conditions of their natural habitat, the cool house with plenty of shade and fresh air during the summer months provides the ideal environment. As these orchids do not produce pseudobulbs, the thick leaves spring directly from a creeping rhizome, so the plants should never be allowed to become dry. Good drainage at the root is also important. Most species flower during winter and spring.

Masdevallia coccinea
○Cool ❀Winter/Spring

This species produces leaves 30cm (12in) in length, and the flower spikes are often much taller. These bear a single flower of 7.5-10cm (3-4in), with sepals that taper sharply towards the tips. The colour varies from lilac to deep crimson.

Above: *Masdevallia coccinea* *Photo x 1*

Masdevallia chimaera
○Cool ❀Winter/Spring

Because this species is inclined to grow in pendent form and down into the compost, it is a good idea to grow the plant in a basket, where the flower spike can come through the sides.

The flowers open one at a time, in succession, on a single spike. Each flower can be from 15-30cm (6-12in) measured vertically, sepals terminating in long tails. They are cream coloured, lightly or heavily spotted with a deep reddish-purple and covered with short purple hairs. The lip is larger in this species, orange-pink in colour, and hinged so that it rocks when the flower moves.

Above: *Lycaste virginalis* Photo x 2/3

Above: *Laelia cinnabarina* Photo x 1

Above: *Masdevallia chimaera* Photo x 2/3

Above: *Maxillaria porphyrostele* Photo x 1/3

Masdevallia simula

○Cool ❀Winter/Spring

This species is a true miniature orchid and is one of the smallest of the genus, the entire plant not growing above 5cm (2in). The flowers, which nestle among the foliage, are very small, not more than 1cm (0.5in) across, and yellowish-green in colour, spotted with red.

Maxillaria

Some 300 species of this very diverse genus are known. They are widely scattered throughout tropical America and almost all are epiphytic. This genus is well known to the grower, not only for its interesting flowers, but also for the variety of their scent.

Both plants and flowers differ in size, the latter resembling in shape those of the *Lycaste* genus. Plants produce either clusters of pseudobulbs with broad leaves that develop from a horizontal rhizome, or narrow pseudobulbs which are well spaced on a creeping rhizome that tends to grow upwards away from the pot; the latter have very thin, grass-like leaves.

The majority of these orchids will do well in the cool and intermediate house, although individual species may require particular cultural conditions.

Maxillaria porphyrostele

○◐Cool/Intermediate ❀Winter/Spring

This species is very easy to accommodate as it will grow into a specimen plant without needing too much space. It is best grown in a wire or wooden basket, because it grows prolifically and in time will not only cover the top of its container but also grow over the sides. Each leading pseudobulb can produce a number of short flower spikes, which carry a yellow flower of 4cm (1.5in) diameter. The tips of both sepals and petals are incurving. The flowers are long-lasting, and appear from winter to spring.

Maxillaria luteo-alba

○◐Cool/Intermediate ❀Spring/Summer

This plant is taller than *M. porphyrostele,* growing to a height of 38-50cm (15-20in). The flowers are about 7.5cm (3in) across, with sepals and petals that are white at the base, turning to yellow at the tips.

Maxillaria tenuifolia

○◐Cool/Intermediate ❀Spring/Summer

In this species a creeping rhizome, which grows almost vertically, produces small oval pseudobulbs at 2.5-5cm (1-2in) intervals. The flowers, 2.5cm (1in) across, are dark or bright red speckled with yellow. The plant has a very strong scent similar to that of coconut. Like *M. luteo-alba,* the flowers usually open during the spring and summer.

Miltonia

Twenty species of this deservedly popular genus have been recorded. The majority are very sweet-scented and flower throughout the year, often more than once. They divide roughly into two natural groups. In the first group are plants from Brazil, which produce yellowish-green foliage and flattened pseudobulbs, well spaced on a creeping rhizome. These orchids require intermediate conditions and more light than plants in the second group, which grow in the higher regions of Colombia. Apart from their silver-green foliage, these Colombian miltonias are similar to odontoglossums; they grow well in the warmest spot of the cool house.

Miltonias are commonly known as 'pansy orchids' because their very rounded flowers resemble pansies.

Miltonia clowesii

◑*Intermediate* ❀*All year*

This is a Brazilian plant, with pseudobulbs, whose leaves reach a height of about 50cm (20in). The flower spike, which may be up to 60cm (2ft) in length, grows from the base of the pseudobulb and bears six to ten flowers, each about 6.5cm (2.5in) across. The sepals and petals are of equal size, reddish-brown and barred with yellow. The lip, in direct contrast, is white with a pinky-mauve blotch on its upper part.

Miltonia spectabilis

◑*Intermediate* ❀*All year*

Another Brazilian species, this orchid resembles *M. clowesii*, but the flower spike grows to no more than 25cm (10in) in length and bears fewer, slightly larger, flowers which are white or pinky-white, with a broad, flat, purple-lip.

Miltonia spectabilis var. *moreliana* is a distinct variety of this plant, and is more often seen today than the pure species. Its flower is an overall deep purple in colour with a lighter hue on the lip.

Miltonia endresii

●*Warm* ❀*All year*

This species is a representative of the Colombian group. The flowers, each up to 6.5cm (2.5in) across, are carried on a slightly arching spike. They are very flat and white, with a small purple blotch at the base of each sepal and petal. The lip has a yellow centre, or 'mask'.

Oncidium

This is one of the largest and most popular genera, with over 750 known species, coming from South, Central and parts of North America. Almost all are epiphytic but, owing to the very wide range of natural habitat, very variable in cultural requirements. None of the cultivated species likes to be too wet at the root, and an open compost, such as a coarse grade of fir bark, is ideal.

The genus is related to *Odontoglossum*, with which many species grow readily. Others prefer the warmer conditions of the intermediate house with more light and humidity. Oncidiums are very varied, both in vegetation and flower.

Oncidium papilio

◑*Intermediate* ❀*All year*

Often referred to as the 'butterfly orchid' because of its resemblance to that insect, the flowers of this species open on the end of a long slender stem and sway in the slightest air movement. Only one flower opens at any one time, but in succession, so that the plant is in flower for many months. The flowers, which can be up to 13cm (5in) across, are a mixture of chestnut-brown and yellow. This plant grows best on a raft suspended from the roof of the intermediate house, where it will get that little extra bit of light.

Oncidium longipes

○◑*Cool/Intermediate* ❀*Summer*

This is a small-growing species, ideal for growing on into a specimen plant in the small greenhouse in cool or intermediate conditions. Short flower spikes which carry three or four flowers, about 2.5cm (1in) across, are produced freely from the base of a small pseudobulb and appear during the summer. They are bright yellow, barred with reddish-brown and have a solid yellow lip.

Oncidium flexuosum

○*Cool* ❀*All year*

This is a cool house species, which is at its best grown on a raft or cork-bark because of its climbing habit. It produces thin, wiry spikes of 60-90cm (2-3ft), that carry branches of tiny yellow and brown flowers, often more than 100 to a spike. This is one of the best-known 'beginners' plants.

Oncidium incurvum

○*Cool* ❀*Summer/Autumn*

Although in growth more suited to pot culture, this cool house species resembles *O. flexuosum* in producing long branching spikes of flowers, each 1.25-2cm (0.5-0.8in) across. Unlike the majority of oncidium flowers, which are yellow and brown, these are white, barred and blotched with violet-purple; and both sepals and petals are much twisted. This orchid often produces its flower spike and buds many months before the flowers open.

Pholidota

This is a small group of plants allied to *Coelogyne*. The 40 species known come from China and Southeast Asia. All produce small flowers and therefore tend

Above: *Miltonia spectabilis* Photo x 1

Above: *Miltonia clowesii* Photo x ⅔

Above: *Pholidota chinensis* Photo x ¾

Above: *Oncidium papilio* Photo x 1½

to be regarded as insignificant, but beware of such generalities, as beauty is often found in small subjects.

Many of the species have brownish bracts that cover the flower buds during development. These are formed in two rows down each side of the pendant spike and resemble the rattle of a rattlesnake, hence the common name of 'rattlesnake orchid'.

These plants are best suited to the intermediate house, requiring moisture, warmth and light while in full growth. Both species listed here flower during spring and summer.

Pholidota chinensis

Intermediate *Spring/Summer*

In this species small globular pseudobulbs grow from a creeping rhizome to produce two short, but rather broad leaves. The flower spike of about 20cm (8in) comes from the centre of a developing growth; its upper section droops, bearing the 1.25-2cm (0.5-0.8in) flowers, which have fawn sepals and petals, and a pure white lip. The plant is seen at its best when grown on to produce many flower heads.

Pholidota imbricata

Intermediate *Spring/Summer*

This is a larger plant than *P. chinensis,* with oblong pseudobulbs and a single leaf up to 30cm (12in) in length. The yellowish-white flowers are smaller, 1cm (0.5in) across, and grow very close together on the spike.

Pleione

Until recently orchid growers had not taken this genus seriously, unlike the alpine growers who cultivate pleiones with great success. The 20 known species are found growing close to the snowline of the Himalayas, and also in parts of China and Formosa. The Himalayan species are probably better suited to the conditions of an alpine house, but others do well in the cool section of an orchid house.

The plant consists of a single, squat, roundish pseudobulb, which lasts for only one year. New growth springs from the base of the pseudobulb, and in its early stages produces a flower spike from its centre. This spike bears one or two flowers, up to 10cm (4in) across, which are very similar to those of a cattleya.

When the flower has died away, a pseudobulb develops at the base of the new growth and the parent pseudobulb shrivels. The new growth should be complete by the late autumn, when the broad but fairly short leaves turn yellow and drop. The pseudobulbs should then be stored for the winter in a cool dry place. In the early spring take them from their pot, remove all old bracts and roots, and reset them, about half-buried in a fine but well-drained compost. Watering should be very light to start with. To produce a good show put a number of pseudobulbs into one pot.

Pleione formosana

○Cool ❀Summer

This is the common species, which has flowers ranging from pure white to pale pinky-mauve. In all variations the broad lip is frilled, and in the coloured forms spotted with red-purple.

Pleione praecox and *P. humilis,* the former being darker in colour, are also good subjects for introducing growers to this genus.

Polystachya

The majority of the 150 known species of *Polystachya* come from tropical Africa. While the flowers are generally small, the plants flower freely under cultivation, and most of the species are both strongly and sweetly scented.

These plants are subjects for the intermediate house. Being epiphytic, they require a well-drained compost, but plenty of moisture at the root while the plant is in active growth. Moderate protection from the full sun is also required. Polystachyas undoubtedly do best when left undisturbed for several years.

A notable feature is that the flowers appear upside-down on the spike, the lip being uppermost with the two sepals, normally at the base of the flower, forming a hood over the rest of the flower.

The three species described here often flower more than once in a year, and can be seen at any season.

Polystachya pubescens

◑Intermediate ❀All year

This species produces narrow, tapering pseudobulbs which grow to a height of 5cm (2in) and have two or three short leaves. The flower spike comes from the apex of the pseudobulb and carries 6 to 12 bright yellow flowers, each up to 1.5cm (0.5in) across, the upper sepals and lip of which are lined with red.

Polystachya ottoniana

◑Intermediate ❀All year

This species is vegetatively similar to *P. pubescens,* the 7.5-10cm (3-4in) stem bearing a single flower, or occasionally two flowers. The flowers are white with a trace of purple on the sepals, and a yellow blotch on the lip.

Polystachya luteola

◑Intermediate ❀All year

This species is larger than the two named above. Each lead often produces more than one flower spike, which bears many small yellowish-green flowers.

Promenaea

Although there are only about 12 recorded species of this Brazilian genus, only two or three of which are found in present day collections, it is nevertheless popular with orchid growers, because the plants are short and compact and produce many flowers. They are ideal subjects for growing on into specimen plants.

The plants are epiphytic and grow best in intermediate conditions, with heavy shade during the summer months. They are intolerant of stale conditions at the root and, ideally, should be repotted in well drained compost every year.

In both species the flowers appear during the summer and are long lasting, remaining in good condition for up to six weeks if kept cool.

Promenaea stapelioides

◑Intermediate ❀Summer

This plant develops clusters of small, rounded pseudobulbs with short, greyish-green leaves, together standing no more than 10cm (4 in) above the pot. One or two flowers are produced on a short stem from each of the leading pseudobulbs. They are quite large for the size of the plant, up to 5cm (2in) across. The sepals and petals are green or greenish-yellow, heavily barred and spotted with deep purple. The lip is an overall dark purple, sometimes almost black.

Above: *Promenaea stapelioides* Photo x ½

Promenaea xanthina

◑Intermediate ❀Summer

This species is alternatively named *P. citrina* and is identical vegetatively to *P. stapelioides.* The flowers are citron-yellow in colour with a few tiny red spots on the lip.

Rangaeris

This genus contains only about six known species, and although not often seen today, they are certainly worthy of a place in any mixed collection. They are all epiphytic, native to tropical Africa, and their vegetation is similar to that of the vandaceous orchids, with pairs of straplike

Above: *Polystachya pubescens* Photo x 4

Above: *Rhynchostylis retusa* Photo x ¼

Above: *Pleione formosana* Photo x 1½

Above: *Rangaeris amaniensis* Photo x ¼

leaves growing from a central stem. Rangaeris are subjects for the warm house, enjoying full sunlight at all times, though care should be taken to avoid scorching of the leaves. Also, the plant will benefit from a liberal spraying, especially of its thick aerial roots, during the summer months.

The two species described below are ideal subjects for bark or raft culture. Their delicately scented flowers appear during the spring or summer.

Rangaeris amaniensis

●*Warm* ❀*Spring/Summer*

This is a delightful species, producing six to eight long-lasting flowers on each of several spikes. The flowers, about 2.5cm (1in) in diameter, are star-shaped, and have a triangular lip with a narrow spur hanging from the base to a length of 10 to 13cm (4-5in). They are all-white, turning to cream with age.

Rangaeris muscicola is similar but slightly smaller.

Rhynchostylis

Four species make up this well-known and popular epiphytic genus, and all are seen in present day collections.

Their natural habitat is Malaysia and Indonesia and, consequently, they enjoy conditions in the warm greenhouse, similar to those of the strapleaf vandas, which they resemble vegetatively. Because the flowers grow densely in cylindrical fashion on a pendent raceme or spike, they are commonly known as 'foxtail orchids', although this name is also given to other orchids that produce their flowers in similar fashion (for example, *Aerides fieldingii*).

The majority of the thick, waxy and highly fragrant flowers produced by the following species appear from winter to spring and only last for two to three weeks, but if well grown the plants flower more than once in a year.

Rhynchostylis retusa

●*Warm* ❀*Winter/Spring*

This species produces a plant up to 60cm (2ft) in height with a pendulous spike of 38-58cm (15-20in) which carries many tiny flowers, each up to 2cm (0.8in) in diameter. These are basically white but may be lightly or heavily spotted with magenta-purple. The hook-shaped lip is solid magenta.

Rhynchostylis gigantea

●*Warm* ❀*Winter/Spring*

This is similar to *R. retusa* in growth, but much shorter, rarely growing to more than 15cm (6in) in height. The flowers are sometimes a little larger, about 2.5cm (1in) in diameter, and range from pure white to an overall pinky red, but are more often a mixture of the two.

Sobralia

This genus contains 30 to 35 very handsome species, most of which are indigenous to tropical America. They are terrestrial plants producing long, slender, reedlike stems up to 2.5m (8ft) tall, although they are usually much shorter under cultivation. Leaves are produced along almost the full length of the stem.

The flowers, which are produced from the apex of the stems, are very similar in shape and general form to those of cattleyas. They only last for two or three days, but to compensate for this there is a quick succession of blooms from each stem, and a plant with a number of leads can be in flower for many weeks.

Sobralias like the conditions of the warm house, with full sunshine and plenty of fresh air. During the growing season they must be kept very moist at the root, whereas, when the plant is at rest, over the winter months, it should be kept drier, but never allowed to dry out.

The three species listed here flower during late spring or summer.

Sobralia macrantha

●Warm ❀Spring/Summer

This is one of the taller-growing species, and is perhaps the best known. When well grown, it can reach the maximum height of 2.5m already mentioned, but often even very good plants do not develop much above 1m (39in). The flowers are 13-15cm (5-6in) across, deep or pale purplish-mauve, with a yellow throat to the lip.

Sobralia leucoxantha

●Warm ❀Spring/Summer

This species is not as tall as *S. macrantha* but produces flowers of the same size. These are white, the lip having an orange-yellow throat and frilled edges.

Sobralia xantholeuca

●Warm ❀Spring/Summer

This is perhaps rarer than the other two species. It has slightly larger sulphur-yellow flowers, with deeper markings on the lip.

Sophronitis

There is no finer sight in the greenhouse than a plant from this genus in full flower. Although only six species of this miniature epiphytic orchid are known, all of which come from Brazil, it has always been well represented in orchid collections, and its alliance with cattleyas has produced some of the most striking of the intergeneric hybrids.

In their natural habitat these plants grow mainly in areas of high humidity and shade, and therefore are subjects for the cool or intermediate house, with good shade during the summer months. They seem to grow best on a raft or cork-bark, but will also grow in a pot. Perfect drainage at the root is essential. Unfortunately, even in ideal conditions of cultivation, sophronitis plants seem to have a lifespan of only a few years, after which they deteriorate quickly. They may live for seven or eight years if you are lucky; however, most die within three or four years. They offer a challenge to the grower, with success bringing great rewards.

Both of the following species flower during the late winter or spring.

Sophronitis coccinea

○◑Cool/Intermediate ❀Winter/Spring

Formerly known as *S. grandiflora* this orchid is vegetatively similar to a tiny cattleya, growing no higher than 8cm (3in). The single flower, 6.5cm (2.5in) across, is produced on a short stem that grows from the top of the pseudobulb. The petals are broader than the sepals and all the segments are bright scarlet, with the lip marked or lined with yellow.

Above: *Sophronitis coccinea* Photo x 1

Sophronitis cernua

○◑Cool/Intermediate ❀Winter/Spring

This species is even smaller than *S. coccinea*, but the pseudobulbs are set further apart on a creeping rhizome. Two to four flowers are produced on a short spike, each about 2.5cm (1in) across. These range in colour from rose to vivid red, with a yellow-orange centre to the lip.

Stanhopea

About 25 species of this fascinating genus have been described, although some may be variants rather than species. They are particularly remarkable both for growth habit and their unusual flower shape. All are epiphytic and come from tropical America.

The flowering habit of stanhopeas is unusual in that the flower spike, which develops from the base of the pseudobulb, grows directly downwards through the compost to flower beneath the plant. For this reason, these orchids must be grown in wire or wooden-slatted baskets, or in purpose-made pots that have holes in the walls and base to prevent the flowers being trapped within the container. Unfortunately, these highly fragrant flowers last for only about three days; nevertheless, the plants are of enormous interest and worthy of a place in any mixed collection.

Stanhopeas are among the easiest orchids to grow, requiring the conditions of the intermediate house with moderate shade and moisture at the roots at all times. These two species flower during the late summer and autumn.

Stanhopea wardii

◑Intermediate ❀Summer/Autumn

In common with the other species, *Stanhopea wardii* produces a 30-38cm (12-15in) broad, leathery leaf from the top of an oval pseudobulb. The flower spike, when it has emerged from the plant container, carries three to nine flowers. The buds develop very quickly and the flowers (up to 10cm [4 in] across when fully open) vary from pale lemon to orange, dotted with brownish-purple, with a large blotch of the same colour on each side of the lip. The very strange shape of these flowers suggests a large insect hovering in flight.

Stanhopea tigrina

◑Intermediate ❀Summer/Autumn

With two to four flowers on each spike, the flowers of this species tend to be larger than those of *S. wardii.* The basic colour is ivory or pale yellow, while the sepals and petals are heavily blotched with maroon-purple.

Trichopilia

About 30 species of *Trichopilia* are known, although only a few of these are available to growers today. Despite this, they remain very popular, partly because they are not difficult to cultivate and also because of their very showy flowers, which are large in comparison with the size of the plant. The plants are epiphytic and are found mainly in South America. They produce very fragrant flowers that last well—often up to four weeks—and which appear in winter and spring.

The plants, which never grow very tall, develop flattened pseudobulbs that may be rounded or elongated, and a solitary leathery leaf. Intermediate house conditions suit them well, with good shade during the summer months. The plants benefit from generous moisture at the root in full growth. After flowering, these orchids should be allowed a long period of rest in much drier conditions.

As most species produce drooping or pendent flower spikes they should be accommodated in baskets or on rafts suspended from the greenhouse roof.

Above: *Stanhopea wardii* Photo x ½

Above: *Trichopilia tortillis* Photo x ½

Above: *Sobralia macrantha* Photo x ⅓

Above: *Zygopetalum intermedium* Photo x ½

Trichopilia suavis

Intermediate *Winter/Spring*

This species produces a short, semi-arching spike, which bears two to five flowers of about 10cm (4in) in diameter and cattleya-like in appearance; the basic colour is white or cream, with rose-pink spotting on the sepals and petals, and heavier blotching of the same colour on the broad lip.

Trichopilia tortillis

Intermediate *Winter/Spring*

This plant carries a single flower, up to 13cm (5in) across, on a pendent spike. The sepals and petals, which are narrow and twisted throughout their length, are brown, bordered by a narrow yellow-green band; the trumpet-shaped lip is white with some rose-red spotting.

Trichopilia fragrans

Intermediate *Winter/Spring*

One of the larger species, *Trichopilia fragrans* produces arching sprays of two to five 10cm (4in) flowers. The sepals and petals are white with a greenish tinge, and the lip is white with yellow markings in the throat.

Zygopetalum

This genus comprises 20 species, most of which come from Brazil. They are mainly terrestrial, producing rounded pseudobulbs with long but fairly narrow leaves. One of their great attractions is the contrast between the colour of the sepals and petals and that of the lip.

These are plants for the intermediate house and require good light, with plenty of moisture at the root when in full growth. Air movement around the plant in conditions of high humidity is very important, otherwise the leaves soon become badly spotted; and, for this reason, they should never be sprayed. Both of these species flower during the winter, producing heavily scented flowers that last for four or five weeks.

Zygopetalum intermedium

Intermediate *Winter*

Often known as *Z. mackayi*, this plant produces an upright flower spike 45-60cm (18-24in) in height, from inside the first leaves of a new growth. The spike bears four to eight flowers each 7.5cm (3in) across. The sepals and petals are of equal size, and bright green blotched with brown. The lip, in contrast, is broad, flat and basically white, heavily lined with purple.

Zygopetalum crinitum

Intermediate *Winter*

This is similar to *Z. intermedium*, although in some forms the blotching on the sepals and petals is very much darker and the markings on the lip are almost blue.

GLOSSARY

Words in *italics* refer to separate entries within the glossary

Adj. = Adjective
Cf. = Compare
Pl. = Plural

Adventitious Usually applied to roots, or any growth produced from a site other than the usual or normal.

Aeriel Living without contact with compost or the ground.

Anther The part of the *stamen* containing *pollen*.

Anther cap The cap covering the *pollen* masses.

Articulate Jointed; possessing a *node* or joint.

Asexual Without sex.

Asymmetrical Not symmetrical; without regular shape.

Axil The upper angle between a stem or branch and a leaf.

Back bulb Old *pseudobulb,* usually without leaves.

Bifoliate Having two leaves.

Bigeneric Involving two *genera* in the parentage of a plant.

Bisexual Two sexed, the flowers possessing both *stamens* and *pistils*. (cf. *unisexual*).

Bract A reduced leaf-like organ protecting a flower stalk.

Bulbous Having the character of a bulb.

Calceolate Slipper-shaped.

Callus The protective tissue covering a cut or bruised surface.

Cellular Composed of cells.

Chlorophyll The green pigment in plants, essential for the manufacture of food.

Chlorotic Excessive yellowing due to a breaking down of the *chlorophyll.*

Chromosome A structure within the cell nucleus, which carries the *genes*.

Clone An individual plant raised from a single seed, and all its subsequent *vegetative propagations.*

Column The central body of the orchid flower formed by the union of the *stamens* and *pistil.*

Crest A raised, fringed or toothed ridge found on the *lip*.

Cross-pollinate The *pollination* of one flower with the *pollen* from another flower. (cf. *self-pollination*).

Cultivar An individual plant in cultivation, including its *vegetative propagations.*

Deciduous Losing leaves at the end of the growing season.

Diploid Having the normal complement of a double set of *chromosomes* in the cell nuclei.

Division The means by which a single *cultivar* is divided into two or more plants.

Dorsal Pertaining to the back or outer surface. (cf. *ventral*).

Ecology The study of organisms in relation to their environment.

Endemic Occurring only in a given area, and not elsewhere.

Epidermis Outer layer of cells.

Epiphyte A plant that grows on another plant but is not a *parasite,* as it obtains nourishment from the air.

Eye The bud of a growth.

Family A group of related *genera*.

Filiform Long, slender or thread like.

Fimbriate Fringed.

Flaccid Soft and limp.

Fragrans Sweet scented.

Gene The unit of inheritance, located at a specific site on a *chromosome.*

Genetics The study of heredity and variation.

Genus A subdivision of a *family,* consisting of one or more *species* which show similar characteristics and appear to have a common ancestry. Adj. generic. Pl. genera.

Grex A group, applied collectively to the progeny of a given cross between two plants.

Habitat The locality in which a plant normally grows.

Hirsute *Pubescent,* the hairs being coarse and stiff.

Hybrid The offspring resulting from the cross between two different *species* or hybrids.

Hydroponics A method of growing plants using nutrient solutions alone.

Inbreeding *Self-pollinating.*

Indigenous Native; not introduced.

Inflorescence The flowering part of a plant.

Intergeneric Between or among two or more *genera*.

Internode The part of a stem between two *nodes*.

Keel A projecting ridge.

Keiki A plantlet produced as an offset or offshoot from another plant. (A Hawaiian term used by orchidists.)

Labellum The *lip*, or modified *petal* of an orchid flower.

Lateral Of or pertaining to the side of an organ. (cf. *terminal*).

Lead A new *vegetative* growth.

Linear Long and narrow, with parallel margins.

Lip The *labellum*, usually quite distinct from the other two *petals*.

Lithophyte A plant which grows on rocks. Adj. lithophytic.

Mericlone A plant produced by *meristem* culture.

Meristem *Vegetative propagation* of plants by cultivating new shoot tissue under special laboratory conditions.

Monofoliate Having only one leaf.

Monopodial Growing only from the apex of the plant.

Mutation A departure from the parent type; a *sport*.

Natural hybrid A *hybrid* produced by chance in the wild.

Nectary A gland or secreting organ that produces nectar.

Node A joint on a stem.

Nomenclature A system of names or naming.

Ovary The central female part of a flower.

Parasite A plant that lives on and derives part or all of its nourishment from another plant. Adj. parasitic. (cf. *epiphyte*).

Pedicel The stalk of an individual flower.

Pendulous Hanging downwards, or inclined.

Petal One of the three inner segments of an orchid flower, which is not modified to form the *lip*.

Pistil The seed-bearing organ of a flower consisting of the *ovary, stigma* and *style*.

Plicate Pleated, or folded like a fan.

Pollen The fertilizing grains borne by the *anther*.

Pollination The transfer of *pollen* from the *anther* to the *stigma*.

Pollinia The masses of pollen grains found in the *anther*.

Polyploid Containing one or more additional sets of *chromosomes* beyond the normal *diploid* number.

Proliferation Offshoots; the growth of buds that normally remain dormant.

Protocorm A tuber-like structure formed in the early stages of a plant's development.

Pseudobulb The thickened portion of a stem, but not a true bulb.

Pubescent Covered with fine hairs or down.

Quadrigeneric Pertaining to four *genera*.

Raceme A simple *inflorescence* of stalked flowers.

Recurved Curved downwards or backwards.

Rhizome A root-bearing horizontal stem, which, in orchids, usually lies on or just beneath the ground surface.

Rib The primary vein of a leaf.

Rosette A cluster of leaves arranged around a short stem.

Saccate Pouched, or bag-like.

Saprophyte A plant which lives on dead organic matter. Adj. saprophytic.

Scape A flower stalk without leaves, arising directly from the ground.

Self-pollination The *pollination* of a flower by its own *pollen*. (cf. *cross-pollination*).

Semiterete Semicircular in cross-section; semicylindrical. (cf. *terete*).

Sepal One of the three outer segments of an orchid flower.

Sheath A tubular envelope protecting the developing *inflorescence*.

Species A group of plants sharing one or more common characteristics which make it distinct from any other group. Adj. specific.

Spike A flower stem.

Sport A deviation from the usual form, a *mutation*.

Spur A hollow tubular extension of the *lip*.

Stamen The male organ of a flower, bearing the *pollen*.

Stigma The part of the *pistil* which is receptive to the *pollen*.

Style The part of the *pistil* bearing the *stigma*.

Symbiosis The close association of dissimilar organisms, with benefit to both. Adj. symbiotic.

Sympodial A form of growth in which each new shoot, arising from the *rhizome* of the previous growth, is a complete plant in itself.

Synonym A surplus name, arising when a *species* has been given two or more names.

Systemic A pesticide that is absorbed by the plant and poisons the cells against pests.

Terete Circular in cross-section; cylindrical. (cf. *semiterete*).

Terminal At the end of the axis (cf. *lateral*).

Terrestrial Growing in or on the ground.

Transpiration The loss of water from the plant tissue by evaporation.

Tribe A group of related *genera*.

Trigeneric Pertaining to three *genera*.

Tuber A thickened, normally underground stem.

Unifoliate With one leaf.

Unilateral Arranged only on one side.

Unisexual Having flowers of one sex only. (cf. *bisexual*).

Variety A subdivision of a *species;* a group of plants that differ slightly from the main *species* type.

Vegetative propagation The increasing of a particular plant by *division*, or by *meristem* culture.

Velamen The thick layer of cells covering the roots of *epiphytic* orchids.

Ventral The front (cf. *dorsal*).

Verrucose Covered with wart-like projections.

Virus An infectious agent which increases in living cells causing disease.

Whorl An arrangement of leaves or other organs in a circle around an axis.

FURTHER READING

Arditti, J., *Orchid Biology: Reviews and Perspectives, 1,* Cornell University Press, New York and London, 1977.

Birk, L.A., *Growing Cymbidium Orchids at Home,* L.A. Birk, California, 1977.

Blowers, J.W., *Pictorial Orchid Growing,* J.W. Blowers, Maidstone, 1966.

Bowen, L., *The Art and Craft of Growing Orchids,* Batsford, London, 1976.

Cohen, B. and Roberts, E., *Growing Orchids in the Home,* Hodder and Stoughton, London, 1975.

Curtis, C.H., *Orchids – Their description and Cultivation,* Putnam, London, 1950.

Darwin, C., *The various contrivances by which orchids are fertilized by insects,* John Murray, London, 1862.

Dodson, C.H. and Gillespie, R.J., *The Biology of the Orchids,* Mid-America Orchid Congress, Tennessee, 1967.

Freed, H., *Orchids and Serendipity,* Prentice-Hall, New York and London, 1970.

Hawkes, A.D., *Encyclopedia of Cultivated Orchids,* Faber & Faber, London, 1965.

Kramer, J., *Growing Orchids at your Windows,* D. van Nostrand, New York, 1963.

Kramer, J., *Orchids: Flowers of Romance and Mystery,* Harry N. Abrams, New York, 1975.

Nicholls, W.H., *Orchids of Australia,* Thomas Nelson, Sydney, Australia, 1969.

Noble, M., *You Can Grow Orchids,* M. Noble, Florida, 1964.

Northen, R.T., *Orchids as House Plants,* Dover Publications, New York, 1955.

Northen, R.T., *Home Orchid Growing,* Van Nostrand Reinhold, New York, 1970.

The Orchid Stud Book, Hurst & Rolfe, London, 1909.

Paul, M., *Orchids – Care and Growth,* Merlin Press, London, 1964.

Reinekka, M.A., *A History of the Orchid,* University of Miami Press, Florida, 1972.

Richter, W., *Orchid Care: A Guide to Cultivation and Breeding,* Macmillan, London, 1969.

Rittershausen, P.R.C., *Successful Orchid Culture,* Collingridge, London, 1953.

Rittershausen, B. and Rittershausen, W., *Popular Orchids,* Stockwell, Devon, 1970.

Rittershausen, B. and Rittershausen, W., *Orchids – in Colour,* Blandford, Dorset, 1979.

Sander, D.F., *Orchids and their Cultivation,* Blandford, London, 1962.

Sanders' Complete List of Orchid Hybrids, Royal Horticultural Society, London, 1966, available from the American Orchid Society, Cambridge, Massachusetts.

Sessler, G.J., *Orchids – and how to grow them,* Prentice-Hall, New York and London, 1978.

Skelsey, A., *The Time-Life Encyclopedia of Gardening: Orchids,* Time-Life Books, Virginia, 1978.

Sunset Books, *How to Grow Orchids,* Lane, California, 1977.

Swinson, A., *Frederick Sander: The Orchid King,* Hodder and Stoughton, London, 1970.

Thompson, P.A., *Orchids from Seed,* Royal Botanic Gardens, Kew, 1977.

Waters, V.H. and Waters, C.C., *A Survey of the Slipper Orchids,* Carolina Press, N. Carolina, 1973.

Williams, B.S., *Orchid Growers' Manual,* Wheldon and Wesley, Herts, 1894; reprint Hafner, Connecticut, 1961.

Withner, C.L., *The Orchids: A Scientific Survey,* The Ronald Press, New York, 1959.

Withner, C.L., *The Orchids: Scientific Studies,* Wiley, New York and London, 1974.

Veitch, J. and Sons, *Manual of Orchidaceous Plants,* H.M. Pollett, London, 1887.

Journals

Orchids, The American Orchid Society, West Palm Beach, Florida, USA

Australian Orchid Review, The Australian Orchid Council, Sydney, Australia

Die Orchidee, Deutsche Orchideen-Gesellschaft, Frankfurt, Germany

Orchids in New Zealand, The New Zealand Orchid Society, Wellington, New Zealand

The Orchid Digest, The Orchid Digest Corporation, Orinda, California, USA

The Orchid Review, The Orchid Review, PO Box 38, Ashford, Kent, TN25 6PR, England

The South African Orchid Journal, The South African Orchid Council, University of Natal, South Africa

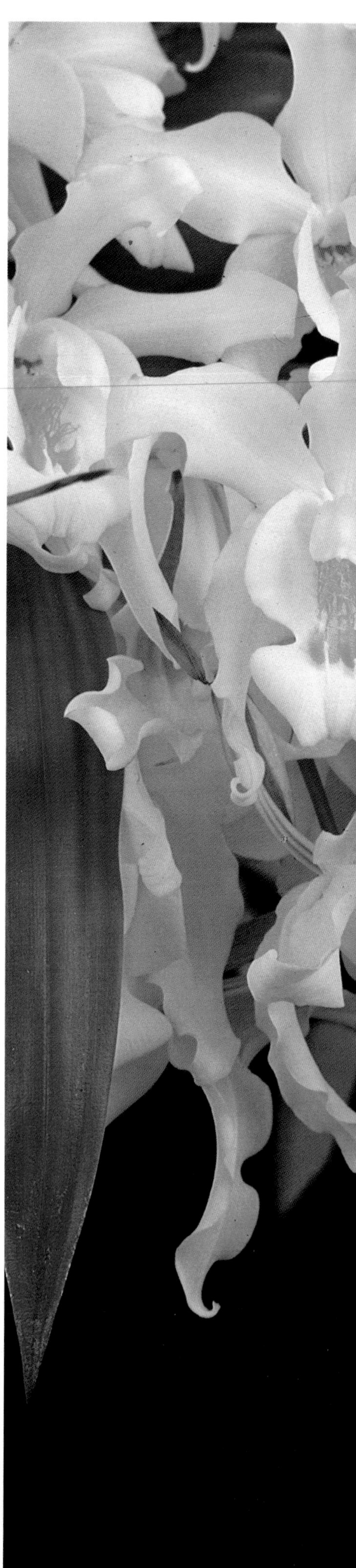

Sources of Plants

Adelaide Orchids Pty., Adelaide, South Australia

A.J Keeling & Sons, Westgate Hill, Bradford, W. Yorkshire, B04 6NS, England

The Beall Company, Vashon Island, Washington, USA

Burnham Nurseries Ltd., Forches Cross, Newton Abbot, Devon, TQ12 6PZ, England

David Stead Orchids, Lofthouse, Wakefield, W. Yorkshire, WF3 3PA, England

Deva Orchids, Pen-y-ffordd, Chester, Cheshire, CH4 OJY, England

Duckitt Nurseries, Darling, Cape Town, South Africa

Equatorial Plant Company, Barnard Castle, Co. Durham, DL12 8PD, England

Floricultura, Haarlem, The Netherlands

Greenaway Orchids, Puston, Weston-super-Mare, Avon, BS24 6TL, England

Ivens Orchids, Sandridge, St Albans, Hertfordshire, AL4 9LB, England

J & L Orchids, Easton, Connecticut, USA

Jones & Scully Inc., Miami, Florida, USA

Kultana Orchids, Bangkok 4, Thailand

Lemförder Orchideen, Lemförde, Germany

Mansell & Hatcher Ltd., Rawdon, Leeds, W. Yorkshire, LS19 6LQ, England

McBean's Orchids, Cooksbridge, Lewes, Sussex, BN8 4PR, England

Only Phalaenopsis, Leighton Buzzard, Bedfordshire, LU7 8UU, England

Orchideen Hans Koch, Unna, Dortmund, Germany

Orchids by Hausermann Inc., Elmhurst, Illinois, USA

Phoenix Orchids, Southowram, Halifax, W. Yorkshire, HX3 9QT, England

Plested Orchids, Sandhurst, Berkshire, GU47 0QD, England

Ratcliffe Orchids Ltd., Owslebury, Winchester, Hampshire, SO21 1LR, England

Royden Orchids, Great Missenden, Buckinghamshire, HP16 0JD, England

Santa Barbara Orchid Estate, Santa Barbara, California, USA

Stonehurst Nurseries, Ardingly, Sussex, RH17 6TN, England

'T' Orchids, Bangkok 4, Thailand

Vacherot & Lecoufle, Boissy-Saint-Léger, France

Valley Orchids Pty., Reynella, South Australia

Whitmoor House Orchid Nursery, Cullompton, Devon, EX15 3NP, England

Wichmann Orchideen, Celle, Germany

Wilhelm Hennis Orchideen, Hildesheim, Germany

Wondabah Orchids Pty., Carlingford, New South Wales, Australia

Woodstock Orchids, Great Brickhill, Milton Keynes, MK17 9AS, England

Zuma Canyon Orchids Inc., Malibu, California, USA

Above: *Cymbidium* Elmwood *Photo x ½*

GENERAL INDEX

Figures in *italics* indicate illustrations in place of, or in addition to, a reference in the text. Figures in **bold** type indicate major treatment of a subject.

INDEX TO PLANTS

Above: *Oncidium cheirophorum* Photo

CREDITS

Picture credits
The publishers wish to thank the following photographers and organizations who have supplied photographs for this book. Photographs have been credited by page number and position on the page: (B) Bottom, (T) Top, (C) Centre, (BL) Bottom left, etc.

Photographs
A-Z Collection: 109(B)

Alec Bristow: 128(TC), 131(TR)

Gloria Cotton: 170-1

Eric Crichton: Endpapers, Half-title, Title page, Copyright page, Contents page, Foreword, 12(CL), 13(CR), 15(TR,CL), 16(T), 24-5, 31, 33-4, 36, 39(TC), 45, 49(C), 50, 53(T, CR), 54-5, 63(B), 64-5(C), 66-7, 68(TC, C), 70-1, 75(B), 82-5, 87-9, 92(B), 93(B), 94(T), 95, 98-9, 103-5(CL, BL, TR), 106-109(T), 110-111, 116-25, 128(L,CR), 129(TC,L), 130 (T,B), 131(TL,CL,B), 132 (T,BR), 133(B), 134-5, 137-141(T,BL,BC), 142-59, 161, 164-9, 172(TL,B), 173(B), 176-80(R), 181(B), 182-3(T), 184(TR,CR,BC), 185(T), 186(B), 187(TR), 188(T), 189(T), 190-1(T,CR), 192(T), 193-4(T,B), 195(T), 196-7(CL,CR,B), 200-1, 202, 207
©Salamander Books Ltd: 14(C), 15(CR), 26-7(L, RHS Lindley Library), 28-9(R, RHS Lindley Library), 30, 32, 41(T), 46, 49(T), 51(TL), 53(CL), 56-7, 59, 60-1, 62(L), 63(T), 65(T), 68(R), 69, 72, 74-5(T), 76-81, 90-92(C,TR), 94(B), 96-7, 104, 162-3

Derek Fell: 114-5

Alan Greatwood: 129(B), 141(BR), 180(TR), 181(T), 183(B), 184(B), 185(B), 186(T), 187(TL), 188(C,B), 189(B), 191(LC,B), 192(B,C), 194(C), 195(B), 197(T,CR)

Jack Kramer: 40-1

Mansell Collection: 27(CR), 29(TL)

Charles Marden Fitch: 174(T)

John Mason: 12(BR), 13(TL), 20(B), 38-9(T)

National Monuments Record: 34(B)

J.R. Oddy: 172(TR)

Orchid Society of Great Britain: 132(BC), 133(C,R)

Alwyn Y. Pepper: 21(TR)

Herman Pigors: 173(T), 174(B),175(T,B)

Ratcliffe Orchids: 44

Gerald Rodway: 105(BR), 128(BR), 130(CR)

Edward Ross: 12(T), 14(CR), 18-19, 22-23, 39(C)

B.J. Wallace: 21(TL)

Peter Ward: 13(TR), 20(T)

Tom Wheeler: 58

Joyce Wilson: 42-3, 47(R)

Artists
Copyright of the drawings on the pages following the artists' names is the property of Salamander Books Ltd.

Lydia Malim: 11, 14-16, 19, 43, 72-4, 76, 81, 83-4, 86, 93-4, 101-2, 112, 126-7, 134, 146, 160, 170, 179

Diana MaClean (Linden Artists) 17,162

Brian Watson (Linden Artists) 35, 38, 48, 52

Acknowledgements
The publishers would like to thank the following individuals and orchid nurseries for their help in supplying material for a major portion of the photographs in the book.

Eddie Anderson, Derek Cotton, Gloria Cotton, Ben Darby, Alan Day, Alan Greatwood, Josephine Kelleher, David Leigh, Molly Pottinger, Sir Robert and Lady Sainsbury: The Bucklebury Collection, Eric Young, Brian Williams, Burnham Nurseries Ltd, Keith Andrew Orchids Ltd, Mansell and Hatcher Ltd, McBeans Orchids Ltd, Neville Orchids Ltd, Phalaenopsis Ltd, Ratcliffe Orchids Ltd, Twyford Laboratories Ltd, Vacherot & Lecoufle, Wyld Court Orchids.